Adorno and Literature

Adorno and Literature

Edited by

DAVID CUNNINGHAM

and

NIGEL MAPP

continuum

Continuum International Publishing Group
The Tower Building, 11 York Road, London SE1 7NX
80 Maiden Lane, Suite 704, New York, NY 10038

www.continuumbooks.com

© David Cunningham, Nigel Mapp and Contributors 2006

First published 2006
Reprinted 2006
Paperback edition 2008

British Library Cataloguing-in-Publication Data
A catalogue record for this book is available from the British Library.

ISBN: PB: 978-0-8264-0368-1

Library of Congress Cataloging-in-Publication Data
A catalog record for this book is available from the Library of Congress.

Typeset by Aarontype Limited, Easton, Bristol

Contents

Notes on Contributors

Timothy Bewes is Assistant Professor in the English Department at Brown University, Providence, Rhode Island. He is also an editor of the journal *New Formations*. His publications include the books *Cynicism and Post-modernity* (1997) and *Reification, or the Anxiety of Late Capitalism* (2002).

Andrew Bowie is Professor of German at Royal Holloway College, University of London, and has published widely in the areas of modern German philosophy, literature and music. His books include *Aesthetics and Subjectivity* (1987; second edition 2003), *From Romanticism to Critical Theory: The Philosophy of German Literary Theory* (1997) and *Introduction to German Philosophy: From Kant to Habermas* (2003). He has recently completed a book entitled *Music, Philosophy and Modernity*.

Howard Caygill is Professor of Cultural History at Goldsmiths College, London. Among his many publications are *Art of Judgement* (1989), *A Kant Dictionary* (1995), *Walter Benjamin: The Colour of Experience* (1998) and *Levinas and the Political* (2002). He is currently completing a book on the philosophical and medical aspects of the body.

David Cunningham is Lecturer in English Literature at the University of Westminster in London, and an editor of the journal *Radical Philosophy*. He has published previously on Adorno, Beckett, surrealism and con-temporary music, amongst other topics. He is also co-editor of the collection *Photography and Literature in the Twentieth Century* (2005) and is presently writing a monograph on the concept of an avant-garde.

Paul Fleming is Assistant Professor of German at New York University, and is the author of *The Pleasures of Abandonment: Jean Paul and the Life of Humor* (2006). His major research interests are in eighteenth-century poetry and poetics, and in critical theory and aesthetics. He has published on Adorno, Hölderlin and Jean Paul, and is the translator of Peter Szondi's *An Essay on the Tragic* (2002).

Eva Geulen is Professor of German Literature at the University of Bonn in Germany, and co-editor of the *Zeitschrift für deutsche Philologie*. She is the author of *Das Ende der Kunst: Lesarten eines Gerüchts nach Hegel* (2002), which is to be published in an English translation in 2006, and of *Giorgio Agamben zur Einführung* (2005). She has published widely on German literature and philosophy, including Adorno, Benjamin, Nietzsche and Thomas Mann.

Timothy Hall is Senior Lecturer in Social and Political Thought at the University of East London. His recent publications include an essay on Lukács in *The Palgrave Guide to Continental Political Philosophy* (2005). He is currently writing a book on Lukács and Adorno, and is co-authoring a book entitled *The Modern State: Theories and Ideologies*.

Simon Jarvis is Gorley Putt Senior Lecturer in English Literary History at the University of Cambridge. He is the author of *Wordsworth's Philosophic Song* (2006), *Adorno: A Critical Introduction* (1998) and *Scholars and Gentlemen: Shakespearean Textual Criticism and Representations of Scholarly Labour, 1725–1765* (1995), as well as, in verse, *The Unconditional: A Lyric* (2005). He is also the editor of the forthcoming volumes on Adorno in the Routledge Critical Evaluations in Cultural Theory series.

Robert Kaufman is Assistant Professor of English and Affiliated Assistant Professor of German Studies at Stanford University. He has published widely on nineteenth-century, modernist and contemporary poetry in relation to aesthetic and critical theory, with particular emphasis on lines of aesthetic thought that stretch from Kant through to the Frankfurt School and beyond. He is currently completing a book entitled *Negative Romanticism: Adornian Aesthetics in Keats, Shelley, and Modern Poetry*, and is also working on two other related book projects: *Why Poetry Should Matter – to the Left*, and *Modernism After Postmodernism: Robert Duncan and the Future-Present of American Poetry*.

Iain Macdonald is Assistant Professor of Philosophy at the University of Montreal in Canada. He has published on French and German thought, including the work of Adorno, Heidegger, Derrida and Hegel. He is currently working on a project concerning ethics and phenomenology.

Nigel Mapp is Senior Assistant in English at the University of Tampere in Finland. He is co-editor (with Christopher Norris) of *William Empson: The Critical Achievement* (1993), and has published essays on Derrida, Adorno and de Man. His *Paul de Man: Rhetoric, Aesthetics, History* will be published in 2007.

Stewart Martin is Lecturer in Modern European Philosophy at Middlesex University, and an editor of the journal *Radical Philosophy*. He has published widely on Adorno and aesthetics, and wrote the introduction to the collection *The Philistine Controversy* (2002). He is currently writing a book on the relationship of early German Romantic aesthetics to the philosophy of post-Conceptual art.

Martin Ryle is Senior Lecturer in Continuing Education at the University of Sussex. He has published extensively on contemporary fiction, modernism, and literary and cultural theory, and is the author of, among other works, *Journeys in Ireland* (1999) and (with Kate Soper) *To Relish the Sublime* (2002). He has recently co-edited a collection of essays on the novelist George Gissing.

Kate Soper is Professor of Philosophy at London Metropolitan University, and has written previously on political philosophy, cultural studies and feminist issues (including on Adorno and feminism). Her many publications include *Troubled Pleasures* (1990), *What is Nature?* (1995) and (with Martin Ryle) *To Relish the Sublime* (2002).

Acknowledgements

This volume has its distant origins in a colloquium on Adorno held at the University of Westminster in 2003. The editors would like to thank, in particular, Alex Warwick, Ken Paterson, Simon Jarvis, Andrew Bowie, Stewart Martin and Matt Connell for helping to make the event possible. We would also like to thank Anna Sandeman at Continuum for commissioning the book and for her patience thereafter. Special thanks are due to Paul Fleming for his assistance in translating passages in Eva Geulen's essay. Above all, we wish to thank the contributors for all their enthusiasm, support and hard work, which have made this project possible.

All the essays are previously unpublished with the exception of Robert Kaufman's 'Lyric's Expression: Musicality, Conceptuality, Critical Agency', which appears, in a different form, in *Cultural Critique* 60 (Spring 2005). We would like to thank the editors of *Cultural Critique* and the University of Minnesota Press for permission to republish it here. We also thank Michael Palmer for permission to reproduce the untitled poem ('A man undergoes pain sitting at a piano ...') from his volume *Sun* (San Francisco, CA: North Point Press, 1998).

Abbreviations

References to Adorno in the German are keyed to the complete works, giving volume and page:

GS   *Gesammelte Schriften*, ed. R. Tiedemann *et al.* 23 vols. Frankfurt: Suhrkamp, 1970–.

NS   *Nachgelassene Schriften*, ed. R. Tiedemann *et al.* 30 vols planned. Frankfurt: Suhrkamp, 1993–.

The following are the abbreviations used for the standard English translations cited in the text:

AA   'Art and the Arts', trans. R. Livingstone, in *Can One Live After Auschwitz? A Philosophical Reader*, ed. R. Tiedemann. Stanford, CA: Stanford University Press, 2003, pp. 368–87.

AT   *Aesthetic Theory*, trans. R. Hullot-Kentor. Minneapolis: University of Minnesota Press, 1997.

DE   (with Max Horkheimer), *Dialectic of Enlightenment*, trans. E. Jephcott. Stanford, CA: Stanford University Press, 2002.

EM   *Essays on Music*, ed. R. Leppert. Berkeley, Los Angeles and London: University of California Press, 2002.

H   *Hegel: Three Studies*, trans. S. Weber Nicholsen. Cambridge, MA: MIT Press, 1993.

MM   *Minima Moralia*, trans. E. F. N. Jephcott. London: Verso, 1978.

MP   *Problems of Moral Philosophy*, ed. T. Schröder, trans. R. Livingstone. Stanford, CA: Stanford University Press, 2000.

ND   *Negative Dialectics*, trans. E. B. Ashton. London: Routledge, 1973.

NL1   *Notes to Literature, Volume One*, trans. S. Weber Nicholsen. New York: Columbia University Press, 1991.

NL2   *Notes to Literature, Volume Two*, trans. S. Weber Nicholsen. New York: Columbia University Press, 1992.

P   *Prisms*, trans. S. and S. Weber. Cambridge, MA: MIT Press, 1981.

Q   *Quasi Una Fantasia: Essays on Music*, trans. R. Livingstone. London and New York: Verso, 1992.

T   'On Tradition', trans. E. Geulen, *Telos* 94 (1992–3), 75–82.

Introduction

David Cunningham and Nigel Mapp

Across the humanities and social sciences, there has been a recent surge of interest in the work of the German critical theorist Theodor Adorno. There can be little doubt today that he deserves his reputation as one of the most important and influential of twentieth-century thinkers. For an Anglo-American readership in particular, the publication in English of his last great, unfinished work *Aesthetic Theory*, originally in 1984 and then in a new translation in 1997, has provoked a wide range of extremely productive arguments concerning art and modernity. Few twentieth-century philosophers accord such an important role to art and aesthetics as does Adorno; so it is unsurprising that it should be in relation to questions of aesthetics that much of the most exciting recent work on Adorno has been carried out. In art criticism especially, *Aesthetic Theory* has provided the theoretical ground on which a series of key debates have been articulated and fought out over the last decade. The so-called 'philistine controversy', first sparked in a 1996 article by the art critics Dave Beech and John Roberts in the British journal *New Left Review*, was, for example, a 'controversy' almost entirely organized around competing readings of Adorno's last text (see Beech and Roberts 2002).

And yet, in the midst of this activity, Adorno's literary writings have remained severely under-represented. This is an odd state of affairs, for Adorno clearly considered literature a vital element in his aesthetic theory which, in turn, plays a key role in his thought more generally. The four volumes of *Noten zur Literatur* – the first three of which appeared between 1958 and 1965, while the fourth was posthumously published – are testimony to a constant engagement with literary texts that spans Adorno's entire lifetime as a thinker. Nor are references to literature, or extensive treatments of literary figures and works, limited to these volumes. As such, occluded though they have tended to be, Adorno's literary interests should not be marginalized as minor by-products of his achievement. Indeed, such marginalization is *inherently* problematic in that it reinforces the kinds of generic and disciplinary separations whose rethinking was one of his major concerns. This is not to say that such separations are not real. Certainly they cannot be overcome by mere thought or subjective will. Rather, Adorno seeks to trace the damage they do to thinking, and what social experience they express. Precisely because of their symptomatic suppression, his writings on literature are thus a key site for exploring such claims.

At the same time, a certain thinking of language is embedded in Adorno's understanding of music and visual art, as well as of philosophical interpretation itself. This does not mean that literature may be taken as some hidden 'master-key' for opening up the entirety of his theory. What Adorno terms the 'likeness' or 'affinity' to language shared by *all* art rests upon a conception of language as being itself 'mimetic' or 'expressive', as well as discursive, in character. Yet it does suggest that some kind of 'literary' problematic is thereby centrally implicated in the questions raised by the aesthetic theory as a whole. This is particularly so because of what would seem to be most distinct about the literary work in the context of a general modernist tendency toward abstraction: its *ineliminably* 'discursive' or 'semantic' moment. As Adorno writes of the novel – in 'contrast to painting' – language imposes necessary limits on its 'emancipation from the object' (*NL1*: 31). The literary work is, therefore, exemplary of the sense in which all artworks are 'not only artworks or not artworks throughout' (*AT*: 182).

Why then, until very recently, have Adorno's writings on literature been so neglected in the Anglo-American academy? The critical stock of his close friend Walter Benjamin has, in contrast, been on the rise for some time. As Jean-Michel Rabaté has written, one can hardly keep track of 'the number of recent presentations or books in progress devoted to "Joyce and Benjamin" ... or "Pound and Benjamin" ' (2002: 65). Yet, despite the efforts of Fredric Jameson for one (1971; 1990), Adorno has remained a far more obscure figure; simply ignored or, worse, caricatured as a pessimistic, reactionary elitist. When he *was* recognized by course syllabuses in the past, it was usually through excerpts from the much anthologized chapter on the culture industry from the co-authored *Dialectic of Enlightenment* (*DE*: 94–136) – generally placed in proximity to a text by F. R. Leavis in order to suggest, mistakenly, that much the same critical position is visible in both. It is perhaps the very centrality of Arnold, Leavis and Eliot to the development of English Literature as a discipline that has served to make a certain misreading of Adorno more or less inevitable here. Post-Saussurean literary theory, in reacting against this 'liberal humanism', found in Althusserian 'science' and Foucauldian 'discourse' the properly disenchanting tools it needed; Adorno's dogged retrieval of art's illusory autonomy in the name of cognition and humanity was seen as a residue of the quaint idealism which had now been stripped away.

One of the aims of this volume is to dispel some of the myths concerning Adorno's thinking. Chief among these is this perception of him as a German Leavis, a conservative defender of bourgeois 'high' culture whose insights, such as they are, have now been superseded in our supposedly 'postmodern' times. (We leave aside the question of whether this is an accurate representation of Leavis himself.) For while, as Martin Ryle and Kate Soper acknowledge in their essay here, there is undoubtedly *some* truth in the standard depiction of Adorno as an intransigent opponent of 'popular' forms – as exemplified, notoriously, in his judgements on jazz – what is generally overlooked in the rush to condemnation is the social theory which underpins such arguments. For Adorno, the 'culture industry' is not to be confused with a genuine 'mass culture', but constitutes that which is *done to* culture under capitalism. In this sense, it 'distorts' so-called 'high' culture as much as the purportedly 'popular'. Any attempt straightforwardly to reconcile these two 'torn halves' can, in the face of the real divisions of modern social life, only amount to a false sublation, a pseudo-democratizing of culture.

Similar confusions attend Adorno's arguments concerning the necessary autonomy of the modern artwork. Too readily assimilated to the 'formalism' of post-war American New Criticism in literary studies (or of Clement Greenberg in relation to the visual arts), such arguments do not reflect a simple aesthetic preference or theoretical 'standpoint', but are proposed as an analysis of art's unfolding *social* determination in capitalist culture. Autonomy is thus neither a simple option for cultural production, nor an inherent property of the object itself, but is produced out of the social relations that constitute art or literature. As Adorno writes in the 1962 essay 'Commitment':

> [T]he work of art's detachment from empirical reality is at the same time mediated by that reality. ... By opposing empirical reality, works of art obey its forces, which repulse the spiritual construction, as it were, throwing it back upon itself. There is no content, no formal category of the literary work that does not, however transformed and however unawarely, derive from the empirical reality from which it has escaped. (*NL2*: 89)

What Adorno understands by 'aesthetic theory' is thus crucially different from conventional ideas of philosophical aesthetics. For art and literature must be taken here, in all their aspects, to be *essentially* historical.

This may not seem contentious. Yet, unlike the forms of historicism dominant in contemporary literary studies ('new' or otherwise), what this insight does *not* entail for Adorno is a relativistic negation of what he calls art's 'truth-content'. Rather the individual work's 'truth' is to be understood as historically constituted and transformable. Such 'truth' is generated, not by authorial intention alone, but by the artwork's own singular configuration of its materials; materials which have forms of historical experience 'sedimented' in them. As Andrew Bowie points out, it is in the nature of language that it transcends subjective intention, because even its aesthetic forms depend in part upon collective interactions that are prior to and irreducible to the individual subject. Adorno thus makes the bold, and easily misunderstood, claim that works of literature and art stand constitutively in need of philosophical interpretation or criticism. This does not mean, however, that they are in simple need of paraphrase – of translation into concepts – but that only through interpretation of their 'immanent movement', and its historical logic, can their properly *critical* potential be unleashed (*NL2*: 97).

Such an emphatic notion of 'truth' is perhaps inassimilable to the hegemonic forms of literary theory and criticism today – to a deconstructive emphasis on radical 'undecidability', or to a cultural studies committed to the 'demystification' of all truth claims through limitless discursivization. Certainly, Adorno's work refuses the quasi-sociological tendency – frequently reinforced by the moralism of 'identity politics' – to treat the literary work as merely another instance of discourse in general. His thinking of mimesis, of a somatic thinking, of the price of culture's obliteration of nature: many of Adorno's central preoccupations are plain anathematic to postmodern theory. But he does not thereby regress behind it. He shows such would-be radical theory's collusion with social domination, the 'second nature' in which we live, unlivingly. For Adorno, a brusque identification of art with ideology ends up liquidating what in literature holds to the genuinely ethico-political possibility of relating to the other differently. The reasons Adorno has been shoved aside in literary studies themselves suggest why his books should be reopened.

If Adorno is coming into favour today, then, it is surely in part because of his insistence on the possibility of making *value* judgements of literary works. Such judgements for Adorno should not, however, be confused with those of traditional aesthetics. In this respect like deconstruction (which has to some degree helped to clear its path today), the insistence of Adorno's critical theory upon a form of 'immanent criticism' that responds to the singularity of the text is intrinsically hostile to the 'formalism' of any such aesthetics, as it is to the idea of an invariant or limitlessly applicable method through which literary works might be read. The subsumption of literary works under 'preformed schemata', as Adorno phrases it, only means that 'they are no longer recognized for what they are in themselves' (*NL2*: 97).

This collection starts out, therefore, from the singularity of Adorno's *own* readings of literature, seeking, at the same time, to make critically available more of the range of his writings in this area. Where the most widely read secondary texts on Adorno do touch upon literature, they have largely been restricted to passing comments found in *Aesthetic Theory* itself, rather than his essays dealing with particular literary writers and issues. In fact, Adorno's writings on literature are surprisingly varied. Perhaps most famous in the English-speaking world for his disputes with Lukács over the category of realism (see Bloch *et al.* 1977), Adorno's criticism has been generally identified, above all, with readings of the great works of twentieth-century modernism and the avant-garde: Proust, Kafka, Joyce, Beckett. Yet his essays on literature also discuss Homer, Goethe, Hölderlin, Heine, Balzac, Dickens, even J. B. Priestley. (He also attempted a Singspiel based on Mark Twain's *Tom Sawyer*.) Some of his favoured subjects are little known in English, and this may well have contributed to these essays' neglect outside Germany. Nonetheless, they remain vital resources, as do his more familiar texts, for any consideration of why Adorno's work should be of interest to critical theory and literary studies today.

This collection cannot hope to cover the full scope of Adorno's engagements with literature. Rather, it brings together a representative selection of work by some of the most inventive and influential critics and philosophers working in this field. The book is divided into three parts – on general questions of philosophy, aesthetics and literature; on poetry and poetics; and on modernity, drama and the novel – in order to give the reader a clear sense of the range of Adorno's thought and influence. Across these divides, various essays in the collection take up Adorno's own particular readings of literary works, giving the reader a way in to their often difficult arguments – and showing how these may be extended beyond their original subjects. The distinctiveness of Adorno's critical work is profiled through comparisons with several of his most important contemporaries, including Lukács, Benjamin and Kommerell. Other essays here seek to take Adorno's insights into more unfamiliar and unexpected areas – the poetry of Wordsworth, the more contemporary writings of Kazuo Ishiguro, Michael Palmer, V. S. Naipaul or W. G. Sebald. Literature's relation to music (sounded in the very title of *Notes to Literature*) and to the visual arts, as well as Adorno's broader reflections on language, are explored, as are the relations of his work to a number of other influential theoretical positions, including those of Heidegger, Derrida, Nancy and Deleuze. It is our hope that this book communicates, with both rigour and enthusiasm, a sense of what Adorno's work can offer to literary criticism.

WORKS CITED

Beech, D. and Roberts, J. (2002), *The Philistine Controversy*. London and New York: Verso.

Bloch, E., Lukács, G., Brecht, B., Benjamin, W., and Adorno, T. W. (1977), *Aesthetics and Politics*, ed. R. Taylor. London: New Left Books.

Jameson, F. (1971), *Marxism and Form: Twentieth-Century Dialectical Theories of Literature*. Princeton, NJ: Princeton University Press.

— (1990), *Late Marxism: Adorno, or the Persistence of the Dialectic*. London and New York: Verso.

Rabaté, J.-M. (2002), *The Future of Theory*. Oxford: Blackwell.

PART I:
Philosophy, Aesthetics and Literature

1

Literature and the Modern System of the Arts: Sources of Criticism in Adorno

Stewart Martin

Literature is dead! Or so said the title of an exhibition recently.[1] The shock that might once have attended such a claim has dissipated. Its repetition now can only hope to draw on about enough repressed libidinal energy to muster a smile. A groan is more likely. From trauma to comedy to boredom, such is the fate of so much 'avant-gardism', to borrow a term from those who seem to be most bored by this saga. But this particular title is aware of this fate, since the exhibition was actually the occasion of the publication of a book of avant-garde writings, many drawing on gothic themes, and fitted out with a kitschy best-seller cover (Russell [ed.] 2003). Death, that dusty avant-gardist threat or prediction, turns out to be a genre of literature itself here: death as life, avant-garde as gothic. Some more groans no doubt, but nevertheless I think it also has the humour of illumination. Perhaps we should view the conspicuous profusion of interest in the gothic within literary studies recently as a displacement or allegory of literature's own relation to the avant-garde: that it not only survived it, but has found life after death all the more invigorating. Literature can even occupy the chaotic space of the 'visual' arts, and without taking off its jacket! What resonates in this clipping is therefore something of the peculiar circumstance that literature ostensibly finds itself in today. On the one hand, it has the ghostly existence of an art that has been subjected to radical criticisms and breaches of its legitimacy and form, while on the other, this criticism has not so much dissolved literature, as massively expanded and enriched its scope and relevance.

The compositional experimentalism of Mallarmé, Hugo Ball's sound poems, the montaging of image and text in Breton, Lettrism's metagraphs, Situationist graffiti, Lawrence Wiener's concrete poetry – the list of experimental forms that have sought to expand the concept of literature could obviously go on, even if they barely ripple the surface of its mass production and consumption. To this we can add any number of conceptual transformations: Blanchot's dissolution of 'the book' into a transgressive and interminable writing, Barthes's analogous attack on the quasi-theological intentionality of the author, the dissolution of the autonomous work into text and the infinite extension of context and intertextuality, Derrida's critique of the subordination of writing to speech – again, this list could go on. Literature, so often the target of these criticisms, has managed to persist it seems, if not through a straightforward self-identity, then with a certain coherence. This appears to be constituted at the level of culture in general. The apparently chaotic structure of contemporary culture has nonetheless found one of its most convincing characterizations in terms of a generalized textuality or semiotics. A syntax of signs has become one of the most influential ways of interpreting the cultural flux. And if the art of literature has become a conspicuous target for the consequences of this world view, it has also been transformed by it and become, in this expanded form, the art in which this cultural logic is made most manifest. This has served, albeit controversially, to offer literature a privileged place among the arts. In fact, insofar as the general logic of culture is revealed to be linguistic, the linguistic constitution of literature gives it a generic status among the arts. Literature acquires the claim to be art as such, while the other arts are rendered species of it. Moreover, insofar as literature comes to embody the logic of culture in general, its scope may even be generalized to the level of the totality of human activity as such. This passage from self-criticism to absolutization has become a fairly familiar trajectory within today's intellectual landscape, even if it remains controversial in its most extreme formulations.

THE MODERN SYSTEM OF THE ARTS

Despite the contemporaneity of this formation of literature's privileged status among the arts, historical reflection reveals that it emerges from a long and deep tradition. Certainly, if we recognize the heritage of today's expanded conception of literature in the classical Greek conception of poetry or *poiêsis*, then early and canonical precedents are not difficult to find. Here, for example, is Diotima speaking in Plato's *Symposium*:

> You'll agree that there is more than one kind of poetry [*poiêsis*] in the true sense of the word – that is to say, calling something into existence that was not there before, so that every kind of artistic creation is poetry, and every artist is a poet. ... But all the same ... we don't call them poets, do we? We give various names to the various arts, and only call the one particular art that deals with music and meter by the name that should be given to them all. And that's the only art that we call poetry, while those who practise it are known as poets. (Plato 1989: 205b–c)

The correspondence between this expansive conception of *poiêsis* and today's generic conception of literature is striking. But this conjunction is anachronistic in ways that are not immediately apparent, since the expansive character of literature today emerges *after* the formation of the system of five *beaux-arts* – architecture, sculpture, painting, music and poetry – which was only established in the eighteenth century. This was entwined with the institution of art and the arts as an autonomous realm of culture at this time. It was ultimately only with the publication of Diderot and D'Alembert's *Encyclopédie* (1751–72) that this system was canonized, and, as Kristeller has shown in his seminal essay on this topic, the development of a systematic philosophy of the arts in late eighteenth- and early nineteenth-century German philosophy presupposed this recently formed taxonomy (Kristeller 1990).

This 'modern' system of autonomous arts is clearly not as secure today as it was throughout the nineteenth century. It does not have the self-evidence that Kristeller took as the spur for his genealogical critique, writing in 1951–2. His critique may even be seen retrospectively as part of a growing suspicion and anxiety about its legitimacy. Today, it is the plurality and hybridity of the arts that are most striking and it is the crisis of the modern system of the arts that has now become most self-evident. Indeed, the expansive conception of contemporary literature seems to derive precisely from this crisis, filling the gaps left by the decaying boundaries between the arts. To the extent that this is true there is a sense in which we are returning to the situation that preceded the modern system of the arts, when terms such as 'poetry', '*belles-lettres*' and 'literature' were not so delimited, and 'literature' extended from poetry to 'book learning' in general as the medium of all activities of human culture.[2] Thus, if the emergence of the modern system of the arts has been recognized as the emergence of the autonomous legitimacy of art and the arts, then the pervasive decline of this autonomy today – both at the level of the particular arts and art in general – appears to be returning us to a seventeenth-century confluence of literature.

However, once we begin critically to examine this predicament through looking at the highest achievements of the philosophical elaboration of the modern system of the arts – namely, from Kant through to Hegel – it becomes immediately apparent that they provide much less of an obstacle to this generalization of literature than may be thought, since, throughout this period, the system of the arts is understood hierarchically, with poetry as both the highest art and the generic art, in relation to which the other arts are understood as internal specifications. This is already apparent from Diderot and d'Alembert's table of knowledge for the *Encyclopédie* published in 1751, where the fine arts, while characterized most generally according to the cognitive ability of imagination, are unified as forms of poetry.[3]

For Kant, the arts are divided according to a principle that is explicitly derived from the model of language. His tripartite classification of the arts of speech, visual arts and arts of the play of outer sensations – the last of which refers to music and the art of colour – is divided according to aspects of speech, taken in the broad sense involving word, gesture and tone.[4] Speech is therefore the generic principle of art. There is no question of an absolute art for Kant. But there is a hierarchy in which poetry takes first place, insofar as it enables the greatest freedom to the imagination and the expansion of the mind (Kant 1987: 196). However, Kant's primary concern is, of course, with judgement, not art as such. It is the 'Romantic' reaction to Kant that really inaugurates the systematic philosophy of art in an emphatic form, and it is ultimately Hegel who fulfils the ambition of this project.

For the so-called Jena Romantics, poetry, extending to an expanded conception of literature, takes on a privileged form. Moreover, in a departure from Kant, it takes on an absolutized form, particularly in the attempt to elaborate an expanded conception of literature through the overcoming of the separation of poetry and prose. Literature presents what the philosophical or determinate presentation of ideas cannot, namely the absolute as that which is necessarily presupposed in any determination, and therefore not determinable itself. It is in 'aesthetic' rather than determinative forms of language that the absolute is more appropriately presented, insofar as they involve a presentation which is resistant to finite determination and, therefore, disclose the absolute or infinite as that which cannot be finitely determined. As Novalis puts it: 'If the character of a given problem is its insolubility, then we solve the problem by representing its insolubility.' The 'true philosophy could never be represented', whereas, 'literature [*Poesie*] ... represents the unrepresentable' (cited in Bowie 1997: 78). Moreover, this aesthetic apprehension of the absolute in literature extends into an aesthetic apprehension of the world itself. As Friedrich Schlegel puts it in his 1799 *Dialogue on Poesy*: 'All of the holy games of art are only distant imitations of the infinite play of the world, of the work of art that is forever forming itself' (1997: 189). The metaphysical generalization of 'poesy' to cover not only the other arts but the world is emphatic here, and serves to prefigure the formation of literature that we can discern today. It also prefigures its problems, as Benjamin saw in his seminal dissertation on 'The Concept of Art-Critique in German Romanticism' (1919), in which he concluded that the Romantic idea of art (certainly for Schlegel) effectively presupposes literature or poetry, and that:

> this equivocation ... designates a fundamental lack in the Romantic theory of literature [*Poesie*], indeed of art [*Kunst*] generally. Both concepts are only unclearly distinguished from each other, to say nothing of their being orientated toward each other so that no understanding of the peculiar nature and the limits of poetic [*poetischen*] expression vis-à-vis those of the other arts [*Künste*] could arise. (Benjamin 1996: 118)

Schelling does propose an explicit grounding of the arts, which, *contra* Kant, are not assumed as given, but understood as generated through the ideal or real aspects of the absolute, whose unity is nonetheless presupposed in all art insofar as it is art at all. Those arts that tend toward the real are the formative arts of music, painting and the plastic arts; those arts that tend toward the ideal are the verbal arts. Nonetheless, language takes on a privileged place among the arts insofar as it manifests the unity that ultimately grounds them all. Whereas the verbal arts are understood as the 'living word', the formative arts are understood as the 'dead word'.[5]

For Hegel, like Schelling, the arts are grounded in terms of a fundamental unity oriented towards the beautiful as the harmony of sensibility and form, which is the 'idea' of art. The historical forms of art are the symbolic, the classical and the romantic. The system of the arts is true to the eighteenth-century paradigm: first, architecture, which renders external nature cognate with spirit; then sculpture, where spirit is given individuality and, specifically, bodily form. The romantic arts follow, where spirit enters the community and becomes a feature of the interior lives of its members: these are painting, understood as an art of visibility and more specifically of colour (as the idealization of the sensuous spatiality of sculpture); music, as the art of sound or audibility now released from the materiality of visibility; and finally poetry, in which, as Hegel puts it, 'sound, the last external material which poetry [*Poesie*] keeps, is in poetry no longer the feeling of sonority itself, but a sign by itself void of significance [*ein für sich bedeutungsloses Zeichen*], a sign of the idea which has become concrete in itself' (Hegel 1975: 88; 1970: 122).[6] The teleology ends with the transition from this last sensuous mediation of spirit to the medium of thought; the transition from 'the poetry of the imagination to the prose [*Prosa*] of thought' (89; 123), and thereby the transition from the realm of beauty to the realm of philosophy, understood as the conceptual self-determination of the ideal (a passage made via the representational thinking of religion). Thus, despite the necessity of the particularity of the arts, as the necessary mediation of the idea with its sensible determination, these arts are nevertheless structured hierarchically with poetry as the privileged art. Poetry is the highest form of the beautiful because the closest to the freest form of the determination of the idea. Hegel's transition from poetry to the prose of philosophy is a movement that the Romantics sought to suspend. He can therefore be seen as providing the most elaborate presentation of the modern system of the arts, as well as decisively delimiting its sphere of value.

Of course, alternatives to this privileging of poetry and literature emerge from this philosophical tradition. For Schopenhauer it is music that acquires the status of the highest art, and that finds access to the fundamental determination of being to which the other arts are subordinate. Nietzsche inherits this privileging of music, and, at least in his early work, understands it as the primary art through which the repressed ontological stratum, not only of art but of culture in general, is revealed; namely, the Dionysiac. This privilege of music is also instituted in English formalism through Walter Pater, albeit in a far more harmonious manner than that advocated by Nietzsche. This displacement of the privilege of poetry through music is also

crucial to Clement Greenberg's modernist understanding of the system of
the arts, which despite, if not because of, its ritual debunking surely remains
one of the most conspicuous and influential formulations of the twentieth
century. Greenberg's preoccupation with painting has tended to obscure his
commitment to a general theory of the arts. Nonetheless, he is explicit that
his defence of the autonomy of painting is set within the context of a defence
of the autonomy of each of the arts, both from each other and from non-art.
Moreover, he recognizes the generic status of literature from the seventeenth
century to be the historic obstacle to this task. Thus, the exclusion of
'literariness' from all non-literary arts and the specification of the 'medium'
of each art becomes the central task of his criticism. Indeed, he applauds the
displacement of literature through music in the late nineteenth century *only*
insofar as it criticizes the idea of a generic art, and *not* insofar as it introduces
a new form of art in general (Greenberg 1992). Greenberg's historic novelty,
which is often overlooked by his critics, can therefore be seen as an attempt
to renew the modern system of the arts in a critical and radicalized form:
since (1) he understood each of the arts to be under the modernist obligation
of self-critically justifying their autonomy, through demonstrating that they
are formed through what is proper to themselves (their medium); and (2)
through radicalizing the distinction between the arts in such a way as to
avoid the dissolution of this autonomy through a generic art.

   In retrospect, there is something surprisingly traditional about many of
Greenberg's critics since they have not only sought to destroy the systematic
specification of the arts, but have done so through the reassertion of a literary
paradigm through which this dissolution is to be understood. This is very
explicit in the early phases of Conceptual Art, which largely understood itself
as producing a direct and radical criticism of Greenberg. Both Joseph Kosuth
and the Art & Language group (as their name suggested) sought to displace
the specification of each art's medium through the development of a generic
art practice pursued through the examination of the language of art in general
(Kosuth 1999; Art & Language 1999). Arthur C. Danto's renewal of Hegel's
theory of the end of art also claims that artworks are not recognized through
their relation to a particular art, but through their relation to 'the artworld'
in general, which demands a process of linguistically communicated
theoretical reflection in order to justify this relation (Danto 1986). Thierry
de Duve has further subordinated the system of arts to a generic conception
of art, which he elaborates through a rethinking of aesthetic judgement after
Duchamp's ready-mades, understood as an explicitly linguistic act of nomi-
nation (de Duve 1996).

   The foregoing indicates some of the most significant and controversial
coordinates of literature's relation to the crisis-ridden theory of the arts:
specifically, that literature's currently privileged and even constitutive relation to the other arts has deep philosophical and historical roots, despite its
apparent novelty; and that the claim for the radical autonomy of the arts, as

outlined by Greenberg for instance, is more novel than it may appear. Any reconsideration of the theory of the arts needs to confront this situation and respond, not only to the quasi-imperial status of literature, but also to the criticisms (familiar since Greenberg) of the crude insistence on a system of arts that belies the undeniable plurality and hybridity of contemporary art. It is in this context that Adorno's critical theory of the relation of litera-ture to the arts has much to offer. But this must take place through a con-sideration of the ambiguous and even contradictory articulation of this theory within his writings.

LITERATURE AND THE ARTS IN ADORNO

The relation of Adorno's philosophy of art to literature has been ambi-valently received, and as a theory of the arts it has received almost no attention. Despite some influence within contemporary literary theory – particularly through its Marxist variants, such as in Jameson and Eagleton – this has taken place despite his marginal and even antagonistic relation to the huge influence of Saussurean linguistics. Adorno was either ignorant of, or indifferent to, Saussure. Certainly, his conception of language was directed emphatically against the radical conventionalism of Saussure, and towards the critical salvation of a number of more ostensibly theological concep-tions of language derived principally from Benjamin. Furthermore, it is Habermas's notorious criticism that Adorno does not make the transition to the linguistic paradigm along with the mainstream of modern philosophy, as demonstrated canonically by Wittgenstein and Heidegger. If Habermas's influence on literary theory has been limited at best, the significance of this linguistic turn in philosophy for the significance of literary theory and its self-understanding has been immense. And yet, despite all this, Adorno's conception of philosophy is conceived very self-consciously in terms of its linguistic form, and its relation to language and literature is fundamental to his conception of art. Although his writings on music vastly exceed his writings on literature, his conception of art assumes an explicitly linguistic form at times. Art is, as he says at one point in *Aesthetic Theory*, a language of its own kind ('language *sui generis*' [*AT*: 131; *GS* 7: 197–8]). Or, as he remarks in reference to how the similarity of Klee's drawings to scribbled writing resonates with the artistic concept of *écriture*: 'all artworks are writ-ing, not just those that are obviously such' (*AT*: 124; *GS* 7: 189).

This problematic, yet profound influence of language on Adorno's conception of philosophy and art has sustained an intensified demand to bridge the gap between Adorno and various forms of (French) structuralism and post-structuralism. It has also sustained recent attempts either to evade or rethink this relation via the context of early German Romanticism. However, if there is a problem surrounding literature's generic status today, this surely must condition the attempt to think Adorno's relation to literature; and not least because this seems to be a problem that informs his thinking. This emerges perhaps most dramatically in his late essay, 'Art and the Arts', first published in 1967, which is committed to delimiting the generic status of literature within a fluid and critically articulated understanding of the relation of the arts to one another (*GS* 10.1: 432–54).[7] But in order to understand Adorno's relation to these issues we need to understand how they relate to his broader conception of the process of enlightenment.

The full scope of Adorno's understanding of literature is introduced most emphatically in the broad anthropological scope of *Dialectic of Enlightenment*, written with Max Horkheimer, which introduces language as central to the constitution of rationality and subjectivity. Here language is understood to emerge from the primal attempt to overcome fear by controlling it through a unified system of representation, in which shock and its attendant sense of powerlessness are converted into power through knowledge of what caused that shock; a knowledge which will thereby defend the subject from future shocks. The emergence of language is hereby associated intrinsically with the constitution of rationality and subjectivity as an attempt to control nature through its representation. The internalization of this feared power or violence within the subject, as the subject's representation of the world, reveals an economy of domination that persists in the development of reason. This is the target of Adorno's critical self-reflection of enlightenment, which seeks to expose, and absolve, the structure of domination sublimated in reason and the constitution of the subject. Without this critical self-reflection, the classical project of the enlightenment – the attempt to overcome domination by unknown forces of nature – renews what it ostensibly seeks to free itself from: blind subordination to domination or myth.

Within this context Adorno and Horkheimer describe language more specifically as the attempt to understand the world in terms of an essence that stands behind and controls its appearances. This constitutes its sacred character, emerging through the experience of fear as subjection to an omniscient power or deity. Language is therefore defined by a paradox that things are not only what they appear to be:

> If the tree is addressed no longer as simply a tree but as evidence of something else, a location of *mana*, language [*Sprache*] expresses the contradiction that it is at the same time itself and something other than itself, identical and non-identical. Through the deity, language is transformed from tautology into language. (*DE*: 11; *GS* 3: 31–2)[8]

Acquisition of the knowledge of this deity, of the ability to read its language, imbibes its power. Subjection, knowledge and power are therefore fused in language. The sacred origin of language emerges mimetically in forms such

mimesis
symbol
language

as the magical fetish. The fetish is characterized here by its inability to abstract from the object it wants to represent, for instance, by the need for the fetish literally to have something of the object in order to represent it, such as using a person's actual hair. Representation is hereby achieved through a kind of metonymic transubstantiation. This primitive mimesis is contrasted critically with the development of more purely codified systems of language in which there is only an arbitrary connection between the sign and what it represents (as for Saussure). However, Adorno and Horkheimer do not propose this primitive mimesis as simply the truth that has been lost by the development of reason and which needs to be recovered as it was. Rather, it makes explicit the entwinement of representation and domination that is subsequently suppressed by the generalization of domination into a necessary and universal principle of representation (*DE*: 6–7; *GS* 3: 25–7). This is understood as the evolution of abstract forms of representation in which there is a divergence of language's significatory aspect and its substantial or actual aspect, manifested by a divergence of its sign and image functions. The sacred symbol and hieroglyph are identified as two forms of language in which this divergence of sign and image has not yet been completed:

> The teachings of the priests were symbolic in the sense that in them sign and image coincided. As hieroglyphs attest, the word originally also had a pictorial function. This function was transferred to myths. They, like magical rites, refer to the repetitive cycle of nature, which is the core of the symbolic: an entity or a process which is conceived as eternal because it is reenacted again and again in the guise of the symbol. Inexhaustibility, endless renewal and the permanence of what they signify are not only attributes of all symbols, but their true content. (*DE*: 12; *GS* 3: 33)

It is in terms of this primal form of language that the concept of art and the arts is grounded, with poetry as the originary form of art, which breaks down into the other arts through a process of rationalization:

> With the clean separation between science [*Wissenschaft*] and poetry [*Dichtung*] the division of labour which science had helped to establish was extended to language [*Sprache*]. For science the word is first of all a sign [*Zeichen*]; it is then distributed among the various arts as sound, image or word proper [*als Ton, als Bild, als eigentliches Wort*], but its unity can never be restored by the addition of these arts, by synaesthesia or total art [*Gesamtkunst*]. As sign, language must resign itself to being calculation and, to know nature, must renounce the claim to resemble it. As image it must resign itself to being a likeness and, to be entirely nature, must renounce the claim to know it. (*DE*: 12–13; *GS* 3: 34)

The task of the critical self-reflection of the enlightenment for Adorno and Horkheimer is not to try and recover the prelapsarian origin of language or *Ursprache* immediately. Since this origin is identified with a traumatic threat to self-preservation, this is hardly salvation. And since that origin is necessarily mediated by subsequent forms of culture (such as language as it developed), what that origin is can, at best, only be negatively conceived. Rather, the task is to try and make enlightenment self-conscious of the repression that culture engaged in in order to preserve itself, with the promise that such self-consciousness or memory (as for Freud) will absolve culture from the repetition of its internalized trauma. Art is one of the ways in which this process takes place, insofar as it departs from the rationalized reduction of mimesis to a copy of something else, and generates forms of substantial self-relation that contradict the tendency towards abstract forms of communication. Art is therefore a semblance that is not reducible to being the appearance or representation of something else. It transforms its material into something different from and resistant to the abstract form of material, something self-insistent. But it does not therefore present the origin or absolute positively. Its semblance character prevents this and means that it only reveals the repression internalized through the enlightenment, through the mediation of the enlightenment itself. This explains why Adorno is so critical of projects to reveal an originary language positively, or a synaesthetic overcoming of the alienated sensibility of enlightenment rationalization, or indeed a *Gesamtkunstwerk* that would overcome the alienation of the arts from one another. All these projects propose to recover the origin of culture immediately and thereby appeal to it in an inevitably mythic form.

A NEGATIVE DIALECTIC OF THE ARTS

The foregoing underpins, and is clarified by, Adorno's 'Art and the Arts'. Its principal preoccupation is the diversity and hybridization of the arts; the extent to which they belie a unifying concept of art, or a conception of the relation of the arts to art as a harmonious and equitable partition of a unifying concept or substance. (He cites Hans G. Helms's assumption of serial music techniques in the novel, presumably a reference to *FA: M'AHNIESGWOW*, and the affinity of Sylvano Bussotti's musical notation to drawing, among other examples.) Adorno therefore addresses a confluence of the arts that speaks directly to the predicament faced today.

Adorno does not identify this predicament as simply the result of cultural decline, requiring a more regulated disciplining of the arts (in the way that some neo-Greenbergians have implored). Neither does he embrace it as a simple emancipation from the discipline of an ordered relation of art and the arts (a position all too familiar among post-Greenbergians). Rather he diagnoses this situation as expressive of the inherently antagonistic relation of art and the arts. For Adorno, each artwork is bound to a moment of unsublatable particularity, which it attempts to render 'eloquent' or meaningful in the attempt to make art, but which is finally resistant to identity with the ideal of art. This prevents artworks from being completely autonomous or purified of non-art. Each artwork *works* on this particularity and art at the same time, and is constituted by this tension. The forms of this tension constitute the arts, which emerge through the various ways in which the artwork attempts to achieve art. Hence, the situation of modern art is understood as structured by a dynamic model of non-art, artwork, arts and art. Art is not simply a persistent illusion, which should be dissolved according to a nominalism for which the only real thing would be the arts or the artworks, or perhaps even the materials of the artworks. Art as such is at stake in each authentically modern artwork according to Adorno, and the fact that it is not positively or completely fulfilled in any particular artwork is not symptomatic of idealism, but descriptive of the antagonistic and hybrid character of modern art. Nor is this a mystical or unthinkable chaos, since art is hereby rendered dialectical in the emphatic sense that its unity is only derived from the difference of its moments. However, unlike Hegel, this dialectical unity is not positive, insofar as the difference of the arts is not finally rendered identical with the idea of art. For Adorno, the idea of art remains negative, since it is not able to render the particularity of each art internal to the self-determination of the idea of art:

> In contrast to the arts, art is something that forms itself, something contained potentially in each of the arts insofar as each must seek to liberate itself from the contingency of its quasi-natural aspects by going through them. *But such an idea of art within the arts is not positive; it is nothing that one can grasp as simply present in them, but only as negation. . . .* Art has its dialectical essence in that it accomplishes its movement towards unity only by passing through multiplicity. Otherwise art's movement would be abstract and powerless. Art's relation to the empirical stratum of reality is essential to it. If it skips that relation, then what it takes to be its spirit remains exterior, like some outer garment; only immersed in the empirical stratum can spirit become substance. The constellation of art and the arts lives within art itself. (*GS* 10.1: 448)

The relation of art to the arts is therefore a model of what Adorno understands by 'negative dialectics'. The speculative experience of art – that is, the absolute unity in disunity of art and the arts, of concept and particularity – is not just abandoned as an illusion, but sustained negatively, as a semblance of truth. It reveals the semblance of the identity of art and the arts as the truth that they are not reconciled through their identity, but through their non-identity.

What is striking about this account is the radical criticism it implies of the generic identification of literature with art as such. Since, despite the privilege literature or poetry is shown to have elsewhere in Adorno's writings, here such a generic or absolute status is strictly excluded, or at least subject to criticism. Adorno is certainly explicit in this criticism of others, such as Rudolf Borchardt and especially Heidegger who is his principal target here as elsewhere. Heidegger maintains this privileged role for poetry emphatically: it is for him the essence of art. But it is assumed through an ontological conception of poetry [*Dichtung*], which is conceived in much more expansive terms than conventional forms of poetry [*Poesie*]. Indeed, the ontological significance of *Dichtung* is so profound that Heidegger maintains that it seems to exceed all the arts put together:

> Poetry [*Dichtung*] is thought of here in so broad a sense and at the same time in such an intimate essential unity with language and word, that we must leave open whether art [*Kunst*] in all its modes, from architecture to poesy [*Poesie*], exhausts the essence of poetry [*Dichtung*]. (Heidegger 1996: 199; 2003: 76)

Adorno fully recognizes the ontological constitution of Heidegger's expanded conception of poetry. But this is precisely his objection, insofar as this involves a dissolution of the difference of the arts into an immediate essence or origin of art: 'Through that ontologization [of *Dichtung*] ... the distinctions of the arts, the relatedness to their materials, is conjured away as subordinate' (*GS* 10.1: 446). Furthermore, Heidegger's radically expanded conception of poetry still has the retrospective effect of a familiar privilege of poetry even in its narrower sense. As Heidegger himself makes clear, 'the linguistic work, poetry [*Dichtung*] in the narrow sense, has a privileged position in the domain of the arts' (1996: 198; 2003: 75).

Heidegger's reason for this privilege partakes of the same significance of language for the development of human culture that Adorno maintains, although for Heidegger this is conceived according to the ontological programme of revealing the Being of beings, which is disclosed here through the allegorical structure of naming: 'Language [*Sprache*], by naming beings for the first time, first brings beings to word and appearance. Only this naming nominates beings *to* their Being *from out of* their Being' (1996: 198; 2003: 75). The other arts are therefore disclosed in a horizon or space that has always already been 'opened' by language or *Dichtung*. This makes it effectively the generic form of art for the other arts. And although Heidegger acknowledges the arts' specific inflections of art, they remain fundamentally constituted in terms of *Dichtung*:

> Building and forming [*Bauen und Bilden*] ... always happen already, and happen only, in the open region of saying and naming. It is the open region that pervades and guides them. But for this very reason they remain their own ways and modes in which truth directs itself to work.

They are the ever special poetizing [*ein je eigenes Dichten*] within the clearing of beings which has already happened unnoticed in language. (1996: 199; 2003: 75)

What becomes clear from Adorno's criticism of Heidegger is that the critical dialectic of art and the arts is oriented fundamentally *against* the generalization of poetry as art as such, even where it is conceived in the most expanded ontological forms. But, more importantly perhaps, it indicates the extent to which this argument is made in the face of the constitutive significance of language for the emergence of human culture, which, in a number of ways, profoundly inflects Adorno's own conception of art. Adorno's account of 'art and the arts' is therefore not merely a descriptive model of the plurality of the arts in which literature is critically delimited. It indicates a radical critique of the relation of literature to enlightenment that has profound consequences which are perhaps scarcely even elaborated in Adorno's own work. Rather than thinking the significance of art's relation to what the enlightenment represses through an essentially linguistically mediated narrative, what is suggested is a model in which this repression is absolved through the dynamically disjunctive constellation of arts, as that which emerges through what they are not. Thus, rather than treat the antagonism of the arts as a consequence of entrenched alienation, it is conceived as rendering negatively what cannot be rendered positively: that which enlightenment represses:

> Over and above their empty classificatory concept, we have only negatively unified the arts [*Kunstarten*] in terms of content: they all repel empirical reality, and tend towards the formation of a sphere qualitatively opposed to it: historically, they secularize the magical and the sacred. (*GS* 10.1: 448)

What enlightenment repressed lies entwined in magical and sacred forms. For Adorno, modernist art recovers this, and does so in the self-consciousness of its entwinement in enlightenment. Art therefore engages in a secular, critical salvaging, which does not take place through the positive presentation of what was repressed. This would be both impossible without the mediation of subsequent forms and, even if that were possible, would simply repeat the trauma that caused this repression in the first place. Rather, it is presented negatively through the constellation of the arts; through that transformation of nature that each art engages in without being able to make it harmonize with art as such. And yet, through that failure, art generates an image of nature as that which is not reducible to either empirical reality or its beautiful harmonization with the ideal: nature as if it were free of the domination of rationalization. The fact that the relation of art to the enlightenment emerges historically through the significance of language does not become a justification for the privilege of literature. This logic of regression is completely inappropriate here. In fact, this privilege of literature becomes a myth insofar as it insists on this hereditary privilege. As such, the mythic privilege of literature as an art becomes an object that needs to be critically dissolved in order to reveal the fully disjunctive constellation of art and the arts.

CONCLUSION

Adorno offers an alternative, critical account of the modern system of the arts and its contemporary crisis as well as of the position of literature within it. The consequences of this are extensive, not least for the coherence of Adorno's own writings. I conclude by briefly indicating three of these consequences, suggesting some propositions or theses for further examination.

The first emerges from Heidegger's essay on 'The Origin of the Work of Art'. Heidegger prefaces his argument about the world-disclosive character of art by distinguishing the artwork from various conceptions of 'the thing', which are nonetheless traditionally presupposed by the concept of art: a subject with properties, a sensible perception or a formed matter. What is indicated here with respect to Adorno's account is that the attempt to apprehend the non-identity of art and the arts is scarcely satisfied by traditional forms of differentiation such as different sensibilities, or different forms, which evidently immediately presuppose and partake of a unifying concept of art as the totality of sensibility or form. Heidegger uses this criticism of the presupposition of sensibility to justify the move from thinking about aesthetics to thinking about art. Adorno maintains that aesthetics should take place through the examination of particular works, although this is scarcely always true. He therefore seems to pursue the historical trend that Hegel makes explicit in displacing aesthetics with the philosophy of art. But Adorno's refusal to engage in the sublimation of nature he diagnoses in Hegel seems to motivate the persistent thematization of art in terms of sensibility. This is fundamental to his somatic metaphysics of experience. Nonetheless, if the critique of art demands the radical critique of all that had previously been assumed to be nature, then the critique of sensibility, with its presupposition of the embodied subject, becomes central to the questioning of aesthetics as a discourse on art and the arts.

Jean-Luc Nancy raises a second consideration in his essay 'Why are there Several Arts and not Just One?'. Despite a deeper debt to Adorno than he acknowledges, Nancy proposes a distinctive conception of the implications of the problem of the multiplicity of the arts. This involves a plural and finite overcoming of the hypostatized absolutization of art in Romanticism, which he takes to be an essential precondition for the present:

> The romanticism of 'art' – of absolute or total art – consists in hypostatising the Infinite End (Poetry, Fragment, or *Gesamtkunstwerk*). With

that, technique dissolves into the form of the 'genius'. To overcome romanticism is to think rigorously the in-finite, which is to say, its finite, plural, heterogeneous constitution. Finitude is not the deprivation but the in-finite affirmation of what incessantly *touches* on its end: another sense of existence and, by the same token, another sense of 'technique'. (Nancy 1996: 37)

The pluralization of the arts exposes a pluralization of techniques, which enables a dissolution of the hypostatization of an infinite end. This would enable the dissolution of a technique or technology which reduces to mere means all that is not yet that infinitely receding end. The overcoming of instrumental reason is therefore identified with the overcoming of the absolutized end of art. In many respects this elaborates very elegantly the profound consequences of the constellational form of art and the arts for the critique of instrumental reason. Moreover, it makes explicit its ambivalent relation to Romanticism.

Finally, if Adorno's aesthetic theory tends to conceive of the problem of art in conspicuously linguistic terms, then undoubtedly this is enforced by the linguistic medium of philosophizing that Adorno was particularly sensitive to, and his claim that art completes itself through philosophy. Indeed, as we saw from the various theories of the arts that privilege literature – Hegel is clearly exemplary here – this privilege is maintained in part by the proximity of literature or poetry to philosophy, not least because philosophizing tends to be received and pursued in a linguistic form. (Although, for Hegel, philosophy sublates this mediation in a way that, for instance, Novalis rejects or puts down to philosophy's loss.) The consequence of the displacement of literature's privilege among the arts suggests a critical delimitation of what may be considered a literary prejudice in philosophizing, which has been so prevalent in aesthetic responses to the linguistic turn in philosophy. But, given that philosophy cannot abandon mediation by its aesthetic form without the risk of idealism, the implication emerges that philosophizing needs to mediate itself through every art, whether that is music, sculpture or any more hybrid form.

NOTES

1   'Literature is Dead', Cabinet Gallery, London, 26 April to 17 May 2003.
2   Larry Shiner has observed the indeterminate expansiveness in the conception of literature prior to the modern system of art, arguing that, in the mid-1600s, 'terms like "*belles-lettres*", "poetry" and "literature" were still not fixed in their modern sense, and "literature" continued to be used primarily to mean book learning in general. Late in the century, however, an additional meaning began to attach to the term "literature", as reflected in Pierre Richelet's *Dictionnaire françois* of 1680, which defined it as "knowledge of *belles-lettres*" or the work of "Orators, Poets and Historians". Even so, Antoine Furetière, compiler of a competing dictionary a few years later, said of the term "*belles-lettres*" (no doubt with Richelet in mind): "People call humane letters, or

erroneously *belles-lettres*, the knowledge of poets and orators, whereas true *belles-lettres* are physics, geometry and solid sciences" '. (2001: 69)

3   An illustration of this table is published in Shiner 2001: 85.

4   '[W]e can choose ... no more convenient principle than the analogy between the arts and the way people express themselves in speech so as to communicate with one another as perfectly as possible, namely, not merely as regards their concepts but also as regards their sensations. Such expression consists in *word, gesture*, and *tone* (articulation, gesticulation, and modulation)' (Kant 1987: 189–90).

5   'Proposition 73. *The ideal unity, as the resolution of the particular into the universal, of the concrete into the concept, becomes objective in* speech *or* language' (Schelling 1989: 99).

6   Various English translations from the German have been silently modified by the author in what follows. Where this has been done, references to the original German are also given.

7   All translations of this essay are my own. A translation by Rodney Livingstone has recently been published (*AA*).

8   Adorno and Horkheimer associate this emergent paradox with Hubert and Mauss's concept of sympathy or mimesis in their 'Théorie générale de la Magie' (1902–3). See *DE*: 256n.; *GS* 3: 31–2n.

WORKS CITED

Art & Language (1999), 'Introduction [to *Art-Language: The Journal of Conceptual Art*]' [1969], in A. Alberro and B. Stimson (eds), *Conceptual Art: A Critical Anthology*. Cambridge, MA: MIT Press, pp. 98–105.

Benjamin W. (1996), 'The Concept of Criticism in German Romanticism', trans. D. Lachterman, H. Eiland and I. Balfour, in *Selected Writings*, vol. 1, ed. M. Bullock and M. W. Jennings. Cambridge, MA: Belknap/Harvard University Press, pp. 116–200.

Bowie, A. (1997), *From Romanticism to Critical Theory: The Philosophy of German Literary Theory*. London and New York: Routledge.

Danto, A. C. (1986), *The Philosophical Disenfranchisement of Art*. New York: Columbia University Press.

de Duve, T. (1996), *Kant After Duchamp*. Cambridge, MA: MIT Press.

Greenberg, C. (1992), 'Towards a Newer Laocoön', in C. Harrison and P. Wood (eds), *Art in Theory, 1900–1990: An Anthology of Changing Ideas*. Oxford: Blackwell, pp. 554–60.

Hegel, G. W. F. (1970), *Vorlesungen über die Ästhetik I*, in *Werke in Zwanzig Bänden*, ed. E. Moldenhauer and K. M. Michel, vol. 13. Frankfurt: Suhrkamp.

— (1975), *Aesthetics: Lectures on Fine Art*, trans. T. M. Knox, vol. 1. Oxford: Clarendon.

Heidegger, M. (1996), 'The Origin of the Work of Art', trans. A. Hofstadter, in D. F. Krell (ed.), *Basic Writings: Martin Heidegger*. London and New York: Routledge, pp. 139–212.

— (2003), *Der Ursprung des Kunstwerkes*. Stuttgart: Reclam.

Kant, I. (1987), *Critique of Judgment*, trans. W. S. Pluhar. Indianapolis, IN: Hackett.

Kosuth, J. (1999). 'Art after Philosophy' [1969], in A. Alberro and B. Stimson (eds), *Conceptual Art: A Critical Anthology*. Cambridge, MA: MIT Press, pp. 158–77.

Kristeller, P. O. (1990), 'The Modern System of the Arts', in *Renaissance Thought and the Arts: Collected Essays*. Princeton, NJ: Princeton University Press, pp. 163–227.

Nancy, J.-L. (1996), 'Why Are There Several Arts and Not Just One?', in *The Muses*, trans. P. Kamuf. Stanford, CA: Stanford University Press, pp. 1–39.

Plato (1989), *Symposium*, trans. M. Joyce, in *The Collected Dialogues of Plato*, ed. E. Hamilton and H. Cairns. Princeton, NJ: Princeton University Press, pp. 526–74.

Russell, J. (ed.) (2003), *Frozen Tears: The Word is Flesh*. London: ARTicle Press.

Schelling, F. W. J. (1989), *The Philosophy of Art*, trans. and ed. D. W. Scott. Minneapolis: University of Minnesota Press.

Schlegel, F. (1997), *Dialogue on Poesy*, in *Theory as Practice: A Critical Anthology of Early German Romantic Writings*, trans. and ed. J. Schulte-Sasse, H. Horne, A. Michel, E. Mittman, A. Oksillof and L. C. Roetzel. Minneapolis: University of Minnesota Press, pp. 180–93.

Shiner, L. (2001), *The Invention of Art: A Cultural History*. Chicago, IL and London: University of Chicago Press.

2

Adorno's Critical Presence: Cultural Theory and Literary Value

Martin Ryle and Kate Soper

Adorno provides us neither with 'literary theory', nor with a substantial body of detailed critical and historical studies of literature. Essays such as those on Kafka and Huxley in *Prisms*, and on *Endgame* in *Notes to Literature*, illuminate the texts that they discuss, but few methodological generalizations can be drawn up on their basis. Adorno's general critical remarks often have an aphoristic cast, and this is not just a stylistic option: it implies distrust for elaborated and explicit literary-theoretical discourse. Fragmentary formulations suggest an internally conflicted orientation towards writing, criticism and the world, and suggest also that only in fragments can truth, necessarily dialectical, be expressed. 'The whole is the false': the phrase from *Minima Moralia* (*MM*: 50) implies that claims to tell the whole truth belie themselves in the utterance.

What we piece together from our encounter with Adorno is not a system, but a presence, a register, a critical attitude. We shall try to show here how this presence, even in the negative responses it may provoke, can prompt and shape our thoughts when we reflect on the uses and practice of criticism. We begin by reviewing Adorno's critique of 'mass culture', which is the negative corollary of his concern for literary value and of his conviction that art, precisely unlike commercial non-art, must express 'the negativity of the positive' (*NL1*: 35). No doubt, Adorno is insufficiently nuanced and dialectical in his account of the 'mass' subject, and pays too little attention to the role of education: here, his English counterparts, from Arnold through Leavis to Williams, offer a valuable corrective or supplement. This failing weakens further the claims one might make for the directly political pertinence of Adorno's literary aesthetics. Nonetheless, the presence of Adorno as intransigent critic of mass culture can help us hold out against the practice, so general in contemporary academic literary-cultural studies, of treating the work of literary art as one more instance of discourse in general. In our second section we note, beyond his reference to a specifically modernist aesthetic, the broadly Aristotelian provenance of Adorno's largest claims about art, truth and totality: 'Art is magic delivered from the lie of being truth' (*MM*: 222); 'Art ... as art ... stands in an antithetical relationship to the status quo' (*NL1*: 224). Our final section suggests how such claims help us to appreciate Kazuo Ishiguro's novel *Never Let Me Go*, and shows in practice why it is still worth thinking with, and against, Adorno.

THE CRITIC AND THE 'MASS'

Never a central point of reference in Anglo-American literary studies, Adorno's work has become even more marginalized with the advent of a cultural studies perspective.[1] There are two main reasons for this. The first is his disdain for mass culture and the associated focus on literary modernism. The other is the sense that his work has little relevance to the issues of identity politics ('race', feminism, the post-colonial subject) that have become so central to cultural studies of literature (Soper 1999: 67–70; 2004: 49–52). Together, these factors have created an impression of Adorno as an outdated critic, a complex and principled thinker maybe, but something of a dead white male in his ivory tower. However, while the tone of his writing sometimes encourages that impression, it is simplistic to conclude that Adorno is an elitist – unless that term is used to characterize any critical practice that is aesthetically evaluative, rather than quasi-sociological, in selecting and discussing texts.

Adorno's address is often irritatingly donnish and even priggish. It can indeed be difficult to get one's enthusiasm back after reading: 'Every visit to the cinema leaves me, against all my vigilance, stupider and worse' (*MM*: 25). We want, all the same, to defend his exacting approach to art, and to insist that aesthetic discrimination should not be confused with social snobbery. Adorno's dismissal of the culture industry's offerings did not imply that popular taste must inherently and always remain incapable of appreciating art and literature. His contempt for the cultural pap served up to the masses did not entail contempt of those to whom it was served, and who found enjoyment in it. For his essential argument was that the power of enjoying and understanding serious and demanding culture had already been pre-empted for most people by the division of labour and its socio-economic oppressions. The entertainments provided by the culture industry were therefore seen by him as the final insult flung at those whose sensibilities had already been discouraged and blunted. Adorno's aesthetic point of view was always orchestrated by his conviction that mutilation had already done its damage, and that bourgeois society then compounded the offence by attributing to the worker a 'pure' freedom and spontaneity of taste that had in fact never been allowed to develop. Therefore the critic of commodified culture should on no account fall prey to the same error by blaming the victim for the consequences of the theft. Neither, on the other hand, should the critic refuse to recognize the expropriation, or deny the role and importance of art in inspiring that critique and sustaining a sense of what had been stolen.

class - power - taste

However, although this understanding of the 'mass' subject is in principle dialectical, it is in effect static and rigid in much of Adorno's criticism. The objection to his position on mass culture is not that he says rude things about mass-cultural products, but that he is reluctant to engage in any discussion of the complex and fluid relations between class, culture, education and social mobility that have been characteristic of industrialized societies since the late nineteenth century. As a philosopher, Adorno was always resistant to any assimilation of concrete particulars under general concepts or subsumption of the individual in the collective. In his 'negative dialectics' he has been credited with providing the philosophical tools for both respecting 'difference' and advancing beyond the limits of deconstructive readings – and has been taken up by some feminist and post-colonial theorists for this reason (Dayan-Herzbrun, Gabriel and Varikas 2004; Varadharajan 1995).[2] Nevertheless he often writes on culture as if there were nothing within the social spectrum other than the 'mass' of the oppressed on the one hand and the aloof modernist critical thinker on the other. Although he criticizes Huxley's limited and puritanical conception of happiness in *Brave New World* (*P*: 95–117), he reproduces a similar image of complacent and unresisting totality from which only the most exceptional individual will sense his alienation.

Lacking here is any recognition that alongside the growth of the mass culture that Adorno deplored, twentieth-century societies made available to new social groups cultural education and cultural pleasures of the kind he approved. Accepting that his experiences of Nazi Germany and the United States were very different from what, say, Raymond Williams knew in social-democratic Britain, one still wants to say that where Adorno is truculent, evasive or silent, Williams both takes a historical view of these questions and relates them to current, collective experience: the experience of a generation of students, and of the engaged teacher of culture. We have argued elsewhere that emphasis on education, within a broader project of democratic change, provides one credible link – the only one, perhaps – between the specialized world of academic cultural critique and the wide horizon of political change which left-wing criticism, including Adorno's, nominally addresses and invokes (Ryle and Soper 2002). Thus Adorno does not really concern himself with how the enlightenment he claims for modernist writing, and the understanding embodied in his own work as a critic, might shine for ordinary mortals. In his celebrated reading of *Endgame*, he hails Beckett's subversion of existentialist pronouncements on *la condition humaine*. But we are left wondering what survives, after this critical and ontological tour de force, of any commonly accessible understanding of the kind supposedly disclosed by autonomous art. His analysis of art as that which keeps open the possibility of a world in which it might prove universally transfigurative, and ecstasy become the norm, makes it all the more essential that he provide some compelling account of how art might in practice play that role. But while he charges others (Brecht, Benjamin) with unwarranted romanticism for their faith in the possibility of epiphanic proletarian cultural experiences, Adorno errs in the opposite direction by never grappling seriously with the question of how the promise of autonomous art will be redeemed.

Adorno's insistence on the fixed, almost irredeemably negative nature of 'mass' life jeopardizes the claim he nonetheless wants to make about art's redemptive power, because it leaves us wondering who – apart from the critic – is supposed to be able to enjoy or understand art. It also prejudices his reading of literature. Even as he illuminates particular writers and works, he often suggests unhelpfully that writing is, or should be, always and only devoted to the representation of negativity. In 'The Position of the Narrator in the Contemporary Novel', for example, he argues that if novelists want to remain true to their realistic heritage and tell us how things really are, they must abandon a realism that only aids the façade in its work of camouflage by reproducing it. He then adds:

> The reification of all relationship between individuals, which transforms their human qualities into lubricating oil for the smooth running of the machinery, the universal alienation and self-alienation, needs to be called by name, and the novel is qualified to do so as few other art forms are. (*NL1*: 32)

Insight on fictional form is here coupled with so damning a version of fiction's object as to subvert the possibility of the truth the novel is credited with being able to reveal: for how can 'reification' and 'alienation' be represented as such if they are shown as 'universal'? Again, rejecting Lukács's reading of Joyce's use of myth, Adorno writes: 'Joyce does not create a fictional mythology beyond the world he represents but rather tries to conjure up that world's essence, or its essential horror' (*NL1*: 223). While he is right to reject the ahistorical reading, he is surely wrong to read *Ulysses* as a relentlessly 'horrified' view of the world. Joyce was aware of the 'nightmare' that was history, but his sense of how human lives might run their course within it was a good deal more comic and less judgemental than the phrase 'essential horror' implies.

Reluctant to engage in detail with the contradictions and fractures in social-historical reality, Adorno disengages from much of the literary work in which these are more fully reflected. Critical insights such as he attributes almost exclusively to modernist fiction are also at work – indeed, more obviously so – in other and earlier novels. He gives rather little credit to the impact of those realist and naturalist writers (most obviously, Zola) who focused directly on the active participants in social labour and on the commodification of the worker's body and spirit. Are we to understand that the realism of the nineteenth century was always 'affirmative', without critical significance in its own time or since? We note below that Adorno did acknowledge, if only implicitly, the limits of a 'strict and pure' literary aesthetic that could give no account of realism. What we emphasize here is the danger – which has ramifications beyond theoretical aesthetics – that formal 'purity' may encourage and mask a refusal of the impure world. The 'detachment' Adorno prizes in critic and writer (associated with his idea of modernist as against realist writing) is surely a much more equivocal advantage than he suggests when he writes that 'the detached observer is as much entangled as the active participant; the only advantage of the former is insight into his entanglement, and the infinitesimal freedom that lies in knowledge as such' (*MM*: 26). This fails to acknowledge the ignorance that detachment can breed, the knowledge that participation (not excluding participation in impurity) can engender, and the possibility that the 'active participant' may simultaneously be or become the 'detached observer'. Since it follows from Adorno's own analysis that he too, as modernist critic, has only a partial view on the social whole, one is surprised how little he reflects on the insights that the relatively privileged intellectual might gain from the perspectives of other social actors. Too little, in short, is said either about how the modernist sensibility might speak to the masses, or about how the 'active participants', who have their dialectical right to figure in any Adornian critical register, might actually enter into dialogue.

These are substantial objections. Nonetheless, we value Adorno's critical presence just because of what is often seen as its elitism. The founding presumption of his criticism, namely that only a few works are worth serious attention, is a corrective to contemporary readings that are reluctant to make value judgements or that base those judgements mainly on the appraisal of texts as registers of 'identity'. In opposition to those who present the suspension of aesthetic discrimination as favouring a more democratic pedagogy, Adorno suggests that those who refuse to discriminate may be colluding in the continued cultural deprivation that is the basis of 'mass' taste. This sets the critics of aesthetic elitism in a more dialectical (not to say equivocal) light: as lending themselves, despite their progressive claims, to a conservative inhibition of popular access to high culture. In condoning a status quo in which readers are to settle for what they already like, or can identify with, rather than what they might otherwise come to appreciate, this sets a seal of approval on a comfortable rather than ecstatic conception of personal liberation and cultural fulfilment. The upshot is a positivistic idealism, whereby the cultural democracy that has yet to be in any serious sense achieved can supposedly be accomplished through a mere shift of aesthetic perspective: all it demands is a gestalt shift – the revelation that after all, one literary offering is no better than another. So enjoy.

What is more, academic critics of cultural elitism do not excise all difficulty when it comes to teaching; they often expect students to read popular texts through the grid of complex interpretative theory. Equally, they retain a specific cultural authority in selecting which texts are to count as signifiers of 'identity'. There is something contradictory in deploring difficulty in texts while reinstating it at the level of their study. At the same time, we question any critical position that reduces cultural politics to a matter of 'identity', or analyses literary value in terms of what writing can provide by way of self-discovery or personal affirmation. Such an approach offers a restricted conception of what literature has to offer. And just because it favours work presented as consoling or confirming immanent 'identities', it neglects the capacity of literature to summon readers towards a more transcendent point of view which can then afford some purchase on the textual (and social) construction of identity in general. Complex texts can open up for readers a quasi-authorial position from which they partake in the imaginary transcendence of representation (Ryle and Soper 2002: 95–6, 125–6).

Here too, Adorno's critical presence is to be invoked: specifically, his insistence on the 'objectivity' and 'aesthetic difference' that literary art produces, and by virtue of which it creates cognitive insights on a par with (though of course different in kind from) the knowledge we gain from science. Even when a great novel takes the form of extended personal recollection, as in Proust, this subjectivity, Adorno argues, issues in an objectivity that transcends the personal. Although it has no verification except through individual experience of the process of recollection, its 'individually synthesized unity, in which the whole nevertheless appears, cannot be distributed and recategorized under the separate persons and apparatuses of psychology and sociology' (*NL1*: 8). Elsewhere, against Lukács's rejection of Proust, Joyce and Beckett as merely subjective and hence decadently solipsistic and politically regressive, Adorno insists that their writing involves no denial of the object, but aims dialectically at its reconciliation with the subject: as the objective world becomes subject-ivized in the novel, its 'image' exposes, and thereby critiques, its 'aesthetic difference' from reality. The 'great avant-garde works cut through the illusion of subjectivity' to reveal the solitary consciousness as itself a social product, and thus in some sense the consciousness of all (*NL1*: 229–31; see also *MM*: 84, 69–70).

This claim for the 'objectivity' of modernism rests on and supports a more general endorsement of the power of literary art to re-present the world so as to create aesthetic difference (and hence new forms of cognitive awareness) in readers. It is above all because he insists in such terms on the distinctive nature and quality of the work of literary art that we would invoke Adorno's presence against the tendency in the academic study of culture to assimilate any and every kind of writing to discourse-in-general.[3] If one side of this insistence is the critique of mass culture, the other, to which we now turn, is the celebration of art's 'magical' transcendence of the already-known.

'MAGICAL' ART, MODERNISM AND DIFFICULTY

The editors of the collection *Aesthetics and Politics* rebuke Adorno for his 'magical' idea of art:

> The notion of a residual transcendental subject was structurally essential to Adorno's thought, furnishing the only point of leverage in a putatively totalitarian social order. ... No assessment of his aesthetics can overlook this semi-miraculous persistence of the subject in a conceptual schema that posits its complete reification. ... [In his aesthetic theory] the production of 'autonomous' works of art is little less than magical. (Bloch *et al.* 1977: 147)

Such criticism is at once confirmed and subverted by the fact that Adorno himself speaks explicitly of 'magic': 'Art is magic, delivered from the lie of being truth' (*MM*: 222). In the final aphorism of *Minima Moralia*, invoking the redemptive knowledge to be seized from 'perspectives' that 'displace and estrange the world', he describes such knowledge as 'utterly impossible', because it could only be acquired from 'a standpoint removed, even though by a hair's breadth, from the scope of existence' (the standpoint, that is, of the 'residual transcendent subject' he is accused of preserving) (*MM*: 247).[4] 'Magic', 'utterly impossible': these phrases court, but defy, dismissal, openly conceding the aporetic quality of the conceptions they express. The point is made in homelier terms earlier in *Minima Moralia*, where it is said that the critical thinker 'should be at every moment both within things and outside them – Münchhausen pulling himself out of the bog by his pig-tail becomes the pattern of knowledge which wishes to be more than either verification or speculation' (74). It is of course art which for Adorno offers the ideal 'pattern' of a knowledge that transcends the antithesis between mere positivism and mere fancy.

Adorno here refers implicitly to the philosophical tradition, originating in Aristotle's *Poetics*, that claims fiction is 'of graver import' than history: 'The historian describes the thing that has been, and the poet a kind of thing that might be. Hence poetry is something more philosophic and of graver import than history, since its statements are of the nature rather of universals, whereas those of history are singulars' (cited in Daiches 1967: 31). Adorno's insistence that art as art 'remains the antithesis of that which is the case' clearly has this Aristotelian provenance – albeit with a Hegelian inflection: for the term 'antithesis' implies, more strongly than Aristotle's statements of the nature of universals, that we find in art not a perhaps partial mimetic representation, but a total representation in which the world is shown more truly for being 'displaced and estranged'.[5] In suggesting the kind of redemptive knowledge that the subject of literary aesthetic experience can gain, Adorno mostly refers not to 'poetry' (fictive art) in general, but specifically to modernist fiction – often counterposed, notably in his argument with Lukács, to a residual realist tradition. It is in this spirit that he discusses Flaubert, Joyce, Proust, Kafka and Beckett.[6] Such selection of texts and the terms of Adorno's commentary favour the European modernist and proto-modernist fictional canon, which broke with the surface norms of quasi-historical narration that had in general governed nineteenth-century novels. Adorno values modernist writing especially because it eschews quasi-photographic rendering, and he has this in mind when he insists, contra Lukács, that only insofar as art 'became qualitatively distinct from ... immediate reality' can it give us knowledge not of 'existence' but of the latter's 'essence and image' (*NL1*: 224). Techniques of the 'most advanced' fiction, he writes elsewhere, negate the possibility of reading the work as if it were 'a report on the facts'; they 'break through foreground relationships and express what lies beneath them' (*NL1*: 34–5). In this, Adorno anticipates later critics who would note how modernist works displayed their own artifice, and posed, through formal difficulty or strangeness, problems of interpretation that the reader was required to grapple with (Ryle and Soper 2002: 161–2).

Adorno's insistence on the specific difference of literary art is valuable. However, the general application of his underlying preconceptions, as criteria for authentic literature, would leave us with a very limited canon. Adorno himself acknowledged the problem:

> Perhaps the strict and pure concept of art is applicable only to music, while great poetry or great painting – precisely the greatest – necessarily brings with it an element of subject-matter transcending aesthetic confines, undissolved in the autonomy of form. The more profound and consequential an aesthetic theory becomes, the more inappropriate it becomes to such works as the major novels of the nineteenth century. (*MM*: 223)

An 'aesthetic theory' of writing which cannot apply to major literary work is not so much 'profound' as inadequate. In effect, the passage concedes the limitations of a 'concept of art' too insistent on 'autonomy of form'.

Adorno is surely mistaken in valuing this 'aspect' absolutely, as if it marked the belated arrival of literary writing at its 'autonomous' essence. The prominence of the 'formal' in modernist writing is to be understood in part historically: as a means by which modernist writers (specifically, prose fiction writers, whose mongrel form had lacked both prestige and generic definition) differentiated their work from the ever-growing mass of printed words (see Ryle and Soper 2002: 161; Ryle 2005). For Aristotle, in a society where there was in any case relatively little in the way of written culture, 'history' and 'poetry' had been generically quite distinct. The problem for the literary artist in the conditions of large-scale commercial publishing was to create a self-selected audience attuned to, and demanding of, a more exacting art: an audience that would prefer, or might be persuaded to prefer, writing whose problematical form drew attention to artistic representation itself, as offering 'magical' knowledge rather than a quasi-historical 'report on the facts'. This differentiation of texts and audiences was fundamentally connected with the difficulty the work posed. Difficulty, as Allon White observes, served not just to distinguish modernist writing from other literary wares, but to secure for it the appropriate kind of readerly attention:

> Despite a remarkable diversity of intent and effect, modernist difficulty signifies in and by the very act of offering resistance. The formal, structural difficulties of a text, the kinds of de-formation that it uses, are inseparable from the way it produces significance, from its mode of signification. (1981: 16)

The textual difficulties of modernism were indeed diverse. The familiarity with classical and foreign languages and writings that Eliot, Pound and Joyce assumed or pretended to assume in their readers was possessed only by a small minority, but Woolf's innovations in the representation of consciousness, memory and the self, while they used unfamiliar syntax and made unexpected elisions and transitions, did not depend on specialist knowledge. The difficulties in most of Kafka, and in some of Beckett, are less in the textual surface than in the problem of interpretation presented by the work as a whole, including the question of whether it requires some kind of quasi-allegorical decoding.

Some of these kinds of difficulty are more problematic, in excluding less well-educated readers, than others. In general, however, and in any of these cases, modernist writing's 'mode of signification' involves reworking or subverting hitherto prevailing norms. Therefore its reader requires a sense of how literary writing has 'produced significance' in the past, and a readiness to find meaning in what is new. George Gissing's imaginary proto-modernist novel *Mr Bailey, Grocer*, described in *New Grub Street* (1891), is less convincingly imagined in its positive qualities than in its mere negation of established literary convention. It is summoned into being as a gesture of defiance against the commercial book-market, on which it is bound to fail; just because it will repel the average novel-reader, it will attract the experienced, discriminating few who can find pleasure and meaning in the fact of textual difference (Ryle 2005).

Difficulty, because its negotiation requires literary-cultural competence and self-confidence, has been an aspect of modernist writing often criticized as politically problematic. It is certainly a lacuna in Adorno's discussions of modernism that he never properly acknowledges that set of problems. Difficulty can be seen merely to inscribe elitism in the text, making literary work inaccessible just at the point where a sizeable reading public comes into being (Carey 1992). A more nuanced and dialectical version of that objection, which pays serious attention to Adorno (as Carey does not), is offered by Andreas Huyssen in *After the Great Divide*.[7] Huyssen rejects the idea that 'the only possibility for contemporary art [now lies] in a further elaboration of the modernist project' (1988: 43). Discussing the impact of the American series *Holocaust* when shown on German TV, he defends the aesthetic–political uses of the 'emotional identification' that the series encouraged, and which helped make it accessible to a mass audience, but which is ruled out by the 'artistic forms' favoured by 'the historical avant-garde' (108). (The argument assumes that broadly realist forms favour or permit 'identification', which will be inhibited by 'avant-garde' forms that prevent us reading the text as 'fact'. The assumption is tenable, though not axiomatic.) Huyssen's conclusion raises very general questions about mass and minority art and audiences:

> The success of this American TV series in Germany does indeed point to broader aesthetic and political problems. ... The vehemence of some left objections to *Holocaust* would then not only point to the blindness of the German left to the specificity of the Holocaust; it could furthermore be interpreted as a rear-guard struggle to hold on to an avant-garde aesthetic and politics of an earlier period which by now has become historical, if not obsolete, in its claim to universality and rationality. (1988: 114)

This argument and these questions are cognate, evidently, with some of the arguments advanced and rebutted in the 'earlier period' when the avant-garde was at work.

So far as the general question of art's (lack of) political valency is concerned, Huyssen never really establishes a position clearly distinct from Adorno's. He laments the severance of the link that once (he claims) joined artistic avant-garde and revolutionary political practice, but he has no doubt that mourning over its loss is futile (15). He berates academic critics for 'ossifying' (4) the moment of modernism, but cannot himself suggest with any conviction how artistic texts, events or experiences might contribute directly to 'the transformation of everyday life' (15). If the choice is put crudely – to categorize literary art as one mode of pedagogy; as Adornian 'antithesis'; or as a redundant bourgeois fetish – it is hard to know where Huyssen stands. However, he is no doubt right to remind those of us who prefer the more-or-less Adornian alternative that we can hardly claim direct political effect for the writing we admire.

We nonetheless remain wary of the suggestion that the democratically disposed critic should in principle favour work whose appeal to 'identification' is premised on its status as pseudo-'report on the facts'. It is in any case essential to avoid reducing the question of a work's value and meaning to an extrinsic question about its accessibility to this or that audience. Criticism and teaching should be ready in principle to defend, and elucidate, the resistance offered by textual difficulty. Of course this cannot be a matter of approving 'difficulty' as a means to differentiation: one has to show also that the interpretative work that the textual problems elicit will disclose interesting substantive meanings. Such defence and elucidation cannot profitably remain at the level of general formulations, but must engage with particular cases. It is to one such case that we turn in conclusion.

NEVER LET ME GO

Kazuo Ishiguro writes British 'literary fiction'. Having gained a reputation and a wide audience with the success of *The Remains of the Day* (which won the Booker Prize in 1989), he has embarked on a sequence of very original novels: *The Unconsoled* (1995), *When We Were Orphans* (2000) and *Never Let Me Go* (2005). In all of these, we find an unusual combination of formal distinction and substantive social reflection. As with any good writer, it would be a mistake to imply that Ishiguro's books can only or exhaustively be understood in an Adornian (or any other) critical perspective. But the ideas we have been developing here prove useful in identifying what is distinctive about a novel like *Never Let Me Go*. The 'magical' and 'antithetical' qualities we find there, as in Ishiguro's two preceding novels, are created by 'difficulty [that] signifies in and by the very act of offering resistance' (White 1981: 16). These novels simultaneously solicit and baffle interpretation. In the case of *Never Let Me Go*, the more obvious ways of reading the novel fail to produce a coherent set of meanings, and we are led towards some strikingly 'Adornian' (or better, post-Adornian) reflections on the education of the subject in a partial democracy which simultaneously develops and thwarts individuals' aesthetic sensibility and conviction of self-worth.

Ishiguro displays no special erudition. Nor does he write obscure or unusual prose: on the contrary, his style has a markedly neutral, everyday quality. The difficulty and the necessity of interpretation arise, rather, at the level of the novel's meaning as a whole. It is immediately readable, but ultimately puzzling, like the work of Kafka (with whom Ishiguro is sometimes compared) or like *Endgame* and *Waiting for Godot*. This is a more democratically accessible mode than that of most of the major modernists. (Here, Ishiguro's expressive choices are consistent with the ethical and political values this novel affirms.) By such means, Ishiguro has perhaps taken with him, into unsettling fictional territory, many readers first attracted by the more straightforward earlier novels. One might regard the doubleness of his later works, which both comply with and subvert the norms of realist literary fiction, as a compromise, and oppose it to the freer inventiveness of 'magic realism' (including that of a British writer such as Angela Carter) or to an uncompromised and uncompromising avant-garde practice (exemplified by B. S. Johnson in England, and Robbe-Grillet or Wittig in France, perhaps). However, in our view Ishiguro's form in *Never Let Me Go* is best understood in its own expressive terms. Its paradoxical, simultaneous distance from and closeness to the everyday is not just a matter of a compromise with realist conventions; rather, the elements that defy realism are clues that urge us towards the meaning, not of the text, but of the world.

Telling the story of a group of young people brought up in apparently favoured institutional settings only to discover they are clones whose destiny is to become organ donors, *Never Let Me Go* combines realism of psychology and setting with narrative elements that subvert the possibility of realist interpretation. It is unreadable as a 'report on the facts', and becomes increasingly so. We know – and the author knows we know – that institutions of that kind have not existed in Britain from the 1960s to the present, when the novel is explicitly set. However, the novel proves resistant also to some obvious kinds of non-realist reading. The most readily available set of alternative generic conventions would make it a speculative fiction, perhaps set in the immediate future (like Huxley's *Brave New World* or Orwell's *1984*). But if we try to read it that way, we run up both against Ishiguro's insistence that its setting is contemporary with its writing, and against internally implausible and incredible aspects. Why do the characters never make the slightest attempt to escape their destiny? How can a series of such institutions have been kept secret, or how can the society in which they are set accept without comment the presence in its midst of this sacrificial machine? If the novel intends to explore ethical questions about cloning, why are these never raised or discussed in any substantial way, either by the narrator-protagonist or by anyone else? It is a tribute to the compelling quality of Ishiguro's writing that even though few of the reviews have got beyond reading *Never Let Me Go* as a 'novel about cloning' (generally, a humanistic 'protest' about cloning), the reviewers have mostly refrained from raising these rather obvious objections to its plausibility and internal coherence.[8]

Rather than reading 'cloning' as the theme of a speculative fiction, we read it as a narrative metaphor, creating (with other metaphorical elements) not a schematic allegory, but a dreamlike parable. As ever with Ishiguro, the elements that puzzle us until we find their meaning refer not inwards, to the discretely decipherable riddles of a closed text, but outwards. The book's questions are about the life we lead, and refer us both to the trans-historic nature of being (the mortality of the body) and to the particular moment of a collective, social-democratic society whose project was to realize, more fully than ever before, the potential, specifically the creative imaginativeness, of every human subject. What is the purpose of fostering the creative imagination of beings whose fate is to live for a while and then die? What kind of world is it in which not even the evidence of lifelong love can defer what awaits the lovers? In sum, and in complex ways which we can only gesture at here, the novel makes us aware of the almost utopian promise of the world that Ishiguro's generation knew, in favoured places like Britain: 'You were better off than many who came before you. And who knows what those who come after you will have to face' (Ishiguro 2005: 243). At the same time, it makes us aware of the limits of any such promise, which is thwarted in the first place by the inevitability of death – there is 'no truth in the rumour' that love wins immortality (236) – but then also by the anonymous, banal uses to which most lives are put in that same society which, in its collectively provided educational projects and institutions, had appeared to value and foster everyone's unique individuality. These are the 'facts', the ineluctable boundaries of nature but also the self-limiting ordinances of social being (which might be otherwise, and less limiting), that often remain unremarked in fictions that masquerade as 'reports on the facts', but which the readers of *Never Let Me Go* will find disclosed as the meaning of its resistant difficulties, as tragic destiny and as still unrealized possibility, as the 'essence and image' of our world.

NOTES

1   His record as a critic of patriarchy was, however, rather better than many of his period. It was against this background of neglect that Fredric Jameson advocated a return to Adorno (Jameson 1990).
2   Varadharajan has suggested, for example, that where deconstruction has in the end only offered the post-colonial reader a pious respect for 'difference' that ends up in withdrawal and refusal to know the 'other', and thus acts as a block on the development of political critique and solidarity, Adorno refuses to allow otherness to be appropriated by the dominant discourses of subjectivity, but also insists that representation of the other is essential to political recognition (1995: xiv–xv).
3   To trace the origins of this tendency within British literary studies, where it began in an impulse to deconstruct what were seen as bourgeois categories of literature and literary value, would take us too far afield here. But see Batsleer, Davies *et al.* (1985), Eagleton (1984), Jordan and Weedon (1995), and Widdowson (ed.) (1982). See also Ryle (1994), and the subsequent debate between Ryle and Antony Easthope in *Radical Philosophy* 70 (March/April 1995).
4   The concept, or conceit, of one who is simultaneously inside and outside the world that s/he critically judges is a recurrent motif in Adorno: see for example aphorisms 6 ('Antithesis'), 41 ('Inside and outside') and 46 ('On the morality of thinking') in *Minima Moralia* (*MM*: 26, 66, 74), and the essay 'Cultural Criticism and Society' (*P*: 17–34).
5   See *NL1*: 224: 'Art exists within reality, has its function in it, and is also inherently mediated with reality in many ways. But nevertheless, as art, by its very concept it stands in an antithetical relationship to the status quo.'
6   See *NL1*: 30–6. The long essay on Huxley in *Prisms* is a striking exception to Adorno's usual preference for modernist writing (is it possible that he thought Huxley a good writer?), and there are several critical essays on German poetry. But Adorno offers little sustained consideration of the major realist fictional tradition, and clearly believes, contra Lukács, that attempts to write realist fiction in twentieth-century conditions are without value.

7   Huyssen's second chapter is a careful critique of the 'culture industry' thesis, which
     however we have no space to summarize here.
8   To discuss particular reviews is not possible, given the limits of space. For access to a
     large number of reviews in the mainstream British and North American press, go to the
     Ishiguro links at www.completereview.com (consulted April 2005). Our very general
     remarks here do not cover all even of the reviews we have noticed.

WORKS CITED

Batsleer, J., Davies, T., O'Rourke, R. and Weedon, C. (1985), *Rewriting English: Cultural Politics of Gender and Class*. London and New York: Methuen.

Bauman, Z. (1997), *Life in Fragments: Essays in Postmodern Morality*. Oxford: Blackwell.

Bloch, E., Lukács, G., Brecht, B., Benjamin, W. and Adorno, T. W. (1977), *Aesthetics and Politics*, ed. R. Taylor. London: New Left Books.

Carey, J. (1992), *The Intellectuals and the Masses: Pride and Prejudice among the Literary Intelligentsia, 1880–1939*. London and Boston, MA: Faber and Faber.

Daiches, D. (1967), *Critical Approaches to Literature*. London: Longman.

Dayan-Herzbrun, S., Gabriel, N. and Varikas, E. (eds) (2004), *Adorno critique de la domination: une lecture féministe*. Paris: Editions Kimé.

Eagleton, T. (1984), *The Function of Criticism*. London: Verso.

Huyssen, A. (1988), *After the Great Divide: Modernism, Mass Culture and Postmodernism*. London: Macmillan.

Ishiguro, K. (1995), *Never Let Me Go*. London: Faber and Faber.

Jameson, F. (1990), *Late Marxism: Adorno, or the Persistence of the Dialectic*. London: Verso.

Jordan, G. and Weedon, C. (1995), *Cultural Politics: Class, Gender, Race and the Postmodern World*. Oxford: Blackwell.

Ryle, M. (1994), 'Long live literature? Englit, radical criticism and cultural studies', *Radical Philosophy* 67, 21–7.

— (1999), 'The usefulness of cultural studies', in N. Aldred and M. Ryle (eds), *Teaching Culture: The Long Revolution in Cultural Studies*. Leicester: NIACE, pp. 39–51.

— (2005), ' "To show a man of letters": Gissing, cultural authority and literary modernism', in M. Ryle and J. B. Taylor (eds), *George Gissing: Voices of the Unclassed*. Aldershot: Ashgate, n.p.

Ryle, M. and Soper, K. (2002), *To Relish the Sublime? Culture and Self-Realization in Postmodern Times*. London: Verso.

Soper, K. (1999), 'Relativism and utopianism: critical theory and cultural studies', in N. Aldred and M. Ryle (eds), *Teaching Culture: The Long Revolution in Cultural Studies*. Leicester: NIACE, pp. 66–78.

— (2004), 'Adorno, le féminisme et la promesse d'utopie', in Dayan-Herzbrun, Gabriel and Varikas (eds) (2004), pp. 49–60.

Varadharajan, A. (1995), *Exotic Parodies: Subjectivity in Adorno, Said and Spivak*. Minneapolis: University of Minnesota Press.

White, A. (1981), *The Uses of Obscurity: The Fiction of Early Modernism*. London: Routledge.

Widdowson, P. (ed.) (1982), *Re-Reading English*. London and New York: Methuen.

3

Interpretation and Truth:
Adorno on Literature and Music

Andrew Bowie

The idea that interpretation is no longer to be thought of as something which seeks the 'definitive' meaning of a text, be it the meaning the author intended, or the 'deep' meaning that underlies the surface phenomena of the text, has become commonplace in the humanities. The idea of defining meaning is now widely seen as relying on a notion of restoring the 'presence' of absent meaning that has questionable metaphysical consequences, because meaning is construed as a substance that is to be recovered in interpretation. In this context Derrida's two notions of interpretation in the essay 'Structure, Sign, and Play' represent a basic opposition that many assume is now definitive for the humanities. One interpretation – the one to which we are supposed to have said farewell – relies on the presence of meaning in a text that is dug out by the hermeneutic activity of the critic; the other gives up this notion in favour of the idea that meaning is unstable and ever-changing, depending on the contexts to which the signifiers of the text are connected (Derrida 1978: 292–3).[1] Like many kinds of new received wisdom, this theoretical consensus is important for having shaken up a lazy old consensus, but it may have been bought at rather too high a price. Arguably, one reason why attention to Derrida in some circles is being replaced by attention to Adorno is that there is a perceived need to reduce this price.

In some areas of theory in the humanities there has been a move back towards a concern with whether and how interpretations of texts are true, and I think that this has to be a good idea. The reason why is that assumptions about inherent undecidability of meaning can rapidly lead to the eternal recurrence of the same demonstration that any text can be shown to involve moments of undecidability, and thence to a failure to engage with texts as specific historical phenomena. Pragmatist and hermeneutic conceptions of texts as forms of action which can affect other actions have been underplayed or ignored as a consequence of the overriding concern with steering clear of the idea of meaning as a substance, even though most pragmatist and many hermeneutic conceptions do not rely on this idea in the first place. The interesting question is how the kind of truth in question here is to be construed without just falling back into bad versions of intentionalism or historicism, or getting into a philosophical mess with the notion of truth.

How, then, does one arrive at a way of thinking about truth which does not come into conflict with the fact that, as Rorty characteristically and aptly puts it, 'Truth is cheap'? On his largely Davidsonian construal we have to think that most of what people say is true, because we would otherwise be unable to understand when we disagreed with them about the truth of particular utterances. In these terms, if we can understand why someone says something this is very often because we can see why they think it is true. Provided we don't adhere to the probably vacuous idea of truth as correspondence to a reality independent of all that we can think and say about it, this means that true things are said all the time, the evidence for this being that we understand most of what is said most of the time. Truth in this sense is propositional and it merely muddies the waters to move away from this everyday sense of truth that everyone intuitively understands. The advantage of this position is that it brings truth down to earth, making it inseparable from the working of meaning in everyday life.

However, the idea that there is a need for a wider sense of truth than that gathered from the indefinite number of particular assertions we could understand and verify on the basis of their truth conditions, is, in varying ways, common to thinkers influenced by Heidegger's notion of truth as the horizon of world-disclosure, Gadamer's idea of truth as the happening of the work of art, or Adorno's reflections on art and truth. Adorno's pupil, Albrecht Wellmer, who used to wish to reserve truth for the everyday propositional sense, now argues that 'the concept of truth points of its own accord to a normative horizon which always transcends that of an argumentative dispute about the truth of individual assertions' (Wingert and Günther (eds) 2001: 52). Given that we never understand individual assertions in isolation from an indefinite number of other assertions, isolating individual assertions as the basis of our understanding of truth is problematic. What, though, makes an interpretation 'true', rather than 'right', or is there no difference from this perspective? In everyday terms we are familiar with true interpretation in relation to individual assertions and actions, or series of assertions and actions, but what sort of normative horizons do we require for truth in this wider sense? One normative horizon is the aesthetically conceived domain of literature, and I want to argue that one can add music to the idea of such horizons as well, not least because it gives one some useful purchase on how one can talk in a non-essentialist manner about the nature of literature. Indeed, it is the very fact that music proves to be crucial to this kind of approach to looking beyond the limitations of a semantic view of truth which puts Adorno at the centre of this issue and can suggest new paths for the relationship between philosophy and literature.

It is clear that in relation to literature and music we cannot think in the kind of terms which allow the definitive sense that one need go no further in interpretation that we encounter all the time in everyday interpretation. – Q. 'Did you mean this book, or the other one? A. 'That one'. 'OK'. End of story. – The need for a sense of truth which takes in what happens in literary interpretation often leads to a Kantian idea of the truth of interpretation being a 'regulative idea'. This is an idea that orients our thinking as the goal towards which it is striving, without us being able to claim to give an account of it which proves that what it refers to really exists. Interestingly this conception tends to be related as much to the natural sciences as to anything else. Kant uses the notion for the idea of nature as a complete law-bound system: we cannot know that nature really is such a system, but if it were, our cognitions would indeed have systematic coherence. The notion makes sense inasmuch as it involves a continuation of something which is already accepted as generating warranted truths, namely scientific inquiry. Rorty maintains in this respect that:

> A complete and final unified science, an harmoniously orchestrated assemblage of scientific theories none of which will ever need to be revised, is an intelligible goal. Scientific inquiry could, conceivably, terminate. So if a unified account of the causal relations between all spatio-temporal events were all that were meant by 'truth', even the most far-out postmodernist types would have no reason to doubt truth's existence. The existence of truth only becomes an issue when another sort of truth is in question. (Rorty 2000)

Rorty's interest is, though, in the kind of truth no longer associated with philosophy, for which there is 'a way things really are': 'It can therefore replace religion. The striving for Truth can take the place of the search for God' (Rorty 2000). Non-philosophical truth in his sense is connected to how art can make us see the world in new ways which are not reliant on the kind of truth generated by the sciences:

> [A] culture which has substituted literature for both religion and philosophy finds redemption neither in a non-cognitive relation to a non-human person nor in a cognitive relation to propositions, but in non-cognitive relations to other human beings, relations mediated by human artifacts such as books and buildings, paintings and songs. These artifacts provide glimpses of alternative ways of being human. (Rorty 2000)

These latter kinds of relations will include what Adorno means by the 'mimetic', and Rorty's conception here echoes in key respects the most plausible aspects of Adorno's position.

If we think of truth in literary interpretation as a regulative idea, we come up against an instructive problem. Rorty warns about the situation, implicit in the notion of a regulative idea, in which truth is 'an ever-retreating goal, one that fades forever and forever when we move'. This is, he argues, 'not what common sense would call a goal. For it is neither something we might realize we had reached, nor something to which we might get closer' (Rorty 1998: 39). The regulative idea of true interpretation, especially of a literary text, could consequently obscure precisely what matters about such a text, namely what it can reveal in concrete situations of reading that nothing else can (an idea which is compatible in certain respects with the deconstructive view of the effects of recontextualization). One way of seeing the hermeneutic circle entails that one can only know that one has reached the truth as a goal if one already has some access to what it is (hence the dialectic between whole and part in interpreting a text), otherwise there is no way of recognizing when one has reached the goal. Interpretation as regulative idea might therefore correspond to Derrida's first interpretation of interpretation, because the idea is seen as something like a substance inherent in the text, and this is clearly inadequate to literary interpretation. So what is the alternative, if we are still to talk about truth in interpretation?

Adorno is interesting in this context because he attempts to develop the notion of literary interpretation in relation to truth, but he does not do so in terms of truth in the semantic sense. He also, however, develops the notion of true interpretation in relation to music, and does so while employing a version of the notion of a regulative idea, which complicates the issues in instructive ways. In this connection his often-quoted remark that 'interpreting language means: understanding language; interpreting music means: making music' (*GS* 16: 253; *Q*: 3)[2] might seem to invalidate the link I want to make. This opposition will, though, turn out to be only relative, because making music also demands kinds of understanding which are not completely different from those required for literary texts. In what follows I want to suggest that Adorno's approaches to musical interpretation may have something to offer literary interpretation that is not always fully manifest in some of his more direct approaches. This will lead to a way of establishing a bridge between the interpretation of language and the interpretation of music that tells us something important about truth.

To see how the link between literature and music can be made, consider the following remark from 'Parataxis', Adorno's essay on Hölderlin: 'Great music is conceptless synthesis; this is the primal image of Hölderlin's late poetry' (*GS* 11: 471; *NL2*: 130). This remark points to a central aspect of Adorno's thinking. The significance of the 'conceptless' results from his critical approach to concepts, which he thinks of as inherently reducing particulars to a general schematic form, and thus as linked to the dangers of modern rationalization, which overlooks or represses difference in the name of identity. However, he offers a questionable version of this approach, and the objections one can make to it are valid for some other positions which claim that conceptual determination involves a repressive reduction of

difference to identity. If, following Wittgenstein and Rorty, one sees a concept as the use of a word, there is no reason to regard concepts as *inherently*
problematic. There will evidently always be cases of potentially repressive,
reductive usage, but there will also be other cases where apt use of a word
can actually reveal something otherwise obscured or not available. The
basic problem need not therefore be seen as intrinsic to conceptuality,
but has rather to do with the specific nature of the use of words in real
situations. Adorno at times relies on the notion that language is essentially
representational, which would make concepts into something inherently
reductive, but his position has more chance of success if read in a pragmatic direction.

What is needed here is a way of getting at the defensible aspect of
claims like the following, which, as it stands, relies on too rigid a distinction
between signification and mimesis: 'language is, by dint of its signifying
element, which is the opposite pole to the mimetic-expressive, tied to the
form of judgement and proposition. In contrast to music, conceptless
synthesis turns against the medium of poetry: it becomes a constitutive
dissociation' (*GS* 11: 471; *NL2*: 130). Poetry therefore has to oppose the
referential aspect of language, hence the connection of Hölderlin's poetry to
music as the non-referential art which becomes the paradigm of non-
referential, non-representational art in modernity (see Bowie 2003; 2006).

How, then, is this opposition between the referential and the mimetic
to be plausibly construed? Adorno generally refers to referential language
as 'intentional', that is language directed towards an object that involves
classifying judgements. At the same time he often refers to art as 'judgementless synthesis', which suggests the possibility of a mediation between
the extremes of reference/signification, and mimesis, because synthesis need
not be construed as conceptual identification: music is, he says, a 'sign
system for the intentionless' (*NS* 1.2: 239). The significance of this possible
mediation is apparent in the Hölderlin essay when he writes: 'What is
music-like [*musikhaft*] is the transformation of language into a sequencing
whose elements connect themselves differently from in the judgement'
(*GS* 11: 471; *NL2*: 131). Language is therefore able to be used in ways which
circumvent what he regards as problematic in judgement as a form based on
identification.[3] Like judgement, poetic language involves synthesis, but it is
synthesis of a kind which does not reduce its object to already familiar terms,
but seeks rather to arrive at something unique and individual. It should
already be clear that this idea of language involves a holism in which new
understanding results from the nature of the configuration of linguistic
elements, rather than from the sum of the supposed propositional content of
the elements. Wittgenstein refers in the *Investigations* to the idea of a poem
depending on 'something that only these words in these positions express'
and Adorno seeks to unfold the philosophical consequences of such an idea,
which he links to music.

What Adorno means can be made more concrete by looking at a few remarks from his essay 'The Essay as a Form', which connects the idea of the essay to music. Adorno considers the habitual philosophical opposition to rhetoric as a way of characterizing the particular nature of essay form: 'However, the objectionable transitions of rhetoric, in which association, ambiguity of words, diminishing of logical synthesis made it easy for the listener and subjugated the weak person to the speaker, become fused with truth-content in the essay. Its transitions disavow the succinct deduction in favour of connections of elements for which discursive logic has no time' (*GS* 11: 31; *NL1*: 21–2).[4] Wellmer's remark about the need for a wider normative horizon for the understanding of truth suggests that we have to consider how logical connections of elements required for understanding function against a background of connections which is not logically construable: 'the concept of propositional truth cannot be understood if it is not understood in its internal relationship to a (normative) problematization of ways of seeing, background understandings, etc.' (2004: 172). Questioning a way of seeing is impossible in strictly logical terms because logic can only deal with the propositionally constituted elements of a whole, rather than with the connections between these elements which help constitute literary form. Seeing things this way need not, though, lead to the deconstructionist consequence that, because one can always recontextualize a piece of language, its meaning is necessarily undecidable.

Wellmer observes in a Wittgensteinian vein that we do not have to think that 'the meaning of utterances or texts has some kind of being-in-itself beyond interpretation, so that it would only ever be grasped, as it were, hypothetically and temporarily or incompletely; instead this manner of its being grasped – interpretation – belongs to the manner of being of linguistic meaning. Its "esse" is "interpretari"' (2004: 200). This observation points to a crucial link between music and verbal understanding. Adorno's remark that 'interpreting language means: understanding language; interpreting music means: making music' starts to look different if one thinks of interpretation of language in the way Wellmer suggests, such that it is part of our being in the world, rather than being the pursuit of an inaccessible goal: 'languages, properly understood, are only what they are as moments of a practical life-context' (2004: 461). In the case of both music and language, interpretation is a practice which has to be carried out as one of the practices of life; otherwise one is appealing precisely to a constitutively absent metaphysical substance. Indeed, the supposed force of the deconstructive view of interpretation can be seen to be parasitic on such a conception. Deconstruction repeatedly shows the view of meaning as substance to be untenable, without then saying anything much that is informative about the nature of our engagement in the practice of understanding that, as Heidegger shows, is constitutive of our very being.

Evidently the norms for successful interpretation of language and of music are different, but they are not wholly distinct. This becomes apparent when Adorno writes:

> the essay touches on musical logic, the stringent, yet conceptless art of transition, in order to appropriate for verbal language something that it lost under the dominion of discursive logic but which cannot just be left out and can only be overcome by dint of the penetration of subjective expression. For the essay is not simply opposed to the discursive procedure. It is not illogical; it itself obeys logical criteria insofar as the totality of its sentences must come together in a coherent manner. No mere contradictions can be left, unless they are justified as belonging to the matter in hand. ... [The essay] coordinates the elements, rather than subordinating them. (*GS* 11: 31; *NL1*: 22)

This passage takes up an idea that had already appeared in an essay of the early 1930s, 'The Language of the Philosopher', which sought to give an account of philosophy's relationship to language which does not rely on the primacy of conceptual determination characteristic of the sciences. For the philosopher, Adorno maintains, 'there is no hope but to place the words around the new truth so that their configuration alone results in the new truth' (*GS* 1: 369). The '*aesthetic* dignity' of words therefore does not lie in the beauty of their combination, but rather in their capacity to be true:

> Powerless words are recognizable as those which in the linguistic work of art – which alone preserved the unity of word and thing against the scientific duality – conclusively fell prey to aesthetic critique, whereas they up to now were able unrestrictedly to enjoy philosophical favour. ... [A]rt gains the character of cognition: its language is aesthetically only right ['*stimmig*', which has the sense of 'fitting', 'being in tune'] if it is 'true'. (*GS* 1: 369)

The truth of art in this sense has to do with dimensions of language which are not propositional.

Adorno's remarks here do depend, though, in one respect, upon the indefensible notion of the unity of word and thing, which is supposedly lost in science (hence the idea of the 'scientific duality' of word and thing) because science's aim of conceptual determination pays no heed to unique configurations of words. The problem is that such a unity – an essentially theological idea he gets from Benjamin – is a myth anyway, as modern linguistics shows. Despite this not inconsiderable difficulty, there is, however, something to be salvaged from the idea that texts which are not simply translatable into other forms of words – think of the inevitable loss that occurs in paraphrasing a poem – have something to do with an otherwise inaccessible truth.

Adorno's more convincing approach to this idea of truth derives from the sense that words which are predominantly used to identify, and thus to cover a large variety of things which may differ in other respects, rely on a great deal of pre-given, unquestioned assumptions, and so may reinforce existing ways of understanding and relating to the world. Moreover, the fact that a limited number of conventional, iterable linguistic signifiers are the essential basis of communication can inherently make expression into a problem, because the irreducible particularity of what the individual subject needs to express clashes with the necessary generality of the material of expression at the subject's disposal. In 'Parataxis', Adorno writes:

> To the extent to which it is conceptual and predicative, language is opposed to subjective expression, it levels down what is to be expressed to something pre-given and known because of its generality. The poets protest against this. They continually would like to incorporate, even to the point of their destruction, the subject and its expression into language. (*GS* 11: 477; *NL2*: 136)

This remark would seem to move one away from the idea of truth as the objective, because the concern is with the subjective, but it is precisely Adorno's Hegelian refusal to separate the subjective and the objective like this that is crucial. He insists that Hölderlin 'knows of language not just as something external and repressive, but also knows its truth'; this truth is dependent upon the subject's need for expression, but it is 'raised above the subject' (*GS* 11: 477; *NL2*: 136). The nature of language takes one beyond contingent subjective intention and expression because even its aesthetic forms depend upon collective interactions within society that are prior to and irreducible to the individual subject, otherwise there would be no way in which expressive forms could have intersubjective significance.

Adorno claims that both literary works and philosophy aim at 'truth-content': 'One is led to [truth-content] by the contradiction that every work wishes to be understood purely from within itself, but no work can be understood from within itself' (*GS* 11: 451; *NL2*: 112). So the question is how the work relates to what is beyond it, and this is what would allow one to talk of its truth: 'The truth of a poem is not without its construction, the totality of its moments; it is at the same time what transcends this construction, which is a construction of aesthetic appearance: not from the outside by what philosophical content is stated, but by dint of the moments which, taken together, mean more than the construction intends' (451; 112–13). Hölderlin's poetry enacts key ideas of German Idealism concerning the nature of contradiction, for example, but describing how this is the case does not show why his poetry is so significant as poetry. The poetry's truth-content depends on the way in which the linguistic material of the text is organized, rather than on the sum of the propositional meanings, of the kind that might be said to constitute the truth of a philosophical system. The trouble is, of course, that this would seem to leave one with no option but just to repeat or point to the text when asked to communicate its truth. However, if one does not think that truth is exhausted by what can be said in propositions, a form like the essay, in Adorno's sense described above, may be able, by finding appropriate ways of conveying what matters in a literary work, to communicate what a descriptive analysis cannot. Significantly, when we talk about music we have no choice but to resort to pointing to things which we cannot convey – 'Listen to this!' – except perhaps by metaphor, which is itself a kind of 'judgementless synthesis' because it does not identify in an objective manner.

Both music and literature, then, involve what Adorno means by 'judgementless synthesis' because their truth is manifest in the connection of their elements that cannot be reduced to a series of propositions. A way of illustrating one aspect of this is via Adorno's essay on 'Punctuation Marks', which sees punctuation in terms which link it to the gestural side of music:

> In none of its elements is language so similar to music as in punctuation marks. Comma and full-stop correspond to half- and full cadences. Exclamation marks are like silent cymbal-crashes, question marks like the upward movement of a phrase, colons like dominant seventh chords; and the difference between comma and semi-colon will only be correctly felt by someone who perceives the different weight of strong and weak phrasing in musical form. (*GS* 11: 106–7; *NL1*: 92)

Music's significance in our context derives not least from the fact that the idea of realizing it successfully is an aim familiar to most musicians and listeners, and such realization cannot come about solely via what can be verbally stated. Think, for instance, of how conductors use gestures to realize things which they know they cannot describe. These gestures have an important relationship to the fact that music itself, as Adorno puts it, can be seen as a 'language sedimented from gestures' (*GS* 18: 154). As such, the idea of the successful realization of music can be seen as something like a regulative idea, and the question is how this can be connected to truth without falling into the metaphysical trap outlined above. Why might musical practice offer a way of responding to the idea of truth which does not involve a metaphysical version of the claim that truth substantially pre-exists the search for it, and what might this tell us about literary interpretation?

Some of Hilary Putnam's recent arguments about the entanglement of fact and value seem to me able to help make sense of the best of Adorno's approaches to this issue. Putnam rejects the idea that value issues can be assessed from a perspective outside involvement in them, which is the approach characteristic of the reductive 'naturalism' that still dominates some talk about values in analytical philosophy. He talks of 'moral perception', by which he means 'the ability to see that someone is, for example, "suffering unnecessarily", as opposed to "learning to take it"'. There is, he continues 'no *science* that can teach one to make these distinctions. They require a skill that, in Iris Murdoch's words, is "endlessly perfectible", and that, as she also says, is also interwoven with our (also endlessly perfectible) mastery of moral vocabulary itself' (Putnam 2004: 128). In saying this, Putnam is careful to insist that epistemic values and ethical values are not the same, but that they can play equally important roles in our lives.

Putnam does not pay a great deal of attention to aesthetic values, but the comments just cited are clearly applicable to music, where the ability to distinguish, both as player and listener, between what is 'deeply expressive' and 'merely meretricious' involves a further mastery; a mastery which is not just of the vocabulary for verbal expression about music, but of musical vocabulary itself. Putnam's concern, which he shares with Habermas, Brandom and others, is with the intrinsic normativity of communication, which pertains both with regard to the ethical and with regard to the world of objects dealt with by the sciences. In any communicative practice one is committing oneself to an engagement with the norms which inform that practice, and this clearly applies to music as well. In consequence, Putnam avoids Adorno's tendency to regard the language of science as essentially different from aesthetically significant language, and makes it possible to widen the conception of truth in the manner I am suggesting.

The obvious problem with musical interpretation is that agreement about how to do it right or about when it is successful *is* often local and transient. There must, though, for the issue of interpretation to be controversial in the way it is, be some underlying agreement on the aim of getting it right, even between those with opposed views of what this consists in. This situation is echoed by Putnam's claim with regard to ethics: 'There is no recognition of transcendent truth here; we need no better ground for treating "value judgements" as capable of truth and falsity than the fact that we can and do treat them as capable of warranted assertability and warranted deniability' (2004: 110). It is the relationship between the norms informing necessary background agreements, without which truth is incomprehensible, and the norms invoked in contingent disagreements about specific cases, that matters here.

The point is that the *idea* of a right interpretation seems both to be inescapable, and yet also to be at odds with the actual practice of music. Adorno asserts of musical interpretation: 'There is an absolutely right interpretation or at least a finite multiplicity of right interpretations, but it is an *idea*, not even purely knowable, let alone realizable. Interpretation measures itself by the level of its failure' (*NS* 1.2: 120). A key difference between the aesthetic and the scientific realm is that, whereas in the sciences the search for truth can also be construed in pragmatic terms, as problem-solving, which does not require regulative ideas as part of the practice, 'problem-solving' in music – Adorno often talks of music in such terms – does not have an immediate pragmatic aim beyond a success immanent to the practice. Music, therefore, can be said in some circumstances still to involve a kind of regulative idea, of the kind suggested by Murdoch's notion of that which is 'endlessly perfectible'. Adorno puts it like this: true interpretation is 'an idea that is strictly prescribed, but one which is in principle unrealizable, for the sake of the fundamental antinomy of art-music' (*NS* 1.2: 74). Truth as regulative idea and true musical interpretation are, then, both 'in principle unrealizable', but this status has a normative significance in music that is not necessarily obviated by the problematic metaphysical consequences involved in a philosophical description of truth in such terms, and this has consequences for how we can regard literary interpretation.

Adorno's 'fundamental antinomy' has to do with relationships that are vital to his thinking, such as that between score and interpretation, between 'analysis' and 'mimesis', and a variety of other oppositions which relate to the opposition between the semantic and the expressive or mimetic in language. The antinomy is explained when he asserts, with regard to the assessment of how far a score should determine its interpretation, that 'musical notation is, of course, expression of a musical *idea*, which it, so to speak, standardizes, reifies, alters, and which ... is to be awoken, restored. In a certain sense true interpretation *revokes* the notation' (*NS* 1.2: 182) – that is, by escaping the reification inherent in a score as a fixed object, even as it also requires that object. How, then, does a claim like this relate to the assertion that 'interpreting language means: understanding language; inter-preting music means: making music'? The fact is that Adorno deconstructs the difference between the two: 'Whether a phrase is played in a meaningful manner can be precisely converted into technical correlates like accents, pauses for breath, etc. But in order to carry out this conversion one must first understand the meaning of the phrase' (*NS* 1.2: 159). One way of accounting for the understanding of linguistic utterances is, as we saw, that it depends on awareness of the contexts of their appropriate use. This suggests a continuity with what Adorno demands for playing 'in a meaningful manner', which is also about relating a phrase to its harmonic, rhythmic, and other contexts in an appropriate way. Such contextualization is, how-ever, never sufficient, because full musical understanding requires what Adorno calls the mimetic. The key to interpreting music lies, then, in the relationship between the 'mimetic' and the 'analytical', which has close affinities to that between the expressive and the semantic, and this is what makes music relevant to literary interpretation.

The essential point is that interpretation is not just a matter of *knowing* how to do it in a technical sense, and this non-cognitive aspect is what is vital to literary understanding in the sense intended here. Truth in art is not a wholly cognitive issue: 'For what mimetic behaviour addresses is the telos of cognition which cognition at the same time blocks with its own categories. Art completes cognition with what is excluded from it and thereby in turn detracts from the character of cognition, namely its unambiguous nature' (*GS* 7: 87; *AT*: 54). The 'telos of cognition' would in these terms be the ability to unify the general categories of thought with the particularity inherent in any specific object of thought. The idea is, then, that cognition alone is not self-justifying, because it necessarily ignores other relations to things. Stanley Cavell reminds us that there can be demands with regard to how we relate to things which cognition alone cannot fulfil when he talks of Heidegger and Wittgenstein 'throwing into question … philosophy's obeisance to epistemology', in which certainty is 'taken as its preferred relation to objects (as opposed, for example, to recognition, or intimacy, or mastery)' (2005: 245). Art's importance lies in its extending the demand for 'truth' beyond what can be known, in the sense of being classified by concepts, towards other relationships to people and things. Music enacts the dilemma involved in the telos of cognition by requiring general forms, epitomized for Adorno by musical notation, which are analogous to concepts in literature because their function is to identify what they stand for, while also demanding that true interpretation incorporate the particular mimetic moment without which justice is not done to the work.

Music is constituted by a connection of elements, which, unlike the connection in a predicative judgement, is not intended to identify what it relates to, but rather to give a mimetic sense of it that can affect the way we relate to the world. What Adorno means are things like the movement of a melody which conveys a specific feeling or the change of mood occasioned by a beautiful harmonic shift: 'What art as judgementless synthesis loses in determinacy in its particulars, it regains by doing greater justice to that which is otherwise cut off by judgement' (*GS* 11: 270; *NL1*: 232). This way of looking at art and interpretation offers a counter to the potential for arbitrariness in Derrida's second interpretation of interpretation. Musical interpretation militates against the idea that undecidability is the essential result of the most advanced philosophical consideration of understanding, even as what is being interpreted precisely resists any kind of semantic determination. The sense of inadequacy in badly interpreted music brings to the fore a kind of normativity which has threatened to be lost in many areas of the humanities. Adorno's concern with the truth in interpretation that is required if the potential of great music is to be realized should inform our interpretations of literature as well if we are not to fall prey to the attitudes of the culture industry.

NOTES

1   I argue that this is something of a travesty of hermeneutics in Bowie 1997.
2   All translations from the German are the author's own; page numbers have also been given for the standard English translations where available.
3   As Herbert Schnädelbach and others have pointed out, Adorno sometimes conflates identifying things *as* something, which it makes no sense to say is necessarily problematic, with identifying things *with* other things, which can be the source of repressive identification of the kind characteristic of the commodity form (see Bowie 1997).
4   A key source of the ideas of this essay is Benjamin's *Trauerspiel* book, but explicating how this is the case would require an essay on its own. I am interested rather in how Adorno's remarks can be used to construct a position which does not rely on Benjamin's esoteric ideas.

WORKS CITED

Bowie, A. (1997), *From Romanticism to Critical Theory: The Philosophy of German Literary Theory*. London: Routledge.
— (2003), *Aesthetics and Subjectivity: from Kant to Nietzsche*, 2nd edn. Manchester: Manchester University Press.
— (2006), *Music, Philosophy, and Modernity* (forthcoming).
Cavell, S. (2005), *Philosophy the Day after Tomorrow*. Cambridge, MA: Belknap Press.
Derrida, J. (1978), 'Structure, sign and play in the discourse of the human sciences', in *Writing and Difference*, trans. A. Bass. London: Routledge, pp. 278–93.
Putnam, H. (2004), *The Collapse of the Fact/Value Dichotomy and Other Essays*. Cambridge, MA: Harvard University Press.
Rorty, R. (1998), *Truth and Progress*. Cambridge: Cambridge University Press.
— (2000), 'The Decline of Redemptive Truth and the Rise of a Literary Culture'. Online at: http://www.stanford.edu/~rrorty/decline.htm.
Wellmer, A. (2004), *Sprachphilosophie*. Frankfurt: Suhrkamp.
Wingert, L. and Günther, K. (eds) (2001), *Die Öffentlichkeit der Vernunft und die Vernunft der Öffentlichkeit: Festschrift für Jürgen Habermas*. Frankfurt: Suhrkamp.

4

Adorno and the Poetics of Genre

Eva Geulen

'was fürs Genre — !'

Gottfried Benn

I

The notion of aesthetic 'genres' [*Gattungen*] conflates two separate meanings. In German it designates the different arts, such as literature, painting, music and so on, but it also refers to particular sub-genres within one art, such as the novel and drama in literature, or fugue and sonata in music. While these distinctions were once hierarchically organized, so that each of the different arts encompassed a set of particular genres (as in Schopenhauer's aesthetics), this model has pretty much disappeared. Lukács's *Theory of the Novel* (1916), with its hope for a restoration of the epic by the modern novel, may be considered the last gasp of this older type of *geschichtsphilosophische Gattungspoetik* so dear to German Idealism (Szondi 1974). Modernism dissolved the binding forms of particular genres and, under the increasing pressure of new media such as photography, film and, later, video and digital art, attention shifted from genre-theory proper to the relations prevailing among the different arts. It became question-able whether they can be subsumed under a 'generic' notion of art in the collective singular.[1] Adorno for one claimed the irrevocable disjunction between different arts and art as such: 'we must dismiss the naive, logical view that "art" is no more than the generic term [*Oberbegriff*] for the arts, a genus [*Gattung*] that contains different species [*Arten*] within itself' (*AA*: 382; *GS* 10.1: 447).[2]

Jean-Luc Nancy's volume *The Muses*, with its central question 'why are there many arts and not just one single art?', may count as a prominent example of the ongoing importance of this issue, and turns to Adorno's late essay 'Art and the Arts' as one of its earliest expositions (Nancy 1996). In fact, Adorno's rather brief and somewhat tentative text has accrued canonical status among younger theoreticians, who mine it for the building blocks of a theory of art capable of superseding the type of dead-end modernism Adorno had developed in *Aesthetic Theory*. The turn Adorno supposedly took late in life is believed to provide the basis for a theory of art appropriate to the growing number of hybrid and intermedial art forms emergent since the 1960s. In her study on the decline of the avant-garde and the emergence of a network of arts [*Vernetzung*], Christine Eichel pioneered this reading by foregrounding Adorno's concept of the fraying or frazzling [*Verfransung*] of the boundaries of the arts, arguing that Adorno's perception of a growing 'promiscuity' (*AA*: 371) between and among the arts prophetically anticipated the decisive trend in contemporary art. At stake in this claim is not only a new aesthetic theory under the conditions of nominalism, but also the possibility of a new, non-modernist avant-garde (Eichel 1993: 21). Apropos Benedetto Croce's strict refusal of any notion of genre in favour of the individual work, Eichel believes that Adorno has to offer a 'genre-transcending theoretical concept for a consideration of art, which wants to be more than an expedition into the cosmos of an individual work' (15).

More recently, Juliane Rebentisch has criticized Eichel's account, demonstrating that Adorno leaves no doubt that hybridization or fraying result in (authentic) artworks only where these phenomena emerge as a direct consequence of standards already achieved within any particular art form or genre. Despite her criticisms of Eichel, however, Rebentisch remains equally committed to some notion of progress in the development of the arts, even and especially today, in a nominalist age of ubiquity and 'anything goes'. Such an idea of progress hinges upon Adorno's notion of *Material-beherrschung*, or mastery of artistic materials. As Rebentisch observes, however, this does not mean ever-growing technical mastery of raw materials – stone in sculpture, tones in music and so on – but refers, rather, to the formal possibilities already disclosed by previous works in one art. They set the standard, behind which no (authentic) work must fall. At the same time, this notion of *Materialbeherrschung* remains inevitably bound to and circumscribed by the particular generic conditions of any given art. For Adorno, even radical distortion or determined rejection of generic requirements responds to challenges and executes demands which originate in genre (*AT*: 180). As he puts it in properly dialectical terms: 'Whenever artworks on their way toward concretion polemically eliminate the universal, whether as a genre, a type, an idiom or a formula, the excluded is maintained in them through its negation' (*AT*: 351). If Rebentisch wants to retain this idea of aesthetic progress, she has to insist on the continued validity of the category of genre vis-à-vis 'fraying' (even though her account of installation art might very well be closer to Eichel's programme of *Vernetzung*). Rebentisch solves the latent dilemma rather elegantly by suggesting that *Verfransung* is merely 'the emergence of the different arts' constitutive intermediality' (2003: 125). If any given art is already constitutively intermedial, then manifestations of fraying do indeed execute demands of the genre. Whereas Eichel implicitly founds a new hybrid genre, or, better, hybridity *as* a genre on the basis of *Verfransung*, Rebentisch moves intermediality into the position of a meta-genre shared by all the different arts. Hence Eichel and Rebentisch converge in two basic respects. Both partake in the familiar and, as it were, generically modernist aversion to genres because they measure aesthetic progress by the dissolution of genres – within one art and of the arts' distinct identities. And both prove inadvertently that any destruction of genres is bound to generate a new normative concept that functions like a genre, be it called *Verfransung* or 'intermediality'.[3]

Even though dispelling genres altogether might well turn out to be a hopelessly paradoxical endeavour, Rebentisch and Eichel have good reasons to keep their distance from genre and genres. As Clemens Pornschlegel has recently pointed out, genres have become so suspect aesthetically in the course of the twentieth century because they are so politically suspect.[4] Adorno himself sensed how political and aesthetic sensitivities converge in the attack on genre executed by *Verfransung*. Regarding the unfavourable reception of contemporary art, he writes: 'Where boundaries are violated, fear may easily provoke a defensive reaction to miscegenation. The complex assumed pathological dimensions in the National Socialist cult of pure race and the denigration of hybridity' (*AA*: 370; *GS* 10.1: 434). This makes it all the more plausible that Eichel and Rebentisch would want to celebrate all modes of mixing and that they should consider genre exclusively as a problematic rationalizing imposition, a controlling instance which has long run its historical course (Eichel 1993: 21). Rebentisch's ostensible insistence on the dialectical unity of *Verfransung* and genre notwithstanding, she also conceives of installation art as another step in the liberation from 'genre-specific constraints' (Rebentisch 2003: 145). Neither author is thus willing to acknowledge that a strictly negative evaluation of genre as mere limitation and formal restriction actually perpetuates the modernist belief in the inherent value of rejecting generic demands; demands both authors seek to transcend or, at least, modify: Eichel by enunciating a new avant-garde; Rebentisch by seeking to establish 'no-longer-modernist' criteria by which to measure aesthetic progress (Rebentisch 2003: 144). As both map the modernist dissolution of genres onto the dissolution of art forms, they reproduce the very modernist logic of progress they reject as outmoded and no longer applicable to contemporary art.

To be sure, Adorno himself presents the fraying of the borderlines separating the different arts as yet another step in the avant-gardist attack on genres. The contrast between Romantic progressive universal poetry and contemporary *Verfransung* clearly marks the latter as progress. In Romanticism, the arts had moved closer together, '[b]ut their boundaries were scarcely weakened by this. They remained what they were, and this disparateness is not the least important critical reason for the most recent development' (*AA*: 375).[5] Yet it is precisely in this regard that Adorno's late essay still adheres to the (modernist) logic of *il faut être absolument moderne*. This is why his text foils all efforts to mobilize it in the service of a non-modernist theory of art. Nonetheless, the question remains whether Adorno's own sense of genre is in fact exhausted by this model, whether it is ultimately reducible to constraint, limitation – in short: to a resistance to be overcome or eliminated.

Prima vista, genre seems unlikely to play any significant role in Adorno, since he tends to privilege the particular over and against the (in this world, always false) universal. Hence one may indeed expect genres to figure on the side of the resistant weight of tradition which the authentic artist chips away 'like plaster with a hammer' (*T*: 76). This is indeed how genre functions in 'Art and Arts', in the essay on Beckett, and in many other contexts. Yet what Adorno has to say about the disappearance of traditions in general might well have consequences for his assessment of genres: 'There is no tradition today and none can be conjured, yet when every tradition has been extinguished the march toward barbarism will begin' (*T*: 79). This suggests that Adorno may have had reasons to hold on to a notion of genre that is not fully exhausted by negation. To put the claim of the following analysis quite bluntly: genre in Adorno turns out to have quasi-anthropological underpinnings which run counter to the predictable conceptualization of genres within the parameters of his aesthetic theory. The fate of aesthetic genres [*Gattungen*] has subterranean links with the fate of the human species [*Gattung*]; links that should be heard each time the word *Gattung* is encountered in Adorno's work. This other notion of genre is generally less obvious than the manifest, properly dialectical account, but in Adorno's dealings with one particular literary genre it gains surprising prominence.

II

In a passage from *Aesthetic Theory* Adorno renders explicit the aporia that genres share with all traditions under the conditions of modernity: 'The existence and teleology of objective genres [*Gattungen*] and types are as true as the fact that they must be attacked' (*AT*: 201; *GS* 7: 299–300). Accordingly, Adorno is far from relegating genres to the realm of anachronistic forms or mere impositions; much less does he denigrate them as instruments of restrictive rationalization. But he is equally far from affirming Rebentisch's claim that all aesthetic genres are essentially intermedial. Instead, while demanding their destruction, he insists on their objectivity. Genre is accorded no less than a telos.[6] The destruction of genres is no heroic achievement of modern artists, but appears, rather, as the historical unfolding of any given genre's possibilities according to a plan and towards a goal, even if this goal were eventually to be self-destruction. Adorno's suggestion is particularly bizarre because he employs the very terms Kant had used when arguing that humanity was on its way to perfection. It seems as if genres shelter a faith in enlightenment that has been thoroughly compromised by the dialectic of myth and enlightenment everywhere else. Kant could still believe in the 'secret of the perfection of the human species' (Kant 1986: 444), because he assumed that the species as a whole would realize what no individual could achieve. However, this assumption also presupposed that the species as a whole is (potentially) present in every individual, that each individual represents the species *in spe*. This assumption underlies the categorical imperative and its demand never to treat a human being only as a means but also always as an end. In *Minima Moralia*, Adorno's anti-Kantian ethics (see Geulen 2001), Adorno states unambiguously that the individual has lost the autonomy which alone would allow it to represent and to realize the species (*MM*: 38). Under the conditions of the culture industry, the individual is no longer an individual, but the exchangeable exemplum of the ever same. Individuality is as corrupt as universality.

It comes as a surprise, then, that the dialectical relationship between particular and universal should remain unperturbed in artworks. Yet Adorno insists that genre and generic demands assume the role of the universal once attributed to the human species. That much is suggested by another passage in *Aesthetic Theory*, whose beginning still seems rather straightforward: 'The unity of the history of art is the dialectical figure of determinate negation. Only in this way does art serve its idea of reconciliation' (*AT*: 35). However, the subsequent illustration of this unity ex negativo approximates an affirmative, positive statement in the name of genre: 'A meager and impure idea of this dialectical unity is given by the way in which artists of a single genre perceive themselves to be working in a subterranean collective [*als unterirdisch gemeinsam Arbeitende*] that is virtually independent of their individual products' (*AT*: 35; *GS* 7: 60). Whether 'genre' [*Gattung*] here signifies, in the original German, the different arts or genres within one art cannot be determined and perhaps it is not even important. It is decisive, however, that genres figure as an emblem, however weak, not just of unity, in some abstract sense, but of a concrete community. While illustrating the unity of art, Adorno also posits an aesthetic communality which is constituted by those artists who work within the same genre. Their communality is guaranteed by a universal which is not produced by their labours but precedes them and unites the artistic workers into a kind of brotherhood. It is passages like this which suggest that humanity, as species or collective project, and (aesthetic) genres communicate in, as it were, 'subterranean' ways. Aesthetic genres circumscribe a realm where human collectives are still at stake. The question of the unity of art is linked to the question of the unity of humanity by way of genres.

According to Adorno, the dialectic of particular and universal, of general genre and individual work, is immanent to each (authentic) artwork. No artwork can do without universal elements. Sheer individuality does not exist. The concept Adorno frequently employs to explain the universal dimension of individual works is *Sprachähnlichkeit*, a 'likeness' or 'affinity' to language, which characterizes all art: 'That universal elements are irrevocably part of art at the same time that art opposes them, is to be understood in terms of art's likeness to language. For language is hostile to the particular and nevertheless seeks to rescue it' (*AT*: 204; *GS* 7: 304). All art is like language, because language, as the medium of individual expression, is in itself the most general or generic: 'In art, universals are strongest where art most closely approaches language' (*AT*: 205). It is worth speculating why Adorno chose the notion of art's language-character rather than its likeness to music, for in music too a limited set of tones constitutes the general medium for individual expression. Yet there is a fundamental difference, because musical tones are not bound to signification in the same way that words are. What distinguishes linguistic artworks from all other media is that language consists of preordained signification, of set conventional meanings. Language is and remains semantic or, as Adorno puts it in the essay on Beckett, language is 'discursive' to a degree shared by neither music nor painting. This accounts for the prominent role of 'language-character' in his aesthetic theory: 'even where language tends to reduce itself to pure sound, it cannot divest itself of its semantic element, cannot become purely mimetic or gestural' (*NL1*: 262). The tension between universality and particularity is greatest in language, precisely because of the resistance mounted by its discursivity or semanticity. Artworks are said to be like language when they develop and sustain the tension that characterizes the literary artefact: to say the particular in a form that is generic. What Hegel objected to regarding the claims of sense perception in the *Phenomenology of Spirit*, that it wants to articulate the here and now but cannot say it, is exactly what constitutes the peculiarity of language in Adorno's view and is responsible for the prominent position *Aesthetic Theory* accords to *Sprachähnlichkeit*.

Against this background, Adorno's discussions of literature assume particular significance. Especially noteworthy are those involving lyric poetry[7] – less because of poetry's affinities to music than on account of its ostentatious linguisticality, what Adorno calls 'the primacy of language' (*NL1*: 43). Poetry, which came to be known as a genre only in the latter parts of the eighteenth century,[8] is to this day identified as the mode of individual expression, the form in which modern subjectivity gains a voice. If genre has indeed to do with collectivity in some way, then the subjective genre of poetry presents the test case for this thesis. Poetry is therefore the most promising site for exploring the status of genres as well as their relationship to collectivity and language in the force field between quasi-anthropological and historical models.

As others have observed, Adorno is drawn to poets whose formal conservatism and restorative intentions make them initially rather unexpected figures in his modernist canon. Like other pieces on George and Eichendorff, Adorno's essay on Borchardt, programmatically entitled 'Charmed

Language' (*NL2*: 193–210), circles the notion of a lost and essentially irretrievable language whose past possibilities are to be conjured up by and in poetry. However, in the case of Borchardt, the topic of genre is equally important. In the first sentence of the essay, Adorno writes: 'Rudolf Borchardt's work spanned all literary genres and enriched them as genres. His lyric poetry has a key position in his work' (*NL2*: 193). This does not mean that he wrote mostly poetry but that 'the defining form of his poetic response' was lyrical (*NL2*: 193). Lyric reaction is characterized by the poet's subservience, even his self-sacrifice, to language: 'In everything he wrote, he made himself an organ of language' (*NL2*: 193). Adorno argues that in Borchardt's poetry language is given the chance to articulate itself in a quasi-autonomous mode; it takes over as the subject takes itself back and surrenders to the impulses of language (see Fleming 2004). This idea of a receding subjectivity returns in the essays on George and Eichendorff. By emphasizing the lyrical abdication of the speaking subject that gives itself over to language, Adorno modifies the dominant understanding of poetry as the articulation of subjectivity. The essay 'On Lyric Poetry and Society' makes this point emphatically: 'Only one who hears the voice of humankind in the poem's solitude can understand what the poem is saying' (*NL1*: 38). And the voice of humanity can only be heard where the poetic subject surrenders itself to language. As Adorno put it with respect to Eichendorff: 'a renunciation ... of the dominion of one's own I over one's psyche [*Seele*]' (*NL1*: 64; *GS* 11: 78). The generic property of poetry is, then, nothing other than the expropriation of the speaking subject. As a genre, poetry depends on an allegorized notion of language which acts as if it were a subject and comes to speak instead of the subject: Borchardt 'was borne by the experience his whole literary oeuvre was striving for – the experience of language itself speaking, to use a baroque expression. ... the epiphany of language' (*NL2*: 193). He sought 'the transsubjective, objectively binding quality of language, a coherence beyond subjective response' (*NL2*: 195).

Towards the end of the essay, Adorno suggests a causal nexus between the prerogative of genres in Borchardt's poetry and his paradoxical project to conjure up a non-existent language with its missed possibilities: 'In Borchardt the critique of simulated immediacy, along with the will to reconstruct missed possibilities, leads to a primacy of genres over individual works that at first sight appears anachronistic' (*NL2*: 206; *GS* 11: 550). While it is obvious that Borchardt's criticism of false immediacy should lead him to privilege historically distant canonical forms, it is less evident why his reconstruction of language's forever missed opportunities should result in the primacy of genres.[9] Once again the reign of subjectivity plays a role. For the language that Borchardt encounters is not only ruined by commerce and jargon; its devastated state is the symptom of an overall 'bourgeoisification [*Verbürgerlichung*] of the spirit' (*NL2*: 194; *GS* 11: 537), which the elitist gesture and high style of Borchardt's poetry oppose. Such poetic snobbism has become possible and necessary because *Verbürgerlichung* essentially means nothing else than the usurpation of language by bourgeois subjectivity which presses language into the service of subjective (self-)expression. According to Adorno, modern poetry since Baudelaire is therefore in search of 'the Not-I, and grasping the Not-I has become the paradoxical idea of the lyric poem' (*NL 2*: 200; *GS* 11: 544). This is why Adorno praises Eichendorff's poetry, which is said to compensate for the injustice of subjectivity by privileging language. Eichendorff's lyrical subject 'wants to make amends for some of the primordial injustice of being an I at all' (*NL 1*: 64; *GS* 11: 78).[10]

This Not-I is nothing other than the experience of collectivity where the subjects are bound together by a binding [*verpflichtende*] language. Borchardt strives for this dimension by reaching for historically distant forms:

> Borchardt's integration of historical cultivation into lyric poetry expanded the concept of the lyric with an abrupt shove. He thereby provided lyric with layers and types that it had lost with the emancipation of the subject and that regain their timeliness in view of the limitations of a self-oriented subjectivity – without, however, making the slightest concession to the fraudulent notion of a *communal art* [*Gemeinschaftskunst*]. (*NL2*: 205; *GS* 11: 549–50, emphasis added)

To be sure, Borchardt's belief in language as the genius of peoples (*NL2*: 204) is judged as ideological, as is his fixation on the nation (208). Nor is this collective dimension to be confused with politics, which Borchardt (together with Brecht) introduced into poetry. (Adorno remains doubtful of poetry's ability 'to fulfill' such 'collective demands'.) And yet, something that is collective, but not reducible to any of the available ersatz-collectives, is at stake with Borchardt's poetry as it activates long lost layers of language. The means by which Borchardt gains access to those *alte Sprachschichten* are restraint and distance: 'For him, detachment was a technique for mobilizing something long lost' (*NL2*: 198). Philological knowledge intervenes so as to protect his poetry from relapsing into barbarism (203–4). Nevertheless Borchardt's poetry succeeds in restoring a collective dimension. To call Borchardt's poetry restorative is in a sense only saying that the genre of poetry is by definition restorative. As poets restore unrealized possibilities of language, they essentially restore a lost or missed chance of collectivity. This is why a poet so different from Borchardt as Eichendorff pursues the same project: 'Eichendorff's lyric poetry as a whole wants to rouse the dead' (*NL1*: 66; *GS* 11: 81).

While Adorno shies away from naming the precise nature of this collectivity, it finds expression in a series of images and metaphors, all related to river, stream and rushing, which traverse Adorno's essays on poetry like a leitmotif, culminating in the notion of a *kollektiver Unterstrom*, a collective undercurrent, which is said to carry all poetry.[11] This imagery of stream and river designates the autonomy of language from the speaking subject, as in the idea that Eichendorff's poetry 'lets itself be borne along by the stream of language' (*NL1*: 64). In the case of Borchardt, Adorno lifts the image from Borchardt himself who wrote, 'the German language ... began to flow for me [*war mir in Fluß geraten*]' (cited *NL2*: 198; *GS* 11: 541). Adorno quickly appropriates the motif of 'the liquefaction of language [*Verflüssigung der Sprache*]' (197; 540) and adds formulations such as the 'Wortstrom' or 'flow of words' (204; 548) or the claim: 'Language murmurs and rustles through [*durchrauscht*] him like a stream' (193; 536). This stream links Borchardt to Eichendorff: 'Borchardt's "Ich habe nichts als Rauschen" ["I have nothing but murmuring"] could stand as the motto of Eichendorff's poetry and prose' (*NL1*: 69). Poetry's anti-subjective tendencies are said to constitute a *deutschen Unterstrom* in which Eichendorff partakes as yet another poet dissolving his subjectivity into language: 'The subject turns itself into *Rauschen*, into a rushing, rustling, murmuring sound: in short, it turns itself into language' (*NL1*: 68–9; *GS* 11: 83).

The implications of this imagery fully surface in 'On Lyric Poetry and Society', Adorno's most didactic and programmatic exposition of poetry. The essay unfolds the dialectic of individual and society in three successive steps. The first is predictably dialectical: to prove poetry's mediatedness by society, Adorno assures his readers that the poem speaks of society precisely where it does not speak of society. What the poem excludes resounds negatively in the poem. Adorno makes this point by way of Goethe's 'Wanderers Nachtlied': 'its unfathomable beauty cannot be separated from something it makes no reference to, the notion of a world that withholds peace. Only in resonating with sadness about that withholding does the poem maintain that there is peace nevertheless' (*NL1*: 41). But this dialectical solution is supplemented by a second, somewhat different argument concerning the possibility of poetry as a genre: 'the very simple fact that grounds the possibility of the lyric as an artistic genre, its effect on people other than the poet speaking his monologue' (43). Poetry's status as a genre is guaranteed by the fact that it affects others, that those who read and those who write poetry share the same language.[12] In a third and final step, Adorno complicates the issue once more by raising the question of how language can become such a shared medium, capable of address, in the first place.

Lyrical poetry is, of course, the voice of a single individual (who can hope to become the voice of humanity only when it abdicates the privileged position as speaker). The poet is therefore separated from those who do not even come into position to abdicate their subjectivity because they are objects in the strictest sense: 'The others, however, those who not only stand over against the disconcerted poetic subject as though they were objects, but who have also literally been degraded to objects of history, have the same right, or a greater right, to grope for the sounds in which sufferings and dreams are welded' (*NL1*: 45; *GS* 11: 59). This right of a collective larger than the artists makes itself intermittently felt: 'A collective undercurrent [*Unterstrom*] provides the foundation for all individual lyric poetry' and 'participation in this undercurrent is an essential part of the substantiality of the individual lyric as well'. It is this collective undercurrent which sustains language as the medium of community, 'makes language the medium in which the subject becomes more than a mere subject' (*NL1*: 45; *GS* 11: 59). If poetry is the genre that restores language by giving back to language what the subject took from it so as to be who and what it is, then this structure is possible only because of the collective undercurrent which founds language as a poetic medium and poetry as a genre. While this undercurrent has always been there, Adorno observes that it has recently begun to surface more frequently. Brecht's and Garcia Lorca's poetry are considered symptomatic of the 'collective power [*kollektive Gewalt*] of contemporary lyric poetry' (*NL1*: 46; *GS* 11: 59). (Were one to endow Adorno's remarks with prophetic value, one would have to conclude that he anticipated not *Verfransung* but POP.)[13]

To illustrate his overall argument in 'On Lyric Poetry and Society', Adorno selects texts by conservative and restorative poets: Mörike and George. In Mörike's 'Auf einer Wanderung' ['On a Walking Tour'], Adorno quickly isolates the allusions to classical Greece in their juxtaposition to the poem's provincial setting. He concludes his remarks with a surprisingly strong judgement: 'In the briefest of spaces, the lyric succeeds in doing what the German epic attempted in vain, even in such projects as Goethe's *Hermann und Dorothea*' (*NL1*: 48). This poetry – and by extension all poetry – restores not some abstract notion of a pure language but a long lost genre (and perhaps a genre that factually never existed). The little poem reconstitutes nothing less than the epic, which according to Hegel, Lukács and numerous others is the genre characteristic of a collective totality prior to the rise of modern subjectivity.[14] To the extent that Mörike's poem succeeds as epic, it succeeds as something other than itself, but it does succeed as a *genre* nevertheless.

Adorno's reading of George proceeds quite similarly. After emphasizing George's allusions to a historically distant lyrical tone – not classical but medieval in the case of George's poem from the *Seventh Ring* – Adorno claims that the poet achieved 'the folksong, something the German language had been groping for in vain in its greatest masters' (*NL1*: 53). Like the epic, the *Volkslied* is a collective genre. Poetry is thus not one genre among others, but poetry is the genre that rescues and restores bygone or even non-existent, and in this sense phantasmagoric, genres,[15] and, more specifically, it restores those genres which are essentially related to collectivity.[16] By virtue of this retrieval of a collectivity which appears in the guise of genre, poetry is the speech which can become 'the voice of human beings between whom the barriers have fallen' (*NL1*: 54). Adorno retains the schema and the nomenclature of genres as a reminder of art's collective, if you will, political dimension. He articulates the utopian dimension of art – poetry as 'the voice of humanity' – by way of genres. This is not to say that Adorno essentializes genres. That they are not a naturally given but a symbolic order, follows from the close connection he establishes between genres and language. Genres are to art what concepts are to language, 'that which establishes an inescapable relationship to the universal and to society' (*NL1*: 43). Just as concepts are symbolic, so are genres. But this makes them no less normative or binding. The order of genres reflects the order of language and it is this order which guards against the threat of regression that the increasingly frequent surfacing of the collective undercurrent harbours. Adorno is honest (and sceptical) enough not to exclude the possibility that the reason for the surfacing of that latency which sustained and nourished the lyrical tradition might be 'regression, a weakening of the I' (*NL1*: 46; *GS* 11: 59).

To many, Adorno's poetics of genre, as reconstructed here, might itself seem regressive; Romantic or Idealist remnants, hopelessly out of touch with contemporary art. Certainly Adorno's insistence on genres seems odd in the contemporary context of hybridization and intermediality. Yet, from certain perspectives, Adorno's fidelity to genres could also seem unexpectedly pertinent. Pornschlegel has pointed out that postmodern artistic and theoretical praxis tends to be so radically anti-generic because of the trauma that generic taxonomic systems have produced in the totalitarianisms of the twentieth century: 'But with this, postmodernism refers to a notion of terror, which systematically confounds generic ascriptions of identity and annihilation' (Pornschlegel 2003: 260).[17] Adorno holds on to the order that genres impose as a system of classification on art, because their full liquidation might itself amount to annihilation – 'the march toward barbarism'.

Boris Groys has adopted a similar position with regard to an issue closely related to the dominant anti-generic impulse. As is well known, the core of the postmodernist project is the collapse of the distinction between high and low culture: *Cross the Border. Close the Gap*, in Leslie Fiedler's famous formula. In an essay provocatively entitled 'Fundamentalism as the middle road between high and mass culture', Groys argues that the current search for the foundations of a new culture 'in which the serious could turn popular and the popular turn serious' could amount to a new fundamentalism, paradoxically grounded in the lack of any grounds (Groys 1997: 63). He suspects that the determined corrosion of all symbolic orders and distinctions could lead to a total, even totalitarian culture (perhaps not all that far from what Adorno and Horkheimer presented as the culture industry): 'The totalitarianism consists precisely in the attempt to overcome the division of modern art into avant-garde and kitsch, to dissolve this border and produce a homogenous, that is to say total cultural space' (Groys 1997: 67). It is not necessary to draw these extreme conclusions to develop an entirely non-nostalgic sympathy for genres.

NOTES

1   For a summary of genre-theory up to and including the 1970s, see Hempfer 1973. The appearance of Issue 32 of the journal *Poétique* (1977), with Genette's essay 'Genres, "forms", types' (389–421) marked a shift in genre-theory, as did the contributions to the 1979 Strasbourg colloquium on genre, from which Derrida's seminal essay on 'The Law of Genre', and related texts, appeared in English in *Glyph* 7 (1980). For recent discussions, see Lamping (ed.) 1990.

2   Editors' Note: Citations for Eva Geulen's essay were originally given in the original German and then matched to existing English translations. However, where necessary to the essay's arguments, these translations have been modified by the editors with the invaluable assistance of Paul Fleming and in consultation with the author. Where this has been done, or where the German has been interpolated, references to the original German have been given alongside the English.

3   Any instantiation of the anti-generic effect since Romanticism suffers from this paradox, as Todorov has pointed out with respect to Maurice Blanchot. See Beaujour 1980: 16ff.

4   Pornschlegel explains the dominant anti-generic and anti-normative inclinations as 'a response to the totalitarian trauma of a murderous politics of administration ... in which classification and annihilation, that is to say, the right to the annihilation of classes and races, mean the same thing, namely the annihilation of those ill- or badly-born' (Pornschlegel 2003: 256). In a famous essay, Genette argued that these affinities are essentially the fallout from a most problematic confounding of linguistic (trans-historical) with aesthetic (historical) categories which in turn is rooted in a profound misreading of Plato's and Aristotle's discussions of genre (Genette 1992).

5   Such distinctions are bound to accompany the discussions of *Verfransung* as well as intermediality because behind them the political and aesthetic shadow of the *Gesamtkunstwerk* looms large.

6   Of course the reverse is, as always, just as true: 'Probably no important artwork ever corresponded completely to its genre' (*AT*: 199).

7   For a sustained discussion of Adorno's readings in poetry, see the forthcoming book by Ulrich Plass, *Language and History: Theodor Adorno's 'Notes to Literature'* (London: Routledge, 2006).

8   Prior to Moses Mendelssohn's subsumption of all poetry-genres under the name of lyric, canonical forms such as elegy, ode and so on subsisted independently as genres in their own right.

9   Subsequently, Adorno speculates that it might be the crisis of the work that announces itself in the dominance of genre: 'The turn toward genre came to light unexpectedly in contemporary music, some of whose boldest exponents, like Stockhausen, seem to open up the possibility of whole types in every single work, rather than the work being complete in itself in the familiar traditional way' (*NL2*: 206). Clearly, Adorno was acutely aware that the flip side of the individual work is always genre and vice versa. (This is what renders Croce's insistence on the individual work so weak.)

10 In sharp contradistinction to music, poetry since the eighteenth century did not seek 'integration, system, a subjectively created unity in multiplicity, but ... relaxation and dissociation' (*NL1*: 65). For Adorno this difference between literature and music demonstrates once again how a 'concept of culture that reduces the arts to a single common denominator is not worth much' (65) – even if *Verfransung* were to be this common denominator.

11 Because it is equally alluring and irretrievable, childhood figures here as a placeholder for the re-emergence of a collective identity (see *NL2*: 200).

12 Repeatedly, Adorno stresses that Borchardt's poetry is essentially speech rather than text. Whether as barely articulate *Lallen* (babbling, mumbling) or *Rauschen* in

Eichendorff and Borchardt, or as the essential aspect of the poem's dialogism in 'On Lyric Poetry and Society' or in the pathos-laden formula of the 'voice of humanity', the oral and acoustic dimension seems indispensable to Adorno's understanding of poetry. One might suspect that it is owed to Adorno's musical imagination and reception, but other aspects might also be at play and speech has to be understood as address.

13   Interestingly, this would mean Adorno was willing to grant to poetry what he denied to jazz. At least he is honest enough to leave open to speculation whether the collective undercurrent amounts to a regressive relapse into a pre-bourgeois, pre-enlightened mythic state of undifferentiatedness or whether it amounts indeed to a determinate negation of the bourgeois subject. Ultimately, it might be Adorno's own determined indifference that makes it difficult to co-opt him for a non-modernist notion of progress.

14   Hence it is not by chance that years earlier, Adorno and Horkheimer chose an epic, the *Odyssey*, to allegorize the precarious emergence of the very subjectivity that is said to abdicate its reign in poetry. By contrasting Adorno and Horkheimer's treatment of the epic, in *Dialectic of Enlightenment*, with Lukács's *Theory of the Novel*, Scholze not only determines the epic's position on the threshold to myth, but also demonstrates that the epic is the literary genre that produces, in a self-reflexive manoeuvre, the 'lived totality' usually ascribed to the epic (Scholze 2000: 82). Scholze's reading culminates in the interpretation of those passages which deal with the death of the female servants at the hands of Odysseus and Telemachos. Since the authors highlight the caesura, which interrupts the narrative flow at the point in the epic where the women's death is narrated, Scholze argues: 'Only the caesura turns the epic into a self-reflexive form of *Eingedenken* which points to the illusionary character of narrative necessities and to what falls victim to this narrative logic' (87). Her very convincing reading, however, eclipses the last line of the Odysseus-fragment: 'Only as the novel is the epic transmuted into fairy tale' (*DE*: 62). According to Horkheimer and Adorno, Homer's description of the death of the women anticipates the modern novel, and is 'comparable in its inhumanity only to the *impassibilité* of the greatest narrative writers of the nineteenth century' (*DE*: 61). But as the epic turns into a novel, it is the novel in turn which supersedes itself and restores another kind of collective genre in the form of the fairy tale. If poetry restores the epic, the novel might very well restore the epic as fairy tale.

15   Whenever Adorno considers 'missed opportunities', he systematically oscillates between a historical *Versäumnis* and a structural impossibility. A case in point is the famous opening of *Negative Dialectics* (*ND*: 3–4).

16   The means leading to this restorative success are different in each case. Whereas in Borchardt, historico-philological knowledge intervenes so as to guard against a relapse into the barbaric, Mörike's success is due to his peculiar position at the threshold of classicism and modernism. George, finally, retrieves the *Volkslied* by what Valéry called *refus*, to such an extent that nothing remains of the work but the genre, the generic formula: 'The method retains only the patterns, the pure formal ideas and schemata of lyric poetry itself' (*NL1*: 52).

17   Pornschlegel's argument is obviously informed by Pierre Legendre. The collapse of generic classification threatens to result in 'pre-symbolic and psychotic stammerings' (Pornschlegel 2003: 259), what Adorno would have called 'regression'.

WORKS CITED

Beaujour, M. (1980), 'Genus Universum', *Glyph* 7, 15–31.

Eichel, C. (1993), *Vom Ermatten der Avantgarde zur Vernetzung der Künste: Perspektiven einer interdisziplinären Ästhetik im Spätwerk Theodor W. Adornos*. Frankfurt: Suhrkamp.

Fleming, P. (2004) 'The Secret Adorno', *Qui Parle* 15(1), 97–114.

Genette, G. (1992), *The Architext: An Introduction*, trans. J. E. Lewin. Berkeley: University of California Press.

Geulen, E. (2001), 'Mega Melancholia. Adorno's *Minima Moralia*', in P. Uwe Hohendahl and J. Fisher (eds), *Critical Theory: Current State and Future Prospects*. New York and Oxford: Berghahn, pp. 49–68.

Groys, B. (1997), 'Fundamentalismus als Mittelweg zwischen Hoch- und Massenkultur', *Logik der Sammlung: Am Ende des musealen Zeitalters*. Munich and Vienna: Carl Hanser Verlag, pp. 63–80.

Hempfer, K. W. (1973), *Gattungstheorie*. Munich: Fink Verlag.

Kant, I. (1986), 'Pädagogik', *Akademieausgabe*, vol. 9, Berlin: De Gruyter.

Lamping, D. (ed.) (1990), *Gattungstheorie und Gattungsgeschichte. Ein Symposion*. Special issue of *Wuppertaler Broschüren zur Allgemeinen Literaturwissenschaft* 4.

Nancy, J.-L. (1996), *The Muses*, trans. P. Kamuf. Stanford, CA: Stanford University Press.

Pornschlegel, C. (2003), 'Vögel mit Schlangen. Zur Problematik generischer Klassifikation in der Postmoderne', in U. Hubekus, E. Matala de Mazza and A. Koschorke (eds), *Das Politische: Figurenlehren des sozialen Körpers nach der Romantik*. Munich: Fink Verlag, pp. 248–60.

Rebentisch, J. (2003), *Ästhetik der Installation*. Frankfurt: Suhrkamp.

Scholze, B. (2000), *Kunst als Kritik: Adornos Weg aus der Dialektik*. Würzburg: Königshausen & Neumann.

Szondi, P. (1974), *Poetik und Geschichtsphilosophie I and II*. Frankfurt: Suhrkamp.

PART II:
Poetry and Poetics

5

Lyric Poetry before Auschwitz

Howard Caygill

The World of this Spirit breaks into two. The first is the world of reality or of its self-alienation; but the other is that which Spirit, rising above the first, constructs for itself in the aether of pure consciousness. This second world, standing in antithesis to that alienation, is for that very reason not free from it; on the contrary, it is really only the other form of that alienation which consists precisely in being conscious of two different worlds, and which embraces both.

Hegel, *Phenomenology of Spirit*

Adorno's 1951 proposition – 'After Auschwitz to write a poem is barbaric' – provoked much contention and debate.[1] In spite of its forthrightness the phrase was ambiguous: it remained unclear whether it was a judgement of poetry written after Auschwitz, a *Darstellungsverbot* on poems about Auschwitz, or a condemnation addressed to post-war art and culture in general. In his frequent returns to his dictum Adorno made more precise the nature of his claim and its implications. From these it becomes possible to recognize two important implications of the proposition. The first, implied in the idea that Auschwitz marks an 'end' to lyric poetry, is that lyric poetry has a specific history, and that this history could not be continued after the Shoah. At the same time, the horrific circumstances of the end of the history of lyric poetry underline the further implication that the history of the genre is inseparable from specific social and political conditions of possibility. In order to understand why writing a poem is barbaric after Auschwitz it is thus necessary to look at Adorno's view of the history of lyric poetry before Auschwitz and why he held it impossible for this history to continue after this event.

Adorno's formulations of the proposition linking Auschwitz with the end of lyric poetry shifted emphasis significantly between 1951 and 1968. The full first statement in 'Cultural Criticism and Society', written in 1949 and published in 1951, reads: 'Cultural criticism finds itself before the last stage of the dialectic of culture and barbarism: after Auschwitz to write a poem [*Gedicht*] is barbaric [*ist barbarisch*], and that erodes also the knowledge that declares why it has become impossible today to write poems [*Gedichte*]' (*P*: 34 [trans. mod.]).[2] Cultural criticism at the last stage of the 'dialectic of

culture and barbarism' finds itself – consistent with the last stages of the
Hegelian logic of essence – in a predicament where the poles of the dialectic
fall apart *and* identify with each other. Culture tries to detach itself from
barbarism but finds itself falling into identification with it. Adorno situates
the act of writing a poem after Auschwitz within this predicament, claiming that the same dialectic affects the knowledge of why it is impossible
'today' ('after' Auschwitz) to write poems. The knowledge that 'the conditions of possibility for writing poetry' no longer exist is itself part of the
same movement of culture taking distance from but finding itself complicit
with barbarism.

Reading the original statement as a reflexive dialectical proposition
severely qualifies, then, the view that Adorno proposed a ban on writing
poetry after or about Auschwitz. He carefully explains this in a reflection
upon his proposition in the 1962 essay 'Commitment': 'I do not want to
soften my proposition [*Satz*] that still to write lyric poetry [*Lyrik*] after
Auschwitz would be barbaric [*sei barbarisch*]; it expresses negatively the
impulse that animates committed literature' (*NL2*: 87). While the move
from the indicative, 'is barbaric', of 1951, to the subjunctive, 'would be
barbaric', of 1962, does performatively soften the proposition, Adorno is
careful to show the mutual implication of the positive and negative aspects
of the dialectic. He carefully restricts his judgement to the positive and
negative *attitudes* toward the predicament of writing, not the predicament
itself: 'It is the situation of literature [*Dichtung*] itself and not simply one's
relation to it that is paradoxical' (*NL2*: 88). The dialectic is objective to
writing; it is part of the predicament of writing that its flight from barbarism
paradoxically confirms it. Adorno's strongest example of this paradox/aporia
is Schönberg's *Survivor from Warsaw*, in which, for him, the 'victims are
turned into works of art, tossed out to be gobbled up by the world that did
them in' (*NL2*: 88).

Adorno's position in *Negative Dialectics* may seem at first sight to have
softened even further: 'Perennial suffering has as much right to expression as
a tortured man has to scream: hence it may be wrong to say that after
Auschwitz you could no longer write poems. But it is not wrong to raise
the less cultural question whether after Auschwitz you can go on living'
(*ND*: 362–3). Yet on closer inspection this apparent concession sharpens
the original formulation, linking it to the harsh judgement of *Survivor from
Warsaw*; it is barbaric to be concerned about art when the issue is survival.
It is also notable that Adorno's seeming admission of error or exaggeration is
only directed to the first part of his original formulation. The second part of
the dialectical predicament of writing after Auschwitz – expressed modally
as its impossibility – is silently confirmed, and carried over into the reformulation of the categorical imperative: unfree humanity must 'arrange
their thoughts and actions so that Auschwitz will not repeat itself, so that
nothing similar will happen' (*ND*: 365). The predicament of poetry is not

exempt from this imperative – it cannot excuse itself from the responsibility to ensure that the conditions of the possibility of Auschwitz never recur. But if these conditions of possibility are also those of its own existence, then respecting the imperative requires that lyric poetry, as it has been known, must cease to exist.

Adorno emphasizes this point in one of his 1967 formulations – the essay 'Art and the Arts' – where he describes his proposition as one concerning 'the impossibility of poetry after Auschwitz' (*AA*: 387; *GS* 10.1: 452). The reference to Kant – according to whom the 'conditions of possibility of experience' are also the conditions of the possibility of objects of experience – can be interpreted ontologically or ethically. According to the first interpretation the conditions of possibility of lyric poetry no longer exist; according to the second they *should* no longer exist, at least according to Adorno's reformulation of the categorical imperative. Yet it is precisely between these two positions that the proposition about poetry orients itself as a Hegelian determination of reflection. According to Adorno, works of art are by definition objects that exist in breach of their conditions of possibility – their peculiar condition of possibility is that they exceed their conditions of possibility. The impossibility of poetry after Auschwitz is its condition of possibility; yet it must establish a form of existence that affirms this impossibility, otherwise art will affirm the very conditions of possibility of a repetition of Auschwitz, transgressing the categorical imperative.

In these later reflections on the 1951 dictum the understanding of the history of lyric poetry in relation to its conditions of possibility becomes the centre of attention. In another 1967 formulation, 'Is Art Cheerful?', Adorno returned to the impossibility of poetry after Auschwitz in the context of cheerful art, observing: 'Further, such impossibility was sensed almost a century before the European catastrophe in great poetry, above all in Baudelaire, then also by Nietzsche and in the George school's renunciation of humour' (*NL2*: 251; *GS* 11: 604). The view intimated here, that the impossibility of lyric poetry indeed constituted its modern history and was confirmed by Auschwitz, is filled out in a paralipomenon to *Aesthetic Theory* where Celan is discussed in the context of Valéry, Mallarmé and Baudelaire. Unfortunately Adorno did not complete a planned Celan essay, yet even the few elliptical comments in *Aesthetic Theory* show that he situated this poet writing actual but impossible poems after Auschwitz within a history of modern lyric poetry. The oblique references to this history in the last writings remain shorthand and cryptic, but the history to which they allude may be reconstructed from a series of Adorno's writings on modern poetry before Auschwitz, over all of which falls the shadow of the 'European catastrophe'.

An important testimony to Adorno's history of modern lyric poetry is the 1957 radio broadcast 'On Lyric Poetry and Society'. After an opening statement of complicity with the distaste of an imagined audience at the prospect of a sociology of modern poetry, Adorno presents a number of thoughts on the ways in which lyric poetry might be related to its social conditions of possibility. These largely revolve around the thought that lyric poetry is an individual form of expression directed against society, a thought which Adorno – consistent with his Hegelian scepticism concerning abstract revolt – insists is itself social. The separation of the lyrical 'I' from society is implicated in what it refuses:

> The lyric spirit's idiosyncratic opposition to the superior power of material things is a form of reaction to the reification of the world, to the domination of human beings by commodities that has developed since the beginning of the modern era, since the industrial revolution became the dominant force in life. (*NL1*: 40 [trans. mod.])

The individuality of the lyrical 'I' and the desire for a pure language are themselves socially mediated, but in a way, Adorno quickly concedes, that may appear to some to have wholly 'sublimated' the relation of lyric poetry and society out of a fear of 'crude sociologism' (*NL1*: 42).

Adorno responds to the charge of excessive subtlety by approaching again the question of the relation of lyric poetry and society, this time through the double-aspect of language:

> Through its configurations it [language] assimilates itself completely into subjective impulses; one would almost think it had produced them. But at the same time language remains the medium of concepts, remains that which establishes an inescapable relationship to the universal and to society. (*NL1*: 43)

Adorno situates lyric poetry between the two aspects of language, or more precisely through the impossibility of their becoming identified with each other. After some thinly disguised critical comments on Heidegger's 'ontological language theory',[3] Adorno ventures a considered statement of the character of the relation between lyric poetry and society. He prepares for it by restating the incommensurability of the two aspects of language in the sociological terms of individual and society: 'It is not only that the individual is inherently socially mediated, not only that its contents are always social as well. Conversely, society is formed and continues to live on only by virtue of the individuals whose quintessence it is' (*NL1*: 44). The individual and the collective, as well as the individual and collective aspects of language, mutually determine each other without becoming fully identified – they are, in short, Hegelian concepts of reflection. Adorno makes more precise this reference to Hegel as he moves from the sociological terminology of individual and society into the philosophical one of subject and object:

Classical philosophy once formulated a truth now disdained by scientific logic: subject and object are not rigid and isolated poles but can be defined only in the process in which they distinguish themselves from one another and change. The lyric is the aesthetic test of that dialectical philosophical proposition. (*NL1*: 44)

In Hegel's *Logic* apparent oppositions such as subject and object are resolved into a process of mutual reflection and determination. Adorno situates lyric poetry on the crux of this movement which is also that of individual and society and, more proximally, that of expressive and communicative language. Lyric poetry is thus situated between the poles of subject and object, becoming cast as a medium of reflection.[4] It is a medium, however, that is subject to fluctuation according to the balance of power between the two poles.

Adorno's locating of lyric poetry in this way amounts to a deduction of its conditions of possibility. Lyric poetry is possible because of the process of mutual reflection between subject and object, individual and collective, expressive and communicative language. This allows him to embark on a historical typology of lyric poetry according to the various calibrations possible within the general conditions of possibility. At either extreme is the abolition of the conditions of possibility represented by complete identification, of the individual with the social or the social with the individual. One reading of the Auschwitz dictum, for example, might regard the conditions of possibility of lyric poetry as having been abolished by the total identification of the individual with the collective in administered society. In the context of his analyses of lyric poetry Adorno rarely concedes this condition, although intimations of its possibility are an important factor in his interpretation of many of the formal choices adopted by modern lyric poetry. The complex calibrations of individual and collective that he finds in modern poetry are ultimately governed by a predicament of loneliness and loss of self in the collective.

Adorno's historical discussion of the developments of lyric poetry carefully avoids a unilateral developmental narrative. This is possible due to the flexibility offered by the 'conditions of possibility' form of argumentation, which concerns precisely conditions of *possibility* not *actuality*. The number of possibilities of actualization depends on the various calibrations of the conditions, some of which may crystallize into diverse poetic traditions which will intersect and mutually determine each other. In the essay on lyric poetry an exemplary point of such intersection, whose identification and description is indebted to Benjamin, is found in the poetry of Baudelaire. Following Benjamin, Adorno identifies in Baudelaire an esoteric response to the pressure of the collective on the individual, one that separates lyrical from communicative language, purifying the former and removing it from living speech. Baudelaire's use of stylized language is in this view held to have opened a path towards hermetic poetry and the work of Mallarmé. Adorno's judgement of this strain of lyric poetry is forthright: 'The elevated, poeticizing, subjectively violent moment in weak later lyric poetry is the price it has to pay for its attempt to keep itself undisfigured, immaculate, objective; its false glitter is the complement to the disenchanted world from which it extricates itself' (*NL1*: 44–5). According to this judgement, the non-communicative language of hermetic poetry is but the complement of a reified world; however, another judgement is also possible – to regard the construction of a non-communicative language on the basis of subjectivity as the construction of a utopia, a position that Adorno approaches in his final work, *Aesthetic Theory*.

One of the reasons for Adorno's harsh judgement of hermetic poetry is his attempt in the 1957 essay to construct another history of modern lyric poetry. If the refusal of communicative language characteristic of hermetic poetry emerges from a fear of the collective, another tradition is to recognize and give shape to its claims. This tradition, identified by Adorno in Romantic poetry, recognizes that a 'collective undercurrent provides the foundation for all individual lyric poetry', and that this current gives substance to the lyric subject, a development that 'makes language the medium in which the subject becomes more than a mere subject' (*NL1*: 45). This evocation of the collective may take various forms – the 'transfusion of the collective in the individual' represented by Romantic poets' use of folk song, Baudelaire's evocation of the masses, or the evocation of 'humanity'. Common to them all is the thought that lyric poetry acts as a medium between individual and collective, registering possible (and impossible) negotiations of this predicament.

It is after these reflections that Adorno moves, in 'On Lyric Poetry and Society', to a closer analysis of two individual poems, which in the original broadcast he read out. Adorno's reading of the first by Eduard Mörike (1804–75), 'Auf einer Wanderung' ['On a Walking Tour'], begins by noting its image of the promise of happiness that, Adorno confided to his audience, can still befall visitors to small south German towns: '*In ein freundliches Städtchen tret' ich ein / In den Strassen liegt roter Abendschein*' ['I enter a friendly little town / On the streets lies the red evening light'] (cited 47). But it is precisely an image of a *promise* of happiness, not actual happiness, that is at issue.

Mörike's lyric negotiates at many levels the opposition between the near and the far: 'The poem gives the feeling of warmth and security in a confined space, yet at the same time it is a work in the elevated style, not disfigured by *Gemütlichkeit* and cosiness' (48). The simple language and the narrative, Adorno continues, 'artificially bring together [*kunstvoll in Ein zu setzen*]' the 'utopias of the most near and the most far' (48 [trans. mod.]). This logical impossibility is achieved by means of eliding subjective and objective registers – the subjectivity of the traveller entering the town and his 'strength of feeling' as he listens to a voice from 'an open window', a retrospective of the town situated between the heavens and the rushing brook. The image of the promise of happiness is a utopia; it is not a description, but describes an impossible condition of inhabiting the near in the far and the far in the near.

From the analysis of the image of the poem, Adorno moves to consider its language and rhythm, in which he identifies an 'antique element'. The language itself is aligned with the image of happiness, being both modern and near, but also containing elements from afar. The rhythmic pattern of, for example, *'wie von weit her'*, of ancient Greek strophes, and the slightly archaic use of word inversions, distance the poem at the same time as its modern lexicon and syntax bring it close to the reader. A similar effect attends the apostrophe to the muse in the penultimate line – *'O Muse, du hast mein Herz berührt'* ['Oh Muse, you have touched my heart'] – which renders anew the overused word 'muse' by placing it at the end, as if in the light of the setting sun. From this Adorno makes the critical judgement that 'the lyric succeeds in doing what the German epic attempted in vain, even in such projects as Goethe's *Hermann und Dorothea*' (48). After this definitively favourable judgement Adorno proceeds to examine the 'social significance' of such a poetic success. He shows that the poem achieves a result that was largely impossible given the social conditions of the pos-sibility of poetry under which Mörike was writing. He first situates the poem within the context of the German classical tradition which had attempted, 'in the name of humanity', to 'release subjective impulses from the contingency that threatens them in a society where relationships between human beings are no longer direct but instead mediated solely by the market' (49). For Adorno this represented in poetry what Hegel attempted in philosophy, namely, the overcoming in the name of Spirit or the Idea of the contradictions of real life, a reconciliation in the 'high style' which was quickly revealed as hollow. The devaluation of the classical ideal in the face of the market provoked its retreat into the private sphere 'and its images':

> The social force of Mörike's genius, however, consists in the fact that he combined the two experiences – that of the classicistic elevated style and that of the romantic private miniature – and that in doing so he recog-nized the limits of both possibilities and balanced them against one another with incomparable tact. (*NL1*: 49)

For Adorno such an approach towards achieving the impossible poem accounts for many of the misrecognitions of Mörike's work by con-temporaries and posterity. Praising his 'tact', Adorno describes how Mörike is 'aware of the empty and ideological aspects of elevated style as of the mediocrity, petit-bourgeois dullness, and obliviousness to totality of the Biedermeier period, in which the greater part of his lyric work falls' (49–50).

The poem acts as the medium for a fugitive synthesis of Weimar humanism and Biedermeier reality already revealed as historically impossible. Adorno's own imagistic description of this predicament enhances its precarious and precious character. As if on a narrow ridge, precarious and distant, looking down, what remains of the 'high style', namely a 'surviving memory', 'fades away' – '*Verhallend*', as in the fading away of a sound with the wind.[5] At the same time the signs of 'immediate life' also fade; the fading sounds of both are as if brought together by a stray wind, greeting the wandering poet only in their disappearance. Adorno's combination of metaphors of fading sound and vision is by no means coincidental, for the image of happiness that he is evoking is both aural and visual, combining evocation of memory through aural distance with visual presence. This crossing over of image and sound points to an important aspect of his analysis – lyric poetry is literally a meeting point of sound and image. The aural, indeed musical aspect of lyric poetry is emphasized by the extent to which the existence of musical setting for poetry underlined his choice and his mode of poetic analysis.

The predicament evoked in the reading of 'Auf einer Wanderung' is described as already sharing in the paradoxes of lyric poetry in the emerging industrial epoch. Mörike's 'trembling and fragile' solutions are exemplary of those of subsequent lyrical poetry, and Adorno makes an explicit connection with Baudelaire by citing Claudel's description of his style as a mixture of Racine and contemporary journalism.[6] In industrial society, the lyrical idea, when confronted by opposing reality, when not dedicating itself to memories of a romantic past, becomes 'more and more something that flashes out abruptly, something in which what is possible transcends its own impossibility' (50).

Before continuing with Adorno's comments on Stefan George's 'Im Windesweben' ['In the Winds-Weaving'] on which he ends the broadcast, it is necessary to digress into the relationship between the 'romantic' and the 'modern' solutions to the impossible predicament of modern lyric poetry. Adorno situates George's poem in a later stage of the development from lyric poetry's distancing itself by means of aural memory from the present and later lyric poetry's surmounting impossibility by means of flashes of light. Another stage of this development, discussed in another radio broadcast of the same year, was represented by the poetry of Eichendorff (1788–1857). The link between lyric poetry and music discernible in the echoes of Hugo Wolf's Mörike settings for voice and piano (1889) in the reading of 'Auf der Wanderung' is explicitly acknowledged in 'In Memory of Eichendorff' with its coda on Schumann's *Liederkreis*. As in the reading of Mörike, Eichendorff's poetry is located as an intimation of Baudelaire. Citing *Les Fleurs du mal*, Adorno comments that 'Eichendorff's uncontained Romanticism leads to the threshold of modernity' (*NL1*: 64). In addition, Adorno locates Eichendorff in a tradition that runs from *Sturm und Drang*, Büchner, Hauptmann, to Wedekind, expressionism and Brecht.

Mörike's and Eichendorff's anticipations of Baudelaire stage an opposition between what Adorno would later, in his essay 'Valéry's Deviations' (which is dedicated to Celan), describe as the Baudelairean left and right. Citing Pierre Jean Jouve's distinction, Adorno writes:

> What put him [Valéry] there [in the Baudelairean right-wing] is his aristocratic classicistic cult of form with its sinister political implications. This represented one aspect of Baudelaire and in Mallarmé, according to Jouve, became divorced from the social-revolutionary impulses of *Les Fleurs du mal*. The left-wing Baudelaire, in contrast, led to Surrealism by way of Rimbaud. (*NL1*: 138–9)

While this distinction is not entirely to be taken seriously, it does point to different emphases in the 'solutions' to the predicament of modern poetry, before, in and after Baudelaire. Within this scenario, Mörike inclines towards the formal discipline that would, in Baudelaire, combine the language of Racine with journalism, while Eichendorff would incline towards the 'systematic derangement of the senses'.

This at first glance unpromising reading of Eichendorff does in the end carry some conviction. Adorno argues that Eichendorff's work is not subjective, but dedicated to the surrender of the 'I'. He supports his case by citing the lines:

> Ich hör die Bächlein Rauschen
> Im Walde her und hin,
> Im Walde in dem Rauschen
> Ich weiss nicht, wo ich bin
>
> [I hear the little brooks rustling / to and fro in the woods, / in the woods in the rustling / I know not where I am] (cited *NL1*: 65)

While the travelling poetic persona of Mörike rarely loses orientation, that of Eichendorff is lost, disoriented by the *Rausch* of the leaves and of the brook amid the trees. If, in the reading of Mörike, the memory of classical humanism is a fading memory [*Verhallend*], in Eichendorff '[t]he subject turns itself into *Rauschen*, the rushing, rustling, murmuring sound of nature: into language, living on only in the process of dying away [*Verhallen*], like language. ... *Rauschen* was his favourite word, almost a formula' (*NL1*: 68–9). *Rausch* is then distinguished by Adorno as noise from sound – '*Rauschen* is not a sound [*Klang*] but a noise [*Gerausch*]' – which he sees as closer to language than sound (69). *Rausch* disorients the subjectivity of the poet, pointing to an objective reconciliation of speech and object, which may then be transcended through music. Adorno clarifies these thoughts through a reading of Eichendorff's 'Sehnsucht' ('Longing'), noting that the poem moves from the sound of the post horn, a human sound that doesn't disturb the stillness of the land but creates it – a 'profound paradox that the sound, the aura of silence, does not kill the silence so much as make it silence' (*NL1*: 71). Longing to join the travellers in the post on such a night, the poem moves between *Klang* (sound) and *Rausch*, but never reconciles them. The song of the distant wanderers descends from the *Rauschen* of the woods and sings of fairy-tale palaces with maidens awoken by *Klang*, with the poem returning to the *Rauschen* of the brooks in the summer night. Commenting on the *Rauschen* of the woods, Adorno evokes 'the paradox of a light rustling [*Rauschen*] still perceptible virtually only in an inner acoustical space, into which the heroic landscape dissolves, sacrificing the sharpness of the images to their dissolution in open infinity' (72). The longing for such infinity expressed in *Rauschen* recurs at the end of the poem as the song of such longing; *Rauschen* translated into *Klang*: 'The poem circles back to close up as in a musical recapitulation' (72). While the sound of the horn creates empty longing, the interruption of the song of the wanderers by an image of noise creates the conditions for longing to return to itself, the highest idea of happiness in which fulfilment reveals itself as 'longing itself'. If Mörike's 'Auf der Wanderung' evokes the promise of happiness, Eichendorff's 'Sehnsucht' evokes happiness as the fulfilment that remains longing, one achieved through a delicate movement between *Rauschen, Klang* and *Bild*.

The coda to 'In Memory of Eichendorff' intensifies the theme of 'Sehnsucht' – the translation of image and noise into musical sound – into a meditation on the relationship between lyric poetry and its musical setting. Adorno places Schumann's settings of Eichendorff's poems in *Liederkreis* in a lineage of settings of lyric poetry that range from Schubert's *Müllerliedern* and *Winterreise* to Schönberg's *Georgeliedern*; works that succeed through 'construction' in summoning a whole from a set of miniature elements. The setting of such poems is, however, far from incidental to them: 'Rather, they bring out a potential contained in the poems, the transcendence into song that arises in the movement beyond all specificity of image and concept, in the rustling [*Rauschen*] of language's flow' (*NL1*: 73). The musical setting of a lyric poem is thus an important aspect of its actualization, effecting a movement beyond the identities of the possible (the 'imaginable' and the 'conceivable') to the impossible. What is understood as one direction of poetic non-identity or transcendence in 'On Lyric Poetry and Society' – the moment of scintillation that exceeds the image – is now complemented by another, namely the transformation through music of the poetic word.

Adorno's concentration upon the latter finds an important limit case in the work of Stefan George, with whom the 1957 essay concludes. George is important for Adorno as a poet who develops aspects of both Baudelairean 'right' and 'left' lineages; the potential of whose work was activated by musical settings by composers of the Second Vienna School, most importantly Schönberg and Webern. This privileged intersection of modern lyric poetry with the New Music thus provides an important case for Adorno, not only for his propositions concerning the relationship between lyric poetry and society, but also for an understanding of the fate of lyric poetry 'after Auschwitz'. For at stake might be the entire 'transcendence through song' of a particular strain of modern poetry. It is in this context that his harsh comments on Schönberg's *Survivor from Warsaw* should be situated.

The reading of George's poem 'Im Windesweben' is introduced as an example of a later stage in the developing predicament of lyric poetry in an industrial society, one whose audacity 'was rescued from the frightful cultural conservatism of the George circle only when the great composer Anton von Webern set them to music' (*NL1*: 50). The spare and linear setting of Webern's Opus 3 actualized the radical estrangement that informs the poem:

Im windes-weben
War meine frage
Nur träumerei.
Nur lächeln war
Was du gegeben.
Aus nasser nacht
Ein glanz entfacht –
Nun drängt der mai
Nun muss ich gar
Um dein aug und haar
Alle tage
In sehnen leben.

[In the winds-weaving / My question was / Only daydreaming. / Only a smile was / What you gave. / From a moist night / A gleam ignites – / Now May urges / Now I must / For your eyes and hair / Every day / Live in yearning.] (cited *NL1*: 50–1)

Adorno relates the poem immediately to the 'high style', but distinguishes it radically from 'the happiness of near things' put in tension with the high style by Mörike. In the conditions of Wilhelmine Germany the high style cannot appeal to any tradition, 'least of all the legacy of classicism' (*NL1*: 52). Taking distance from and avoiding any taint of language by commerce, George's poem places the subject alone before the reified world. Even the German language is confronted by 'the ear of the German Mallarmé scholar' as if it were foreign:

He overcomes its alienation [*Entfremdung*], which is an alienation of use, by intensifying it until it becomes the alienation of a language no longer actually spoken, even an imaginary language, and in that imaginary language he perceives what would be possible, but never took place, in its composition. (*NL1*: 52–3)

Adorno cites the closing lines, arguing that they seem already to be a citation, 'but a citation not from another poet but from something language has irrevocably failed to achieve' (*NL1*: 53 [trans. mod.]). It is as if George made lines 'that sound as though they were not written by him but had been there from the beginning of time and would remain as they were forever' (53). This impossible task – a parallel is drawn with Don Quixote – is not realized without risk, in this case of the dissolution of the self-distancing subject, one which Adorno alludes to in the references to the eroticism of the poem and its intimations of the poet's subsequent homoerotic cult of Maximin.

Adorno's reading of George complements his reading of Heine in 'Heine the Wound' (1956). The same alienation from language is disclosed in Heine, but with different consequences: 'If the language were really his own, he would allow the dialectic between his own words and the words that are pre-given to take place, and the smooth linguistic structure would disintegrate' (*NL1*: 83). The movements evident in Mörike and Eichendorff are for Adorno absent in George and Heine: George distancing himself from the pre-given words of the collective and citing words never spoken, and Heine adapting language 'with the mimetic zeal of one who is excluded' (83 [trans. mod.]). Both move the language of lyric poetry away from the tension between sound and image towards pure sound, but both find at the limit of this purity an extreme vulnerability where sound touches on noise: George's use of the contraction '*gar*' (*NL1*: 53) and Heine's extravagant and exaggerated virtuosity. 'So great was the virtuosity of this man, who imitated language as if he were playing it on a keyboard,' writes Adorno of Heine, 'that he raised even the inadequacy of his language to the medium of one to whom it was granted to say what he suffered', breaking the 'immediacy of rounded, fulfilled language' (*NL1*: 83). While George removes his language from everyday experience, Heine transfigures this language: 'In Heine commodity and exchange seized control of sound and tone, whose very nature had previously consisted in the negation of the hustle and bustle of daily life' (82). The immediacy produced was fragile, and while Baudelaire would take as his theme the destruction of immediate experience, this would become apparent only much later. Adorno ends his Heine essay with the poem 'Der Heimkehr' ['The Return Home'], which describes an idyllic landscape with a young sentry playing with his rifle. The poem concludes with the brutal line: '*Ich wollt, er schösse mich tot*' ('I would that he shot me dead'). He notes: 'It has taken a hundred years for this intentionally false folksong to become a great poem, a vision of sacrifice' (*NL1*: 85). The conditions of possibility of this poem would only be satisfied a century later, after Auschwitz.

Adorno's proposition that it is barbaric to write lyric poetry after Auschwitz haunts then all of his readings of lyric poetry prior to Auschwitz. What these readings show is that Adorno's understanding of the conditions of possibility of lyric poetry was extremely subtle and open. This underlines the complexity of the proposition. It is not simply a Kantian judgement of taste, one that petitions the *sensus communis* with the claim that writing poetry after Auschwitz is tasteless and barbaric. Nor is it, in any uncomplicated sense, an ontological claim to the effect that the conditions of possibility no longer exist for the production of events previously known as lyric poems. Adorno insists in all his readings that lyric poetry is by definition impossible; it always exceeds its conditions of possibility. Nor is the claim simply ethical, that only those poems may be written which will prevent the repetition of Auschwitz. The poems written previously did not prevent this event, so how can those written afterwards be called upon to prevent its repetition? As impossible events, not fully consistent with their conditions of possibility, how can the effect of the poem be predicted? Heine's murderous sentry only gained full meaning a century later – until then he was epistemologically in advance of the conditions of knowledge that would allow his meaning to be recognized.

While it is difficult precisely to determine the force of Adorno's famous proposition, it does seem to lie between the ontological conditions of possibility and the statement of the new categorical imperative. It points to a break in the history of lyric poetry that makes it impossible ontologically or ethically to justify writing certain kinds of poem any more. The break manifests itself in a number of specific ways. It is no longer possible to write poetry in the name of happiness, the affect guiding most of the pre-Auschwitz poems read by Adorno; instead poetry must now express suffering. But this expression too now has definite limits; the use of image for present experience, and noise/sound for past and future, is now far more complicated. Granted that all lyric poetry is impossible, the question informing Adorno's proposition becomes one of how to select the appropriate form of impossibility to give expression to suffering. A final return to Adorno's examples of artistic success and failure after Auschwitz – Schönberg and Celan – in the light of these considerations might illuminate the appropriate and inappropriate form of expression for suffering.

In 'Commitment' Adorno turns to Schönberg's *Survivor from Warsaw* to show how art should not approach the suffering of the victims of National Socialism. The discussion is already at an advanced level – Schönberg is not being criticized for producing 'cheerful art' or contributing to the culture industry but, rather, for giving inappropriate expression to suffering. Adorno points to the predicament of literature – suffering cannot be forgotten, and giving it aesthetic form requires selective forgetting; but the same suffering also demands art since 'hardly anywhere else does suffering still find its own voice, a consolation that does not immediately betray it' (*NL2*: 88). The criterion at work then is immunity to betrayal – those artistic expressions of suffering are to be prized that most resist betrayal, as illustrated through the vulnerability of *Survivor from Warsaw* to such betrayal. Schönberg's work is criticized for turning suffering into an image – making it narratable through the voice of a survivor bearing witness to state murder. The latitude for betrayal of the victims is described in terms of an 'artistic rendering' of violence which contains 'the possibility that pleasure can be squeezed from it', and the chorus's prayer at the end of the work 'makes the unthinkable appear to have had some meaning; it becomes transfigured, something of its horror removed' (*NL2*: 88). Acknowledging the suffering of the victims in art seems to affirm their suffering and thus perform a further injustice.

While these criteria seem harsh with respect to Schönberg's composition, which offers a witness that moves between the languages of the survivor, the perpetrator and the victims, and which by giving meaning to the event makes it all the more horrific, they do point to what Adorno considered to be the conditions of impossibility of art, in particular lyric poetry, after Auschwitz. Refusal to betray suffering by making it narratable, by making it an object of pleasure, by giving it meaning or otherwise transfiguring it, are satisfied in the few lines on Celan in *Aesthetic Theory*. In a paralipomenon on hermetic poetry, whose German beginnings he locates in Jugendstil and George, Adorno's critical thoughts on this tradition, specifically Mallarmé and Valéry, issue into a reflection upon Celan, 'the most important contemporary representative of German hermetic poetry' (*AT*: 322). He finds Celan's poetry 'permeated by the shame of art in the face of suffering' – art is ashamed before an impossible theme, one that cannot be experienced (that is, contained within our routine conditions of possible experience) and which cannot be transfigured or raised above them, given a higher meaning. Language finds its limit in a return to the theme of noise discussed in the Eichendorff reading. These poems 'imitate a language beneath the helpless language of human beings' (322). This is not the pure language of musical sound aspired to by George, but a noise, a variant of Eichendorff's *Rausch*. Celan's noise that is imitated but not forced into images or translated into sound, whether music or human language, 'is that of the dead speaking of stones and stars'. This language is 'the last possible comfort for a death that is deprived of all meaning' (322). The organic and its promise of reconciliation are refused – what remains is the hermetic reconstruction of 'the trajectory from horror to silence' or from noise to the absence of sound. Such impossible work is for Adorno immune to betrayal since it does not offer any narrative consolation, nor provide an image of suffering, and does not transfigure or give meaning to it. Suffering murmurs through the defamed medium of lyric poetry.

The end of the history of lyric poetry does not mean that it ceases to exist but rather that it cannot continue to exist within its previous conditions of possibility. However, this does not mean that certain lyrical experiences beyond these limits are no longer available; since this history is indeed made up of such impossible moments, they are available to be recognized. Adorno's reading of lyric poetry prior to Auschwitz is conducted from the other side of horror, from beyond an experience unimaginable to the tradition of lyric poetry, a shock that may have proved terminal. In these readings Adorno encountered elements unrecognized or not fully appreciated by earlier readings. His histories of modern lyric poetry thus form part of a renegotiation of the conditions of possibility of such poetry. His readings of Mörike, Eichendorff, George and Celan – to which also might be added those of Goethe, Hölderlin, Baudelaire, Mallarmé, Valéry, Brecht, Borchardt – make them into poems written after Auschwitz. Echoing Benjamin's thesis XIV, in the 'Theses on the Philosophy of History', Adorno's history of lyric poetry is a construction of the past filled by *Jetztzeit* ('now-time') – '*Nach Auschwitz*' (see Benjamin 1973: 252–3). It created a constellation that linked the past of lyric poetry not only with its defamed present but also its possible futures.

NOTES

1   For a useful documentation of the controversy, see Kiedaisch 1998.
2   The well-known translation in *Prisms* breaks up the single German into three short English sentences in a way that disturbs the continuity of the thought.
3   Adorno's critique of Heideggerian poetics is developed further in his reading of Hölderlin, 'Parataxis'. See *NL2*: 109–50.
4   An important and influential earlier statement of this view of art as a mode of reflection is to be found in Benjamin 1996.
5   Nicholsen translates this simply as 'vanish' (*NL1*: 50).
6   The citation of Claudel is curious, for the same observation was made by Benjamin and is the more probable source for Adorno's thought at this point.

WORKS CITED

Benjamin, W. (1973), 'Theses on the Philosophy of History', trans. H. Zohn, in *Illuminations*. London: Fontana, pp. 245–55.
—— (1996), 'The Concept of Criticism in German Romanticism', trans. D. Lachterman, H. Eiland and I. Balfour, in *Selected Writings*, vol. 1, ed. M. Bullock and M. W. Jennings. Cambridge, MA: Belknap/Harvard University Press, pp. 116–200.
Kiedaisch, P. (ed.) (1998), *Lyrik nach Auschwitz? Adorno und die Dichter*. Stuttgart: Reclam.

6

The Truth in Verse?
Adorno, Wordsworth, Prosody

Simon Jarvis

Adorno chose the title *Notes to Literature* quite deliberately. It reminds us of his more extensive commitment, to music, and also implies a possible relationship between music and literature. Yet in Adorno's fragment 'Music and Language' can be found some assertions which complicate this connection:

> It is not for nothing that Kafka, like no writer before him, should have assigned a place of honour to music in a number of memorable texts. He treated the meanings of spoken, intentional language as if they were those of music, parables broken off in mid-phrase. This contrasts sharply with the 'musical' language of Swinburne or Rilke, with their imitation of musical effects and their remoteness from true musicality. (*Q*: 3)

This is not a rogue judgement. In his essay on Stefan George, too, Adorno remarks that '[t]he glib decorative quality that is so irritating in Rilke, the tendency to surrender to verse and rhyme without resistance, is for the most part restrained by reflection in George' (*NL2*: 184). Surprising as Adorno's valuation of Rilke is; unhappy as his dismissal of Swinburne may be for those of us who do not wish to put away those pleasures; what has always troubled me about these sentences is something else: the truly musical poet must renounce music. Yes, literature can in one sense have musicality. But it can only do so if it forgoes musical 'effects'. This implies a sharp distinction between the arts. Although the separations between, say, music, painting and poetry cannot be naturalistically grounded, attempts simply to abolish them in total works of art misfire. Such works treat the historical separations between the arts as though they were accidental. This seems to be the trouble with Swinburne. His verse is thought of as appropriating, with false immediacy, effects belonging to another art.

But aren't 'musical' effects often thought to be part of poetry? The distrust of Swinburne's musicality bears on the way poems are thought about in Adorno's *Aesthetic Theory*. There *Sprachkunstwerke*, linguistic works of art – a term which Adorno finds it hard to replace even as he deplores its awkwardness – fall into an anomalous zone. In order to see the anomaly, we need to recall the way Adorno handles the concepts of 'autonomy' and 'heteronomy' in art. These concepts are not classifications. It is not that some works are autonomous, others heteronomous. Adorno is thinking, rather, about a logic of autonom*ization* which at once frees and impoverishes the artwork. The less often artworks bear magical, political or liturgical functions, the more the idea of their cognitive content comes to look mythical. The embedding in 'common sense' of the notion that artworks have no such content is accompanied by an expansion of the field of their possible properties. In the case of so-called linguistic works of art, however, Adorno appears to suggest that this development is complicated by the fact that in one sense a cognitive content necessarily remains. What works of art say is 'not what their words say' (*GS* 7: 274; *AT*: 184).[1] Yet they do at least say what their words say. '[L]iterary compositions ... are both works of art and, because of their relatively autonomous discursive component, are not only works of art and not works of art throughout' (*GS* 7: 272; *AT*: 182). Interpretation of their historical truth-content or ideological force cannot then proceed only as does Adorno's philosophy of music, by treating the combinations of historically sedimented musical materials as bearing an implicit, alienated cognition which is to be deciphered, but must (one might think) also deal with an explicit cognition whose very explicitness can make it appear as a heteronomous remnant. Such are the difficulties faced by any 'philosophic song' of the kind Wordsworth once declared his 'last and favourite aspiration' (Wordsworth 1991: 1.112).

Because an abstract schedule of difficulties will produce only an abstract solution, I would like instead to approach them – and, therefore, the question of what poetics might today draw from Adorno – with close reference to a specific example: Wordsworth's poem 'Resolution and Independence'.

I

Perhaps, today, Wordsworth's expression, 'philosophic song', strikes us as strange. Socrates instructs Ion: 'Choose, then, whether you will be considered false or inspired?' (Plato 1994: 50).[2] The terms of this choice, a choice between truth and poetry with an excluded middle, are still second nature to us. So we tend to think that composing 'philosophic song' would have to be like constructing a complicated and rather unstable machine. It seems certain that thinking and versifying are essentially different kinds of activity. To attempt both at once could only be a fudge. At every turn verse would choke on a hard word, or thinking be led to founder by some metrical siren.

Yet this might not be the only way of understanding the situation. What if it were possible, not to put thinking into verse, but to think *in* verse? Before thinking was ever called philosophy, much of it was indeed undertaken in verse. Was it accidental to Empedocles' *Katharmoi* to have been composed metrically (Diels and Kranz 1993–6: ll. 354–71)? Or was it rather, we might ask, in no way strange for verse to be the medium of thinking? Pindar, to his first auditors, was not a master of rhetoric, music or feeling, but a 'master of truth' (Detienne 1996). This truth is not something which is contained in verse and could be got out of it by paraphrase. Pindar's truth *is* verse-truth. Our own sense that prose is the natural medium for philosophy does not really testify to anything natural, but rather to something historical: to the defeat of a performative conception of truth, in which truth is the opposite of oblivion and is something done by the poet to somebody else, and its replacement with another set of conceptions, in which truth is the opposite of error and is established through dialogic argument, and has nothing in particular to do with poetry. There is no path 'back' through this history. But there is an unanswered, and to some extent still unasked, question. When the poet's mastery over truth is broken, what happens to his or her relationship to metres and rhythms in which that truth was, not clothed, but embodied? Do those worlds of sound really become mere ornaments, a series of miniature mimeses of whatever the semantic content happens to be at any given point? Or do they rather retain, through the long mutations and mutilations of history and tradition, a recollection of their suppositiously immortal home – an impossible wish to be, not the garments or casket for true thinking, but the very event of truth itself: truth, as it were, 'carried alive into the heart by passion' (Wordsworth 1992: 751)?

Adorno quoted with admiration Borchardt's line referring to the '*Schmerz, in dich zu lauschen*' – the pain of listening (accusatively) *into* you (*NL1*: 193). Might the following be an instance of such a listening *into*?

> A gentle answer did the Old Man make,
> In courteous speech which forth he slowly drew:
> And him with further words I thus bespake,
> 'What kind of work is that which you pursue?
> This is a lonesome place for one like you.'
> He answer'd me with pleasure and surprize;
> And there was, while he spake, a fire about his eyes.
>
> His words came feebly, from a feeble chest,
> Yet each in solemn order follow'd each.
> With something of a lofty utterance drest;
> Choice word, and measured phrase; above the reach
> Of ordinary men; a stately speech!
> Such as grave Livers do in Scotland use,
> Religious men, who give to God and Man their dues.[3]

To listen into, rather than listen to, in this sense: that the poet finds the man's speech so interesting that it is almost impossible for him to hear what he is saying. He tells us that the man answered him with pleasure and surprise, but not what he actually said. As the quality of the poet's attention to paralanguage deepens – not only to the solemn order, and the lofty utterance, but also to the feeble chest and the fire about the eyes – semantic content, and finally word-boundaries themselves, melt away: 'But now his voice to me was like a stream / Scarce heard; nor word from word could I divide' (114–15). The man's 'phrase' is 'measured', not only in the sense that it is 'deeply weighed', perhaps, but also in a more literal sense. Following in such solemn order, it approaches the condition of metre, for which a 'stream' is often in Wordsworth's writing used as a figure (Wordsworth 1977: 76–8, ll. 620–45). (We may recall Adorno's judgement that in Borchardt's poetry '[l]anguage murmurs and rustles through him like a stream' (*NL2*: 193).) At least the effect on the poet, his inability to divide word from word, is just that which he once told us metre tended to have in all compositions, 'to throw a sort of half consciousness of unsubstantial existence over the whole composition' (Wordsworth 1992: 755n.). Here Wordsworth's half-consciousness about semantic content is just what lets him think about all the embodied aspects of speech.

Wordsworth, in other words, is using the leech-gatherer's speech to think with. He is using it to think about his own problem, verse. In one kind of reading, this use would be a misuse. It would be Wordsworth's 'aestheticization' of the encounter. But is that really true? It would be true, only if these embodied or partially material features of language (voice quality, muscular-articulatory apparatus, intonation contours, metre, phrasing) are themselves 'aesthetic': where aesthetic has come to mean, precisely, not cognitive. But what if these features are, instead, inextricably intertextured with cognition? What if it is the case that, as Ann Wennerstrom has recently suggested, prosodic features of language are by no means merely expressive and ornamental, but also essentially entangled with pragmatic and even semantic features (Wennerstrom 2001)? Then to listen to these shapes and tones might be, not just a way of ignoring someone, but a way of finding out something important about them.

What Wordsworth finds out, immediately after the man's words have for him become perfectly empty not only of semantic content but also of their very character as words, is this:

And the whole Body of the man did seem
Like one whom I had met with in a dream;
Or like a Man from some far region sent,
To give me human strength, and strong admonishment. (115–19)

Wordsworth's simile feels uncomfortable. Usually a simile compares one thing with another. This simile, though, comes forward as though comparing something with itself. The whole body of the man was like a man. 'Like a Man', I would cry out – 'he *is* a man!' The effect is not really one of bathos. It is more like that experience which Coleridge wrote of when questioning Wordsworth's theory of metre. On a staircase in the dark, you prepare yourself for a leap of several steps, only to find that you were in fact on the last step all along, and so are brought up short; 'When, therefore, correspondent food and appropriate matter are not provided for the attention and feelings thus roused, there must needs be a disappointment felt; like that of leaping in the dark from the last step of a staircase, when we had prepared our muscles for a leap of three or four' (Coleridge 1997: 220). Here, the second half of the line helps you find your balance. 'Like', in this line, has itself become a sort of transferred epithet. It is not as though the man were a man but as though the man were sent from some far region. Yet the strangeness caused by the repetition of the word 'man' does not go away. It lingers, and it implies that the word 'man' might be, as it were, not quite the same as itself or not quite equal to itself, and so is capable of making a whole simile out of itself, providing both tenor and vehicle.

What could I mean, though, by saying that a word is 'not quite equal to itself'? Here it is helpful to remember Adorno's contrast between 'emphatic' concepts and 'cover-concepts' (*GS* 6: 152–4; *ND*: 148–51). A cover-concept is one which can be used to limit the members of a set. It is descriptive. But an emphatic concept is one which has inside it a promise. It is a promise which cannot be cut out of the concept without changing it. So that the concept of 'art', it could be suggested, is not merely a cover-concept. It does not signify a certain set of properties, any object possessing which could count as an instance of the concept. To call something art is always not only to describe something but also to evaluate it.

The word 'human' stands uneasily at the borders of these two kinds of concept. Even in its apparently most straightforward descriptive use, it is, as it were, coloured by a norm, a value, or a wish: for the 'truly' human, say. In this sense it is a word which is not equal to itself. Even where it is used to designate, for example, the rational component of a rational animal, it is accompanied by an undersense of something harder to name, just because it concerns a wish or a problem rather than an object. How often, then, Wordsworth's uses of this word open this gulf! 'No human fears' (Wordsworth 1992: 164). Inhuman ones, then? 'Last human tenant of these ruined walls' (1979: 72). Then animals or plants may be tenants too? 'A deep distress hath humaniz'd my Soul' (1983: 267). What then was it before?

'To give me human strength, and strong admonishment'. What kind of strength is 'human' strength? How would the meaning of the line be altered if Wordsworth had written: 'To give me strength, and strong admonishment'? It would sound awkward, of course: strength *and* strong admonishment. The addition of 'human' relieves this difficulty. A half-chiasmus is created, with 'strong' and 'strength' in the middle, so that the connection between *strength* and *strong* feels not inadvertent, but like wit. More simply, without 'human', the line would be metrically defective.

It would be too short. But semantically, or in so far as paraphrase is concerned, it is much harder to say how the line would be changed. The meaning of 'human', by the end of this stanza – and, eventually, by the end of the poem, of which this, after all, presents what comes to seem the decisive event, the moment which enables the poet to take the leech-gatherer as confirming his faith in himself as a poet – the meanings of 'man' and of 'human' have not been specified, but sounded out. If the human were only the rational component of a rational animal there would be no difficulty of any kind in knowing what was meant by it. We could all know just by knowing our own presence to ourselves in consciousness. But for Wordsworth, the human does not seem to be something which is readily and straightforwardly known, but rather something fragile or temporary which becomes most visible precisely where it is on the point of being lost. The leech-gatherer is described as 'not all alive, nor dead', and yet, strangely, this does not make him less human, but instead testifies to his seeming to bear 'a more than human weight'. Just so, the human strength which this man-like-a-man gives the poet seems also in some way to be more than human: not to be what, since I am human, I could always in any case produce, my self-conscious reflection on my own mental activity, but rather to be something which, precisely, can never be all my own work: 'a leading from above, a something given' (51), 'from some far region sent' (118).

And as if at once to confirm this sense that the 'human' may be something fragile and temporary, rather than a secure possession, this 'human strength' then disappears as rapidly as it has arrived:

> My former thoughts return'd: the fear that kills;
> The hope that is unwilling to be fed;
> Cold, pain, and labour, and all fleshly ills;
> And mighty Poets in their misery dead.
> And now, not knowing what the Old Man had said,
> My question eagerly did I renew,
> 'How is it that you live, and what is it you do?' (120–6)

The apparent consolation of the previous stanza vanishes. It is not sublated, kept in reserve, or overcome. It is simply erased, as though a cloud had passed over the sun. Cold, pain and labour seem to disperse the very idea of 'human strength' sounded in the previous stanza. They seem to render that idea, precisely, *aesthetic*, by placing its optional 'as if' against a reality of compulsory need. It is as though nothing of any substance had in the event happened at all in the previous stanza, and as though the poet cannot now remember what the point of it was. And this appearance is deepened by the way the poet reacts to this unexplained relapse. *Now* it is important to hear what the man is actually saying. Now stately speech and lofty utterance be damned: how does this man keep alive? And yet perhaps not everything has been erased: since, after all, the question can only feel in this way urgent to the poet because he has begun to get a dim intimation that there might be an analogy between himself and the leech-gatherer. Only because this implicit analogy – which is never at any point made explicit – has already been established through such close attention to the paralinguistic, can asking the man with such urgency how *he* lives and what *he* does, feel like a way of dealing with the poet's fears for his own self-preservation. This feeble chest may utter stately speech: perhaps, then, even an impoverished poet may bring forth mighty verse. To which, as soon as we have got the idea of this analogy, succeeds a further, less edifying connection. Poems are like leeches. They attach themselves to you and suck out your blood. Then you can sell them, for a pittance. What is more, the supply of them is dwindling. Once they could be met with on every side, but not any more. Given this developing connection, it is perhaps not so surprising that, within a few lines, the poet's mind again appears to wander. In the very next stanza he is already pursuing thoughts within himself, so evidently absent that the leech-gatherer courteously leaves a pause in which this inner preoccupation may be pursued.

The poem, in fact, lays before us a series of just those kinds of 'generous fluctuations of feeling' which it has told us about near its beginning:

> But, as it sometimes chanceth, from the might
> Of joy in minds that can no further go,
> As high as we have mounted in delight,
> In our dejection do we sink as low (22–5)

What is characteristically Wordsworthian about this explanation is not so much the lurch from one feeling to another as the insistence on the connection between the two. Excessive joy is not merely replaced by excessive dejection: the one follows 'from' the other. Wordsworth's poetry is recurrently preoccupied with this question, of how to bear an intolerably intense joy. And one of the main ways in which it can be borne, he implies, is through metre.

II

The 'Preface' to the *Lyrical Ballads* famously argues that metre can make intolerably painful passions a proper object of readerly pleasure. The discussion of metre is, of course, well known. But, as Hegel once remarked, just because a thing is well known it does not follow that it is known; and the strangeness of some of what Wordsworth says about metre there has perhaps become familiar only through repetition. There's no time here even to begin to discuss those passages in full. Here I want only to think about one phrase. *How* does metre produce its effects? By 'an intertexture of ordinary feeling', Wordsworth answers (1992: 755). This answer is itself extraordinary. What *is* 'ordinary feeling'? It seems to be, precisely, no particular feeling, but, as it were, the feeling of feeling itself. It appears to be that feeling which is in the background of every other feeling, or which accompanies every other feeling, rather as Kant says that transcendental apperception accompanies all my representations – except that for Kant, apperception is emphatically not a feeling. Ordinary feeling is the feeling of being alive itself. Yet, at the same time, metre is to *supply* this 'ordinary' feeling! Why? Why does it need to? Wouldn't this feeling necessarily always be there in all experience? Perhaps not. Perhaps we have, even for quite long stretches, the experience of going through life as if we don't feel anything, and perhaps especially not the feeling of being alive: the phenomenon which Adorno calls 'loss of experience'. Perhaps we even, as Wordsworth at one point implies, need something as intrusive as an intolerably powerful light – the sun, 'Which while we view we feel we are alive' – to make us feel this feeling (1991: 1.129). Because, for Wordsworth, metre is emphatically a power in itself, and not merely a mode of tempering or restraining other passions. Metre does not, for Wordsworth, merely temper strong feelings. It also resuscitates dead ones.

And for this reason, we need to read 'Resolution and Independence' a second time. If, as I have suggested, the poem charts for us the generous fluctuations of feeling from joy to dejection and back again, and back again, and back again, then it may not only lay these fluctuations out, but also sound them out. We need to read Wordsworth as he reads the leech-gatherer. We need not only, like eager literalists, to interrogate him – 'How is it that you live and what is it you do?' – but also to be capable of becoming absorbed in what we now know cannot be the mere contingencies of lofty utterance and measured phrase. For this reason, rather than making a diagram of the poem's metrico-rhythmical problems, a diagram which, of course, would necessarily leave out or freeze to a mere placeholder the very foundation of both metre and rhythm, the experience of a living subject, I want to start from an experience of one line in it. Somebody's experience of that line: mine, in fact. Very little of our experience of poetry really happens in the way that it tends to get narrated when we are doing what is called 'doing a reading' of it. That's of course one of the virtues of doing a reading. We force ourselves to attend not only to what we have liked to think about, but also to what we have not liked to think about. Yet one of its by-products is a kind of simulacrum of readerly experience: a writing which does not so much describe any experience in particular as it uses an experience to make a story which might be everybody else's too. There's no hope of avoiding that. But the more rapidly everything which the critic fears is merely contingent or idiosyncratic gets crossed out, the less chance any eventual *sensus communis* could have of being fully solidary, rather than merely contractual. If, as Kant supposed, and as I am willing to believe, it is written into the very grammar of aesthetic judgements that they are subjectively universal – unable to compel assent, yet unable not to try to – then I would want to add that the entire subject needs to be at stake in this, and not merely the approbable bits of it (Jarvis 2002). So the fact that much of our experience of poems comes in recollecting them, voluntarily or involuntarily, is not unimportant. It is impossible to make the entirety of a poem appear before consciousness instantaneously. Even if one knows it by heart, it must be recounted. A single line, however, is different. It feels as though it is not only something to be measured out in time, but rather as though it is itself a measure of time, a unit of lived, not pseudo-spatialized, duration. Or, again, it may feel like an explosion or an implosion of any such measure, since, when I think I am remembering 'Resolution and Independence', what I am very often remembering is this one line, 'But thereof comes in the end despondency and madness' (49). The core of my experience of this line is that of someone blurting or stammering out a truth which has long been kept suppressed from the speaker himself. I join it in my mind with another experience, of hearing an eloquent and rational friend recount the process by which he had come to acknowledge a painful incident in early childhood, and of the moment at which this friend, in retelling, not the incident itself, but the story of how he came to remember it, suddenly was back at the same point all over again, and blurted out, without warning all at once on the point of weeping, an angry question to a nurse he had not seen or thought about for thirty years. What makes this experience joinable in my mind with the experience of the line in the poem is not only the distressing content in both cases and the suddenness of its appearance, but the paralinguistic disturbance of measure.

Can I see what it is in the line that shapes this experience? I can engage in all sorts of creative accounting to make the line work as an instance of the kind of line that has been at the corresponding place in the previous stanzas. The line is fourteen syllables, admittedly, but one of those is accounted for by the so-called 'feminine' ending, and there is no shortage of ways in which the other one can be got rid of: if I were a certain kind of eighteenth-century prosodist I could suggest eliding 'despondency'and'; in an Attridgean schema I could call on the exceptional emergency measure of the 'triple offbeat'; in Curetonian rhythmic-phrasing analysis I could construct a tree which would show the 'satisfying' order beneath surface disturbance. Yet, in another way, the plethora of means for solving the problem only shows how difficult the problem is. It is not, in other words, primarily that the line risks being hypermetrical, but that its potential hypermetricality goes along with such metrico-rhythmic undecidability. Even if we restrict the analysis to a crude two-value stress system, of relatively strong and relatively weak stress, and attempt to begin from the provisional standpoint of so-called 'prose rhythm', the line is not easy to read:

But thereof comes in the end despondency and madness

As usual, the polysyllables give us most initial help, because their rhythmic value is much less ambiguous: despondency looks pretty clearly like W S W W, and madness is S W. 'Thereof' is less easy, because it can be stressed either W S or S W, according to preference, and even, for emphasis, S S. Usually, this kind of rhythmic polyvalence is not a problem but a resource for metrical verse, because it allows for metre itself to influence performance, yet here it is not clear how it should so influence it. In the end I conclude that S W, '*there*of', at least does not render the line hopeless. So that I come out, roughly, with this:

W   S   W   (W/S)   W W   S   W S   W W   W   S   W

But thereof comes in the end despondency and madness

In this line of fourteen syllables only four relative stress peaks can with the best will in the world be discerned. At the beginning of the line there is an extraordinary hurry of four relatively unstressed syllables in succession, and another such hurry after the stress peak of the word 'despondency'. Given that the first syllable of 'thereof' is also a weaker stress peak than that on 'despondency', I have the sense of a rush towards these two late peaks in the line: 'despondency', 'madness'. The 'overflow', in other words, is not merely figurative. It joins those other instances of severely dislocated or possibly hypermetrical lines in Wordsworthian lyric at which some joy or pain too forceful to be contained is blurted out: 'Shout round me, let me hear thy shouts, thou happy Shepherd Boy!' (1983: 272); 'And the most ancient Heavens through Thee are fresh and strong' (1983: 107). And, I suggest, the fact that Wordsworth uses the same word, 'overflow', to think about feeling and rhythm alike, indicates to us that the necessarily perpetually unresolved drama of enthusiasm and its regulation in Wordsworth is not conducted solely or even primarily at a 'thematic' level, but also and perhaps even more centrally in the stuff of the poetry itself, at a metrico-rhythmic level.

'A deep distress has humaniz'd my Soul'. The clear implication is that the soul was previously inhuman. Also, that were it to become perfectly and entirely and descriptively 'human', rather than merely humanized, it would be finished off entirely: dead. My two subjects thus far, in reading 'Resolution and Independence', have been the human, and metre. But I think I can now see that they are, for Wordsworth, and, even, for me, too, perhaps, the *same* subject. Wordsworth senses already what Henri Meschonnic formulated thus: not only that 'there is no theory of rhythm without a theory of subjectivity', but also that 'there is no theory of subjectivity without a theory of rhythm' (Meschonnic 1982: 71). The human, we found, in this poem, is not what is always and undisturbably present to itself. It is strange to itself, there most fully when most on the brink of being lost or of disintegrating. And metre, we saw, provides 'an intertexture of ordinary feeling'. It provides the feeling not of any particular feeling but of being, not necessarily a rational animal, but a feeling being. It needs to provide this just because ordinary feeling is something that we precisely do not always have in our possession, but which we can and do lose, as we can and do lose the capacity for experience itself. One name for that capacity, I think, is imagination. Imagination can name our sense that something of some kind has actually happened to us: something that we have *not* made, except in so far as we have been able to *receive* it. In these dislocated lines we hear in this sense the sound of imagination. For this reason, Wordsworth's 'resolution' hardly seems final. The poem tells a story, about coming to a resolution. Yet its own most dislocated and irresolute utterance continues to resound long after it is supposed to have died away.

III

Because prosody is often understood as a name for whatever is musical in the poem, it may represent for Adorno a troublingly liminal area between literature and music. It is characteristic of Adorno's materialism that some of his most extended considerations of the questions usually covered by the concept of prosody should come in his essay on 'Punctuation Marks':

> In none of its elements does language bear such an affinity to music as in its punctuation. Commas and full stops correspond to the half cadence and the full cadence. Exclamation marks are like the clashes of soundless cymbals; question marks, the upward movement of a phrase; colons, dominant seventh chords; and the distinction between the comma and the semi-colon can only properly be felt by one who is capable of perceiving the differing weights of strong and weak phrasing in musical form. Perhaps, however, the idiosyncratic animus against punctuation which developed in the early years of the twentieth century, and from which no attentive observer will wholly dissociate himself, perhaps this was less a protest against an ornamental element than an indication of how sharply music and language diverge from each other. It can hardly be regarded as accidental, on the other hand, that music's point of contact with the punctuation marks in language was bound up with the schema of tonality, a schema which has, in the meantime, disintegrated; and that the new music can well be thought of as striving towards a punctuation without tonality. But if music is compelled to shelter the image of its affinity with language in punctuation marks, it is possible that language, in its mistrust of them, is clinging to its affinity with music. (*GS* 11: 106–7; *NL1*: 92)

Punctuation thus turns out to be a critical topic for understanding the relation between music and language. The 'correspondences' between various punctuation marks and certain frequently recurring musical figures are affinities, rather than severe analogies. Such recurring elements are essential to Adorno's thought about music. For him, there is not only a philosophy of music, but a philosophy in music. Adorno often compares these musical 'ciphers' to the 'basic concepts' of epistemology. The way in which a system marshals its networks of contradictions and antagonisms with the help of certain repeated tropes (for example, the law of the excluded middle or the distinction between thinking and knowing) is compared to the way in which a musical work is marshalled by just the kinds of figure referred to in this essay: dominant sevenths, cadences, question-and-answer phrasing. For this reason Adorno thinks that an apparently non-cognitive system of signs such as music does in fact take on a cognitive content, one which works not only by articulating, within larger arrays, signs which, taken by themselves, mean nothing (just as, in any case, the letters of a word mean nothing at all taken by themselves); but which also works by the relation of these larger arrays – phrases and movements and sonatas – to the entire history of the cognitively resonant materials with which they work. Interpretation of the cognitive content of musical works becomes possible thanks to the affinities in the composition and articulation of substantively discontinuous fields.

Punctuation marks appear, then, to occupy the same place with respect to literature that musical ciphers occupy in music and that basic concepts occupy in epistemology. Like their counterparts, instances of deployed punctuation are possessed of a possible, and necessarily historical, truth-content. The particular early-twentieth-century suspicion of excessive punctuation which Adorno has in mind here is likely to be that of Stefan George and his school, mentioned several times in this short essay. In differing forms, though, the suspicion is one shared by much modern poetry. Adorno provides a compressed critique of this moment. A dislike of ornament is only the ostensible reason for it. More significant is the musical function of punctuation. Minimized pointing emphasizes the autonomy of poetry from music. Yet it does so just as music is creating a way of organizing itself which does not depend upon the recurring ciphers of tonality, but which might instead be understood better, Adorno suggests, by analogy with written punctuation. The consequence of this is that poetry, when it purges punctuation to a bare minimum, may in the event become less, rather than more, sharply distinct from music. In his long essay on Hölderlin's late hymns, Adorno suggests that their difference from identity thinking lasts better than, say, that attempted in concrete poetry, just because Hölderlin does not think he can free himself by what would remain a merely abstract obliteration of syntax (*NL2*: 134–7). Just so, here, it is possible that wiping the page clean of punctuation may offer only an illusory exit from the domination of language. But Adorno's tone is not so clear at this point. If advanced music is right to shelter its resemblance to language, why would it be wrong for poetry to be attached to its own affinity to music?

What emerges here is the aporetic status of language, and, acutely, of prosody, in Adorno's thinking. It's just because Adorno is a materialist that he rejects the culturalistic understanding of language which has so prevailed recently. Language is aporetic just because it can't confidently be assigned to either of the twinned and so mutually dependent pair, 'culture' or 'nature'. Just as Adorno's philosophy of music both depends upon and differs from the language of what is thought of as the natural science of music, so any account of prosody learning from it will both depend upon and differ from the natural science of language. By the same token, it will keep its distance from the dogmatic abbreviation holding that signifiers are 'arbitrary', an abbreviation whose metaphysical content is only further embedded when it is extended to signifieds and to everything else as well. Prosody, liminal with respect to the categories of autonomy and heteronomy, liminal with respect to the categories of culture and nature, threatens to blur some of the lines along which Adorno wants to interpret those aporias. The distinction between musical works (more decisively alienated from cognition and thus more decisively autonomous) and literary works (still harbouring a heteronomous remnant of explicit reference) is founded on a distinction between the explicit and the implicit; a distinction which is, however, continually being undone in Adorno's own demonstrations: of the impossibility of perfectly literal language, of the impossibility of perfectly thoughtless music. So that the real justification for distrusting Swinburne's musicality, if any, would have to be found somewhere else.

In 'Music and Language' Adorno remarked that music was 'demythologized, prayer rid of efficacious magic' (*Q*: 2). Something of this applies to 'philosophic song' too. I want, then, to restate some of the questions with which I began this chapter, not because I think that I am now in a position to answer them, but because of the 'strong admonishment' administered by Wordsworth's poem.

When the poet's mastery over truth is broken, what happens to his or her relationship to metres and rhythms in which that truth was, not clothed, but embodied? Do those worlds of sound really become mere ornaments, a series of miniature mimeses of whatever the semantic content happens to be at any given point? Or do they rather retain, through the long mutations and mutilations of history and tradition, a recollection of their suppositiously immortal home – an impossible wish to be, not the garments or casket for true thinking, but the very event of truth itself?

One answer, of course, goes like this: 'That's ancient history'. Yes! But because verse is not primarily a collection of opinions, ideas and attitudes, but a sort of technique of the body, at once cognitive and corporeal, it requires that kind of historicism which pays attention to protracted duration, as well as to rapid change. Philosophy and verse do not have a merely accidental relationship to each other, as we tend instinctively to feel, but rather a quite particular historical relationship: a war embrace in which verse has been allowed to be inspired so long as it does not make the mistake of claiming to be true. The most illuminating recent discussion by a classicist describes one aspect of this process thus: 'Dialectic is not only the antidote to the death of the words of Socrates: it is also an antidote to the words of the rhapsode. We see a rivalry here in establishing the definitive meaning of *dialegesthai*: ... The Socratic *dialegesthai* of Plato brings back to life the words of Socrates each time they are read, but it does not bring back Socrates himself. ... Rhapsodic *dialegesthai*, by contrast, brings back to life not only the words of Homer. It brings back Homer himself' (Nagy 2002: 32–3). In other words, Plato's *Ion* enters the sanctum of mediumistic rhapsody, strips it of its authority, yet carries off its core function – the immortalization of truth – for a new practice: dialectic!

It is no accident that 'a philosophy of metre is almost altogether lacking in our age' (Agamben 1998: 34). It shows part of what has happened to philosophy and what has happened to metre, for both good and bad. A division of intellectual labour projects its own wounds on to poetry, as though they were the fault of the object, which is then to be punished by having the possibility of its truth thoroughly deleted. Philosophy has excised from poetry something which was once at its heart. Philosophical poetics cannot give it back, but can try to decipher the strange accents in which poetry has spoken ever since. These tunes, rhythms and orchestrations, notes of a damaged thinking.

NOTES

1 Where I have used my own translation from Adorno, I have given the reference to the German original first, and to the standard English translation after.
2 This is Percy Bysshe Shelley's translation of Plato.
3 Wordsworth 1983: 127, ll. 92–105. Further references to this poem will be by line number to this edition.

WORKS CITED

Agamben, G. (1998), *The End of the Poem: Studies in Poetics*, trans. D. Heller-Roazen. Stanford, CA: Stanford University Press.
Coleridge, S. T. (1997), *Biographia Literaria*, ed. N. Leask. London: Dent.
Detienne, M. (1996), *The Masters of Truth in Archaic Greece*, trans. J. Lloyd. New York: Zone.
Diels, H. and Kranz W. (1993–6), *Die Fragmente der Vorsokratiker*. Zürich: Weidmann.
Jarvis, S. (2002), 'An undeleter for criticism', *diacritics* 32(1), 3–18.
Meschonnic, H. (1982), *Critique du rythme: anthropologie historique du langage*. Lagrasse: Editions Verdier.
Nagy, G. (2002), *Plato's Rhapsody and Homer's Music: The Poetics of the Panathenaic Festival in Classical Athens*. Cambridge, MA: Harvard University Press.
Plato (1994), *Plato on Poetry*, ed. P. Murray. Cambridge: Cambridge University Press.
Wennerstrom, A. (2001), *The Music of Everyday Speech: Prosody and Discourse Analysis*. Oxford: Oxford University Press.

Wordsworth, W. (1977), *Home at Grasmere*, ed. B. Darlington. Ithaca, NY: Cornell University Press.

— (1979), *The Ruined Cottage and The Pedlar*, ed. J. Butler. Ithaca, NY. Cornell University Press.

— (1983), *Poems, in Two Volumes, and Other Poems, 1800–1807*, ed. J. Curtis. Ithaca, NY: Cornell University Press.

— (1991), *The Thirteen-Book Prelude*, ed. M. L. Reed. 2 vols. Ithaca, NY: Cornell University Press.

— (1992), *Lyrical Ballads and Other Poems, 1797–1800*, ed. J. Butler and K. Green. 2 vols. Ithaca, NY: Cornell University Press.

7

Lyric's Expression:
Musicality, Conceptuality, Critical Agency

Robert Kaufman

What today could be more bourgeois, more aestheticist, than a poetry and poetics of lyric expressivity? Not much; or at least, that's periodically been the response, across the last century, of key progressive and Left strains in poetry and criticism. Everybody knows that, starting essentially with Romanticism, individualist bourgeois subjectivity sidles up to the social jukebox and pushes the warped button marked *lyric expression* whenever it's time to hear a songful meditation of and about poignant longing, mild dissatisfaction, or carefully delimited negativity. That *lyric* is the mode or genre at issue surprises no one, nor should it, because lyricism, musicality and expression have been formally and historically bound together since well before the advent of Romantic poetry, a binding that has continued through the most modern poetic and musical experiments in and after atonality, dissonance and serialism. During the past few decades of Left artistic and critical activity, the critique of lyric expressivism has often turned to Marxian and, more specifically, to Frankfurt School figures to underwrite renewed attempts to imagine a poetry that could leave expression behind; whether in Language Poetry or in kindred neo-avant-gardist groupings, and with a host of citations in particular to the translated texts of Benjamin's *Passagenwerk* and Adorno's *Ästhetische Theorie*, this has often seemed like a call to abolish lyric musicality *tout court*, though experiments have also toyed with notions of a non-expressive or anti-expressive musicality, even an anti-expressive lyric.

For all the real interest thereby generated, such critical and artistic work has tended to misconstrue Frankfurt approaches to lyric expressivism, as if zeroing in, without context, on Benjamin's quip – often ratified by Adorno – that for all he cared, innerness or inwardness [*Innerlichkeit*] could go fly a kite.[1] In Benjamin and Adorno's more sustained engagements with Romantic, later-nineteenth- and twentieth-century poetry, an exploratory or experimental poetics is virtually at one with the stretching rather than the abjuration of lyric subjectivity and practice. The Frankfurters and the artists historically closest to them tend to regard lyric as literary art's 'go-for-broke-game' ['*Va-banque-Spiel*'], for the lyric must limit itself to working coherently in and with the medium – language – that human beings use to articulate presumably objective concepts, even while the lyric explores in semblance-character the most subjective, non-conceptual and ephemeral phenomena. This theoretical or philosophical difficulty, concerning how simultaneously to think objectively and subjectively, also arises practically as lyric's great problem of form-construction: how – with language alone as medium – to build a solid, convincing artistic structure out of something as evanescent as subjective song and how, into the bargain, to delineate or objectivate the impressively fluid contents of capitalist modernity? How, spontaneously yet rigorously, and with the utmost concision, to make thought sing and to make song think? For the Frankfurters, lyric dramatizes with special intensity modern aesthetic quasi-conceptuality's more general attempt in semblance to stretch conceptual thought proper, precisely in the aesthetic's enactment of a thought-experience that maintains the *form* of conceptual thought without being beholden to status quo concepts and their contents. Lyric's special formal intensity within this larger field of quasi-conceptual aesthetic experience arises from its historically constitutive need to stretch musically in semblance the very medium of 'objective' conceptual thought, language – that is, to stretch language quasi-conceptually, mimetically, all the way toward affect and song, but without relinquishing any of the rigour and complexity of conceptual intellection, so that in a semblance-character vital to the possibility of critical agency, speech can appear as song and song can legitimately *seem* to be a logical, purposeful speech-act (see Kaufman 2002; 2004).

All this is perhaps a long way of saying that Benjamin's and Adorno's much-celebrated theory and practice of the constellation, far from being an antidote to immersion in the literary and aesthetic, just might for them be the most profound work *of* the aesthetic, the literary and, above all (because of its medium and that medium's relationship to conceptuality), the poetic in lyric mode. For Benjamin and Adorno, experimental nineteenth- and twentieth-century lyric stands as the initial foundation and ultimate instance of how, *pace* more orthodox historical materialism, constellative form seeks the kind of thought that by definition attempts to exceed determination by extant concepts while still aiming to configure or construct something potentially objective or universal; thus the constellation operates as an intellectual attempt non-deterministically yet also non-arbitrarily to locate and dynamically connect elements (historical, socioeconomic, cultural) that are not initially given as relational but that, when animated – constellated – into conjunction, create or reveal a signifying force field neither instrumental nor arbitrary. This is, of course, almost precisely Benjamin's sense of what genuinely experimental lyric does; it is likewise and even more explicitly Adorno's oft-quoted definition of such lyric: 'a subjectivity that turns into objectivity' (*NL1*: 43; *GS* 11: 56). So it is hardly accidental that, again and again, Benjamin and Adorno will temporally suspend or interrupt their considerations of the substantive referents pertaining to the constellations under construction in order to emphasize the formal aesthetic dynamics *of* construction and its twinned Other, mimetic semblance-expression. Such charged momentary suspension is the very calling card of aesthetic experience, and of lyric especially, whose go-for-broke wager involves reconfiguration of the forms of its linguistic medium (and from the perspective of lyric theory and practice, this will mean making the constellation – the heavenly, intelligent, *geistige*, or critical sphere – sing its music and allow its song to be heard). In a dance-tension of thought and affect, constellation seeks, at least in semblance, to restore to thought-experience what the invaluable tool of conceptual abstraction perforce has excised from thought, namely, concrete, particular, conceptually undetermined *experience* (*ND*: 162–6; *GS* 6: 164–8). It is not happenstance that among the aesthetic and lyric problems Benjamin and Adorno love to attend to are those that seem precisely and self-consciously to constellate this theory of constellation itself. These may indeed be some of the most fascinating moments in their work, but, arguably and on their own authority, the issues will be even more intensely presented by poets attempting implicitly or explicitly to enact and rediscover the bases of constellation theory and practice in the making of and response to lyric art.

Because Benjamin, Adorno and artists adjacent to them all undertook militant defences of constructivism, it has seemed to many that their constructivism must have placed them in opposition to mimesis, semblance-projection and expression – starting and finally ending with the instance of lyric. This supposition has become an uncritical article of faith, decoupled from historical or aesthetic contextualization, for significant numbers of neo-avant-gardist poets and critics. Yet from Benjamin to Brecht to Adorno, that was emphatically not the case, as some recent critical reconsiderations have made clear (Huyssen 2002; Jay 2004). Indeed, precisely this question of expression and its relation to expressive subjectivity will not only mark the later rift between Adorno and the Darmstadt 'hyperconstructivist' composers; it had already marked Adorno's ultimate reservations about Schönbergian serialism (which for the Darmstadters still bore too many traces of lyric semblance, expression and subjectivity, while for Adorno it retained too few).

Following from Benjamin's work on Baudelaire and the modern 'withering' of experience, Adorno offers what is perhaps the most acute and sustained analysis of the relationships between expression and experience. He notes that the abandonment of expression, however radically intended, is tantamount to the acceptance of the unavailability of historical experience, individual and collective. On some level, the continuing struggle for expression – whether or not successfully achieved – is the precondition for the sense of critical agency, because even the negative glimpse of a receding 'aura' or experience offers some sense of what aura, experience and expression are, and some sense of the meaning of their apparent banishment from contemporary social life (whereas an ostensibly hard-nosed acceptance of such unavailability simply leads to forgetfulness about what it is like to experience the reflective preconditions for critical agency, which leads in turn to acceptance of their disappearance). Far from this merely entailing the disappearance of the alleged pseudoemotions of bourgeois culture, what is at stake is an awareness of history as such; 'experience' here is inextricable from history, which Adorno repeatedly underscores when he states that the struggle for expression in art is the struggle to express historical experience, above all, the historical experience of human suffering.[2]

To make the content of such experience and suffering available in semblance to the affective life and consciousness of others, artworks must seek or develop the formal means to express the resources of their media. These means have frequently been grasped as artistic 'languages' because of the fundamental relationship between language and conceptuality: 'What makes existing artworks more than existence is not simply another existing thing, but their language' (*AT*: 104; *GS* 7: 160). That's why literature, and lyric in particular, so often serves as model for the necessarily formalist act that expresses – that ultimately sings – the capacity for expression itself. 'There is good reason that where this term ['expression'] has been technically employed longest and most emphatically, as the directive *espressivo* in musical scores, it demands nothing specifically expressed, no particular emotional content. Otherwise *espressivo* could be replaced by terms for whatever specific thing is to be expressed' (*AT*: 104–5, 111–12, *GS* 7: 160, 170–1).

All this helps explain why – again following the early Benjamin – Adorno understands expression as semblance or mimesis, mimesis grasped not as transcription but as an attempt provisionally to know something of the otherness outside the subject, an effort proceeding through consciously undertaken fictions that begin, à la Aristotelian imitation, with bodily gestures aiming toward a non-identical notion of what otherness of various kinds might be. It also helps us see why, particularly in the modernity that appears to make historical experience recede from view, mimesis or expression, rather than being something that ought to be abandoned, needs to be coaxed or constructed all the more urgently into form. Hence Adorno's repeatedly invoked, ceaseless dialectic of construction and expression and his severe critique of the unintentionally reactionary consequences of one-sidedly antimimetic or anti-expressive styles of constructivism, because banishment of semblance and expression prevents the mimetic process from allowing for or stimulating the emergence and shaping of materials that may subsequently, post-aesthetically, begin to be conceptually enunciated as critique.[3] This has come to seem a specifically Adornian view; it is not. Nor is it, even in Adorno, a necessarily 'high-art' view, though it is a view that assumes that works of art and culture, if they are to contribute to critical agency, will likely be of a certain intensity and density, which usually means that, whatever else they are, they'll have to be pretty damn good (see Huyssen 2002).

But Left and neo-avant-gardist doubts may remain when it comes to anything as subjectivist as expression, not to mention poetic lyric expressivity itself, and those doubts might lead some again to join their voices to that old and not-so-old cry: 'Forget Adorno! How about Brecht?' Well, here the latter is, writing in his *Arbeitsjournal*, thinking in exile about modernist lyric, its prehistories, and the future of his own poetic production. It is 8 August 1940; Brecht is in exile in Finland while German bombs are falling on London during the Battle of Britain. Immediately behind him is his collaborative rereading with Benjamin of Percy Shelley and hence a re-thinking of lyric, aura and commitment:

> i skimmed a small volume of WORDSWORTH in [Matthew] arnold's edition, came on '*She was a Phantom of delight*' and was moved by this now remote work to reflect how varied the function of art is [*wie vielfach die Funktion der Kunst ist*], and how dangerous it is to lay down the law. (Brecht 1993: 90–1; 1994: 417)

What Brecht has at hand is a 1927 reprint of Matthew Arnold's canonical 1879 *Poems of Wordsworth* (Brecht 1994: 661). Here is the poem as it appears in Arnold's edition, placed in the section Arnold titles, following Wordsworth's own previous editorial practice, 'Lyrical Poems':

> She was a Phantom of Delight
> When first she gleamed upon my sight;
> A lovely Apparition sent
> To be a moment's ornament;
> Her eyes as stars of Twilight fair;
> Like Twilight's, too, her dusky hair;
> But all things else about her drawn
> From May-time and the cheerful Dawn;
> A Dancing Shape, an Image gay,
> To haunt, to startle, and waylay.
>
> I saw her upon nearer view,
> A Spirit, yet a Woman too!
> Her household motions light and free.
> And steps of virgin liberty;
> A countenance in which did meet
> Sweet records, promises as sweet;
> A Creature not too bright or good
> For human nature's daily food;
> For transient sorrows, simple wiles.
> Praise, blame, love, kisses, tears, and smiles.

And now I see with eye serene
The very pulse of the machine;
A Being breathing thoughtful breath,
A Traveller between life and death;
The reason firm, the temperate will,
A perfect Woman, nobly planned.
To warn, to comfort, and command;
And yet a Spirit still, and bright
With something of an angel light.
                    (Wordsworth 1927: 148–9)

One of the wonderful convergences here is that this lyric, though extra-ordinarily familiar, has received surprisingly little commentary or criticism of note. Yet in his artistic, aesthetic and critical response to Wordsworth's poem, Brecht's largely unknown comments begin to sketch the lineaments of a fascinating mix of literary-aesthetic and political criticism of both Wordsworth's lyric and modernist poetry. Moreover, Brecht's comments should perhaps help unsettle standard views about what would constitute a Brechtian stance toward lyric, aura and expression. In short, Brecht is led to reconsider the elements, in poetry and the other arts, which have frequently and rightly been understood since Romanticism to underwrite that pre-sumably baleful phenomenon, aesthetic autonomy. As he continues: 'there are indeed some petty bourgeois tendencies which are directed towards the perpetuation and consolidation of the petty bourgeoisie as a class, but within the petty bourgeoisie there are also other kinds of tendencies that conflict with those' (Brecht 1993: 91; 1994: 417).

From this real, admittedly mild, departure from some of the stricter Marxian orthodoxy he'd recently confronted in the Moscow-based Left exile journals, Brecht moves toward an affectionately mocking but also self-mocking recognition: the English petit bourgeois are reported, Brecht notes, to have been heroically resisting Nazi bombardment in a manner parallel to earlier Left internationalist defences of the Spanish Republic; but if those reports are a bit rhetorical, so too, Brecht indicates, may have been earlier, overhasty condemnations (by Brecht and others) of the poetic and extra-poetic 'petty bourgeois idyll':

the individual petty bourgeois currently patrolling the fields of en-gland equipped with a shotgun and a Molotov cocktail ('as used against tanks in the Spanish civil war', so a general assured us on the wireless), has up to a point legitimate enough grounds for blaming his wordsworths; yet it is just in dehumanized situations like these that *'a lovely apparition, sent / to be a moment's ornament'* helps to conjure up other situations more worthy of the human race. (Brecht 1993: 91 [trans. mod.]; 1994: 417)

Of course aware of the trajectory of the British poet who, having been liberal or progressive, turns Tory and thus, Brecht believes, gives petit-bourgeois antifascists 'grounds for blaming [their] wordsworths', Brecht nevertheless finds the lyrical, auratic, musical thread of the poem that takes the reader to an elsewhere that, far from inculcating escapism, apparently helps make humane agency, thought-feeling and resistance possible. In a focusing of attention worthy of his formidable poet's ear and eye, he immediately concentrates – to the apparent exclusion of everything else – on the arresting lines found in the first stanza. It may be no great stretch to speculate that Brecht thereby suggests a critical interpretation that would underscore how the subsequent entrance into the poem of a rather heavy-handed doctrinal language of gender quickly begins to predominate, and contributes to or even causes the poem's effective loss of much of the magical lightness that had marked its earlier lines: the lightness of the eight-stress rhyming couplets seems to begin disappearing with the entrance into the poem of an impulse to move toward what threatens to become a thumping monotone, or at least toward some stiffness and clanging (none of which appears to prove attractive to Brecht, though it should be noted that something of the poem's initial gracefulness returns in the final couplet). It would be a notably Shelleyan view for this perhaps most self-consciously Shelleyan of radical modernist German poets to find Wordsworth's didacticism and Angel-in-the-House gender ideology weighing down his finer artistic impulses and gestures; at any rate, Shelley's (and Byron's) jibes at what they deemed Wordsworth's buttoned up, conservative moralism and its effect on his music are highly relevant to what Brecht now notices about 'She Was a Phantom of Delight' (though Brecht also clearly inherits the Shelley–Byron acceptance of, and attraction to, traditional associations of lyric-auratic spectrality with the feminine). Perhaps knowing that his strong, spontaneous response to Wordsworth's phantasmatic lyricism brings him awfully close to that intriguing or infuriating nemesis named Adorno, Brecht begins – or continues – a one-step, two-step dance toward and away from (but mostly toward) the power he sees and values in the poem. Not surprisingly, Brecht first engages in a self-cautioning, differential-stressing analysis: 'certainly ours is a time when the poem no longer serves to *"haunt, to startle, to waylay"*'. But since Wordsworth's poem clearly *has* served 'to haunt, to startle, to waylay' him – into the critical activity of grappling with the relationships between lyric magic or aura and the sociohistorical – Brecht immediately issues an aphorism or axiom that may be the most Adornian he ever pronounced: 'art *is* an autonomous sphere, though by no means an autarchic one' (Brecht 1993: 91; 1994: 417). The power of Wordsworth's spectral lyric, and Brecht's response to it, has turned into an argument for aesthetic autonomy – and if that in itself doesn't demonstrate considerable, unexpected comfort about a term that might cause worry for its apparent relationships to bourgeois culture and economics, Brecht intriguingly goes on to distinguish autonomy from *autarchy*, the latter being the term then current in modernist liberal, Left German discourse about economies, like Germany's, that sought to address problems of modernization not so much via genuinely forward-looking capitalist (let alone socialist) development but through essentially dictatorial command-and-directive policies. At the level of poetry and aesthetics, Brecht is concerned to insist that 'ours is a time' when a certain lyric aura (or an approach/response to it) must – to be distinguished from the smoke and mirrors effects of the waylaying propaganda inimical to critical agency – allow its haunting to work differentially, with and through a sense of charged absence (in this case, the absence during war or under fascism of 'situations worthy of the human race'), rather than through an ostensible, and overwhelming, immediacy and presence. Certainly that very differentiation is what Brecht, recently rereading Shelley, Baudelaire, Rimbaud and others with Benjamin, had seen as militating toward the reasons that lyric aura, with its inherent opposition to literal immediacy and full presence, was somehow formally inextricable from an insistence on the historical and on the imagining of a present in excess of what is available through extant social concepts.[4]

These Wordsworth-and-lyric-generated thoughts lead Brecht to the projection of three remarkable 'theses' centring around experience, expression and individual (though not exactly individualist subjectivity), with care taken to value those concepts and practices but to distinguish them from essences or ideas already at hand, ready to go without any spur from artifice or construction. Brecht contends, in these theses, that what is involved is a move from a passive reflection-notion of lyric expression to a more active sense of what lyric expression entails:

> 1) possible criterion for a work of art: does it enrich the individual's capacity for experience? (an individual, perhaps, who goes ahead and is then overtaken by the masses moving in a predictable direction.)
>
> 2) it may enrich the capacity for expression, which is not the same as the capacity for experience but more like a capacity for communicating (perhaps the question is to what extent the how linked to the what, and the what bound up with specific classes).
>
> 3) poetry is never mere expression [*Lyrik ist niemals blosser Ausdruck*]. its reception is an operation of the same order as, say, seeing and hearing, ie something much more active, writing poetry must be viewed as a human activity, a social function of a wholly contradictory and alterable kind, conditioned by history and in turn conditioning it. the difference lies [is located] between 'mirroring' and 'holding up a mirror' [*Der Untershied liegt zwischen 'widerspiegeln' und 'den Spiegel vorhalten'*]. (Brecht 1993: 91 [trans. mod.]; 1994: 417–18)

Brecht speculates here about a continuum of activity, historical conditioning *and* acknowledged, necessary engagement of agency: a particular human being makes specific decisions about when, how, why and where to hold the mirror, and in relation to whom, or to what object. Poet and reader, rather than simply choosing one of two extremes (passive reflective mirroring versus active, self-conscious holding or placement or manipulation of a mirror), are instead now thought of as participating in a process of experimentally discovering and working within the whole spectrum of possibility that 'lies' or 'is located' 'between' those two poles.

There remain volumes to say about artistic creation and aesthetic reception, about how particular poems and other works are made and received within this spectrum between mere passive mirroring and the almost infinite modes, contexts and degrees of conscious construction that can be involved in holding up a mirror. Brecht observes that an irreducible musicality in or attendant to lyric's semblance-character (in this instance, Wordsworth's) animates or makes possible the sense of and capacity for expression, or for what might be called the critical, necessary illusion or semblance of expression (simply another way, perhaps, of saying 'aesthetic experience'). Yet for all the recognition – up to and including by Brecht himself – of the historical imbrication of expression and musicality in lyric, there would appear to remain something mysterious though acknowledged, even necessarily taken for granted, about how lyric's semblance-projection of musical speech can stimulate expression and the sense of agency. Ideas about stretching – language stretched toward song; such stretched language creating a feeling of expansiveness that presumably, in the post-aesthetic moment, remains as an awareness of the emergence of materials (starting *with* that formally stretched language) that might then allow for the emergent construction of new concepts themselves, not to mention the new social dispensations that could correspond to them – such ideas, and far more complicated ideas about artistic techniques and aesthetic response, are surely indispensable.

Nonetheless, though it will hardly solve the mystery of the workings on us of melos, rhythm, tone and pitch, it might prove useful to overlay the discussion of lyric's artistic techniques and aesthetic effects with a rather more physiological registration of lyric musicality's artificing ability to stretch or exaggerate something or someone into, or toward, expression. I have in mind, for example, the highly successful practice employed by speech therapists who work with stroke patients struggling with aphasia, in which sentences that cannot yet be spoken, or that can be spoken only with difficulty, are intoned or sung aloud by the patient, which can then with astonishing rapidity contribute to the reacquisition of the ability to speak such sentences. It is perhaps unnecessary to stress the importance of this experience of stretched or exaggeratedly constructed speech, this language pushed into song, this remarkable reconstruction of the ability to speak when speech ability had vanished, this reconstructed ability to experience expression and to begin again to express experience. One wants simply to observe that such practice has proved vital for the process of recovering the ability to speak and for the capacity to know that crucial aspect of one's own agency. And in the context of a discussion about how musical intonation works to reconstruct otherwise impossible *speech*, it is hardly irrelevant to remember how Benjamin raises this reconstructive dynamic to the second power with his great insight – fully adopted by Adorno – that Baudelaire's modernity is marked by an artistic commitment to sing *song*'s now-apparent impossibility, musically to reconstruct expressive experience in poetry precisely from the absence of auratic, reflective and expressive experience (the kinds of experience that together constitute the precondition for critical agency).

Speech and critical agency in relation to musicality return us to a final moment of poetry and poetics, aesthetics and critical theory – a moment decidedly after Brecht's. Yet the poet I'd like to consider will reanimate for us striking aspects of Brecht's earlier concerns; in particular, the real struggle with the ways that barely bygone eras of art and theory – and only apparently bygone practices and notions like expressive subjectivity – turn out to demand further histories for themselves. One of the most challenging and talented poets working in English to extend modernist experimental traditions as they engage with Left political commitments and aesthetic and critical theory, Michael Palmer has since the 1970s produced a much-admired and often-imitated body of work, an *oeuvre* known perhaps especially for its unabashedly lyric yet rigorous and experimental character.[5] Here I'll offer a terribly compressed discussion of an untitled poem taken from the 37-page sequence called 'Baudelaire Series' from Palmer's 1988 volume *Sun*.

> A man undergoes pain sitting at a piano
> knowing thousands will die while he is playing
>
> He has two thoughts about this
> If he should stop they would be free of pain
>
> If he could get the notes right he would be free of pain
> In the second case the first thought would be erased
>
> causing pain
>
> It is this instance of playing
>
> he would say to himself
> my eyes have grown hollow like yours

my head is enlarged
though empty of thought

Such thoughts destroy music
and this at least is good
                    (Palmer 1988: 19)

Moving subtly through these lines one hears so many echoes from Primo
Levi, from Else Lasker-Schuler, Wallace Stevens, Edmond Jabès and Paul
Celan, that it may take a while longer for the dominant, dissonant key to be
heard: this poem is not only deeply informed by its own transformations
of materials from social and literary history, philosophical aesthetics and
critical theory, by its posing of art's possible engagements with incomprehensible and inexpressible suffering; it also happens to be a poem about
Adorno. Ever-restless and self-reflective philosophical thought here meets
inconceivable damage and the 'damaged life' that seems to make art
impossible or irrelevant, but where the 'instance' of art, the confrontation
with it, just might also begin to convey 'that which happened' (Celan's
designation for the Holocaust), to convey how much is broken. And this
very negative knowledge 'at least is good'.

The poem's formal casting – its dissonant sound-and-rhythm off-
rhyming of *pain* and *playing*, its strange wavering between numb recitative
and charged ghost song, its overall architectural shaping and pitiless
grammatical machinery – is so acute, simultaneously so elegant and so
rigorously logical, so invitingly asphyxiating, that each new level of grim
joke unfolds precisely as any ability to experience even dark humour is
pulled from beneath us. (Included in that ghost song are hints and echoes of
familiar metres and rhythms, simultaneously invoked and fractured; in the
poem's longer lines, for instance, one hears play with and against iambic
pentameter and – not surprisingly for a poem within a sequence titled
'Baudelaire Series' – the alexandrine, in its classical twelve-syllable form or,
transposed, as so often in the history of English-language translations and
borrowings, into six-accent lines.) In the poem's fiction, the twentieth
century's greatest and most musical practitioner of Marxian dialectics has
finally and masterfully integrated Wittgensteinian language games into his
Hegelian structures of self-cancellation, but only, we know, because given
'that which happened', he will go on – after the moment or instance
imagined in the poem – infamously to pronounce 'barbaric' what he once
(following the lead of his now-lost friend Benjamin) thought to be
language's greatest possibility: its utopian vocation as lyric. 'To write a poem
after Auschwitz is barbaric' (*P*: 34 [trans. mod.]; *GS* 10.1: 30); 'All culture
after Auschwitz, together with its urgent critique, is garbage' (*ND*: 367
[trans. mod.]; *GS* 6: 359). All of which we read about, and recognize in
Palmer's poem: the (negative) knowledge not only of the world but of poetry

and art as well comes now in the poem, just as the (negative) knowledge of music arrives in the poem's barely withheld and barely given musicality, at a piano that is played or not played with a rather altered sense of what might be meant by 'refrain'. Music thus 'plays' its own historically unique role as an art form, even as it plays a related but different role in relation to the other arts (lyric poetry in particular) and to the play between music and philosophy in the life and work of the historical figure Theodor Adorno; but music in the poem plays too in the figuring and reconsideration of poetry's own impasses in the situation linked perhaps most famously with Adorno and Celan. (Palmer has in fact indicated, in a number of interviews and comments made during public readings, that part of the origin of this poem involved a profound experience of rereading – with Celan and others of course in mind – Adorno's *Minima Moralia*, and of gazing at the famous photo, reprinted on the English translation's back cover, of Adorno at the piano keyboard, seeming both to play and to be suspended in – or from – play.)

Palmer's poem summons up another famous scene of Marxism and pianism – in fact, a remarkable counterpoint to his own imagined instance:

> At Yekaterina Peshkova's in Moscow one evening, listening to Isaiah Dobrovein playing Beethoven's sonatas, Lenin said: 'I don't know of anything better than the *Appassionata*, I can listen to it every day. Amazing, superhuman music! I always think with a pride that may be naive: look what miracles people can perform!'
>
>   Then screwing up his eyes and smiling, he added rather sadly:
>
>   'But I can't listen to music often, it affects my nerves, it makes me want to say sweet nothings and caress the heads of people who, living in a filthy hell, can create real beauty. But today we mustn't caress anyone's head or we'll get our hand bitten off: we've unfortunately got to hit heads, hit them without mercy, though in the ideal we're against doing any violence. Ahhh – it's hellishly difficult!' (Gorky 1932: 52, [trans. mod.])

Rereading *that* episode at the piano, of Lenin indelibly rendered by Maxim Gorky, leads one to speculate about how recently – and how diabolically – Adorno and Horkheimer might have been perusing their Gorky when they sketched Odysseus the ur-bourgeois, the 'primal modern' plugging his crewmen's ears against the art songs of the Sirens, thereby preparing not Utopian equality but all subsequent divisions of labour (not to mention divisions between labour and pleasure) (*DE*: 3–80; *GS* 3: 19–99). A measure of the Gorky text's iconic status comes across in the Yugoslavian film-maker Dusan Makavejev's anecdote about the first showing in the Soviet Union, 20 years after its 1971 release, of his wild mix of Wilhelm Reich and Sergei Eisenstein, *W.R.: Mysteries of the Organism*. Makavejev reported that, during the last year of the USSR's existence, a packed cinema house in Moscow laughed uproariously at every joke the film directed at the system and at its unsparing representation of figures from Marx to Lenin to Stalin. But near the film's conclusion, where Makavejev makes a People's Artist star ice skater – who just happens to be named Vladimir Illyich – recite word for word Lenin's lines about the *Appassionata* from the revered Gorky text, the boisterous viewers fell into stunned silence; barely a sound, let alone a laugh, was heard from the audience throughout the rest of the film. (Makavejev's film, by the way, was released the year after the posthumous publication of Adorno's *Aesthetic Theory*, which itself spirals round and round Beethoven's *Appassionata*.)[6]

Indeed, if silence is also what Palmer's poem ultimately suggests as 'Adorno's' compositional method for pianistically revising the Gorky–Lenin–Beethoven *Appassionata*, that suggestion itself starts retrospectively to seem bizarrely preordained when one remembers those pages where Adorno himself seizes on the *Appassionata* amid a crucial demonstration of how experimental artistic process brings together labour, constructivism and fantasy (or imagination) in ways allowing for 'the transformation of the existing' (most immediately, for the transformation of art's own existing materials). The *Appassionata* actually turns out to be Adorno's premier example of how artistic 'fantasy shifts whatever artworks absorb of the existing into constellations through which they become the other of the existing, if only through its determinate negation' (*AT*: 173–4; *GS* 7: 259–60).[7]

But to return from Bolshevik and Frankfurt sonata-reception to *sonnet*-form, to poetry's genre of the 'little sound' and its experimental progeny. For Palmer's untitled poem is an experimental modern sonnet, a test case for how a poet thinks anew about radically working and reworking sonnet-form (including the raising and unsettling of expectations about the form itself, as with the above-discussed play with traditional sonnet metres like iambic pentameter and alexandrine, which are evoked, transformed and then all but disintegrated as the poem proceeds), about how the poet experiences anew the form's unique and curious compression, its spaces, its range of musical possibility; how the sonnet surprises and instructs poet and reader by and in the necessity of its twist or turn; how all this becomes inseparable from engagement with the poem's historico-political and ethical materials. Here the whole formal poetic tradition weirdly yet rightly works a path into the poem's content, so that the way history itself converges back upon the age-old problematics of the sonnet is writ large. How do those fourteen lines present and solve, present and intensify, or interestingly refuse to present, a problem – and what is the problem here, in relation to our overarching concern with expression? One tried-and-true crux would be where and how the poet places the *volta* or turn (classically, at or around the eighth or ninth line, in the sonnet's transition from octave to sestet). And sure enough, in 'A Man undergoes pain sitting at a piano' we have, just at that juncture, the raising of the stakes by what looks to be a typically postmodernist gesture of undecidability, the 'play' of language and chance. Palmer not only makes the *volta* into a nodal point of language and hazard; he goes so far as to focus the *volta* onto the thematically and historically laden word *playing* itself. The poem's turn then leaves it unclear whether the man has been playing and thinking or only thinking about playing; whether the playing is the play of thought or music, or both, or neither; whether this line belongs at all to the consciousness of the man or whether it is somehow the poem's line.

Yet what should seem – formally – to be not only a triumph of the sonnet-form's literary history but, even more specifically, of the Baudelairean-modern trajectory of a playfully *art pour l'art* resolution now thrown onto *play* itself at the pressure point of a *volta* in its turn located at the site, with-in the poem's fiction, of a musical instrument made *to be played* (the piano): all this (along with the philosophical undersong-assumption of Kantian, Schillerian, Stevensian, Marcusean or Derridean versions of dynamic 'suspension of purpose' in favour of imaginative free play) instead feels rather like triumph's undoing. For the poem's devastating, suffering-induced and pain-producing sense of paralysis appears to bring aesthetic play-experience to the brink of withering critique, indictment and con-viction on charges of causing or being accessory to terrible repression. But the poem turns out not quite to be a critique of aesthetic freedom as the joyful and/or shattering realization of a human quiddity that exceeds mere instrumentality. Because while Palmer presents something like the photo and sonic negative of such free, imaginative, aesthetic play, the negation responds more emphatically to the poem's omnipresent sociohistorical content (the Holocaust and its aftermaths; related cases of genocidal terror) than to what might be deemed its form-content (including the structure and experience of aesthetic play and the provisional suspension of material-instrumental interest or purpose, which the poem mediates and partially enacts via its play with another aspect of its form-content: the materials of sonnet-form and the latter's history).

That is, the poem invites us to see how its shaping of the underlying sociohistorical content makes over, in grave or grotesque register, the signs that would otherwise here more likely be associated with the form-content of aesthetic experience itself. What Kant and others famously called the 'enlarged mentality' enabled by aesthetic judgement (where the sense of agency emerges from an intellectual-affective process emphatically felt *not* to be bound or determined by extant concepts, in contradistinction from less affective or non-affective acts of intellection) here appears to cede its rights to the very sign 'enlargement', finding that those rights have been usurped, or apparently rendered null, by the sociohistorical content that via starvation and related horrors has produced a perversely 'enlarged', 'hollow'-eyed 'head' that seems to bear no relationship to the emancipatory workings of aesthetic vacancy or aesthetic emptiness (in which the aesthetic thought-feeling has been emptied of, or left vacant vis-à-vis, the determining power of extant concepts, allowing the subject to experience as-yet conceptually undetermined thought).

It is worth further emphasizing that Palmer has taken this lifeblood of poetry and art – the classical emptying/suspension of, or turn from, 'ordinary, material purpose', and the concomitant turn toward the creative imagination's free play – and imprinted it perfectly in reverse onto the *volta*'s pivot, which 'in turn' will be further, historically, *turned* or *twisted*: a *volta* in the history of the *volta*. The *volta* has been, in a word, *tortured* (though not, first-blush appearances to the contrary, by art or aesthetic experience – and there's the rub) into a deadening 'play': into the inability really to play in ease, into an Adorno sitting at but no longer able to play the piano, or alternatively, an Adorno who now plays seriously by being unable to play, unable to 'play along', as the Frankfurters often put it ['*nicht mitmachen, nicht mitspielen!*'], and hence an Adorno who now rediscovers the aesthetic's purposeless play only in resistance to what an earlier understanding of play itself would seem to have degenerated into in the face of incomprehensible pain and loss. To turn still to once-reliable instruments of art that have offered so much to the conceptually undetermined, affective-intellectual activity denominated *aesthetic* – instruments like the piano (or like the instruments one works with to make, speak and otherwise experience a poem) – might be to instrumentalize precisely those special, artistic-aesthetic instruments intended to resist mechanistic instrumentalization.

Another formulation may prove helpful. The poem's tying together of aesthetic experience and suffering initially leads one to feel that the former has produced or contributed to the latter (not least because of the poem's stated recognition that no particular aesthetic mode or stance will directly, perhaps not even indirectly, ameliorate human suffering, a recognition that is itself always, in an at least secondary manner, 'causing pain'). But as it offers its strange blank music, the poem gives us to understand that its central problem actually has not been caused by that old Kantian fiction of aesthetic experience and dilated subjectivity, wherein the subject defamiliarizes his or herself, imaginatively suspending in constructive semblance his or her sociomaterial purposes and interests, experiencing (likewise in semblance) a provisional, play-enshrining, 'purposeless' freedom theorized as the ground for a non-coercive intersubjectivity. Taking into itself recent history's nightmare turn or inversion, the poem does appear to regard some sort of historical suspension, in charged relation to the question of subjectivity, as having caused mass acts of barbarism. Yet the history at issue involved a suspension not *by* or *for* but emphatically *against* subjectivity; the great problem was hardly the aesthetic's suspension of *instrumental purpose* in favour of individual and collective subjects' *freedom*, but just the opposite. The poem's dark, underlying sociohistorical content involves an extremely *purposeful* and hence by definition *un*aesthetic, intensely instrumental and instrumentalizing *suspension* of human subjects' *freedom*: a historically un-speakable suspension – a literal elimination – of subjectivity, the purpose-ful, instrumental elimination of millions of human subjects.

History's *volta*, then, is what has turned, twisted and tortured the later-modernist literary existence of the sonnet's own, more properly poetic, *volta*. Or rather, mass torture and genocide in recent history now leads the subject, within aesthetic experience, first to question urgently – in inappropriately casual but relevant parlance, 'to be tortured by the question of' – whether aesthetic play-experience is any longer warranted, beneficial, to be desired (or whether its semblance-character would at best exhibit a terrible callousness toward real and overwhelming suffering); then, the focus on artistic-aesthetic response seems to lead the subject toward what he or she starts to see as baleful, exaggerated concern with the aesthetic itself, to the point where it retrospectively begins to look as if the aesthetic or its self-absorption has been a cause of the very historical suffering at issue; next, the subject discovers an emerging awareness that concern with the efficacy (vis-à-vis the primary historical content) of certain known artistic forms, styles, tones and generic conventions may somewhat misleadingly have slid into the analysis of sociohistorical causation; finally, in a manner that is, or at least begins from, a resolute negationalism ('such thoughts destroy music and this at least is good'), the subject finds a mode of aesthetic activity that seems to engage the task at hand, the expression in semblance of the underlying experience.

All this bespeaks the necessity of articulating separately the poem's sociohistorical content and form-content; but also the necessity of reuniting them finally as a third, fused, new content, namely, the fate or career of aesthetic – and above all, lyric – expression in the face and aftermath of modern genocide. The Beckettian 'I can't go on, I'll go on' becomes a self-sacrificing, self-regenerating law of poetic form all over again. The *volta* or turn has itself so drastically been turned that *turn* threatens to disintegrate and lose meaning, as if the whole history of sonnet-form has been led against its own will to this grim moment where the sonnet becomes nothing *but* turn, yet where turn or *volta* itself has almost simultaneously gone up, not in the flames of Petrarchan, Dantean or Shakespearean erotic and philosophical tension, but in the smoke of something else entirely. Nonetheless, the very apprehension of these processes depends precisely on, and thus revivifies, *volta*- and sonnet-history at what had appeared their moment of grave historical inadequacy and disappearance. And what's true of Palmer's *volta* is no less true of what follows it: after the poem's earlier lines had offered trace-hints of pentameter and alexandrine, the sestet's bitterly reduced lines seem to have given up those metrical ghosts, appearing to incorporate them, if at all, only by mute reference to what is no longer present. However eloquent this dwindling that serves to 'destroy music' (which on reflection 'at least is good'), it is not the full story. For, read as one sentence or phrasal unit (an option encouraged by the capitalization of the word 'Such' that begins the final couplet), the poem's last two lines just happen to contain the twelve syllables of an alexandrine – and are, moreover, quite susceptible (as in a number of Palmer's own public readings of the poem) to being enunciated with the five accented beats of iambic pentameter. Again, the ostensible situational incapacity of aesthetic play and its sympathetic imagination – once having been registered – paradoxically gives way to a further stretching in which the apparent destruction of music, having been placed on the table, turns out to provide a way into a music (pianistic in the poem's fiction, lyric-poetic in terms of the art of the poem itself) that, by its willingness to risk muteness, might begin to do justice to the subject matter and its human subjects. 'Muteness' might involve a spectrum extending from the meta-phorical muteness of what cannot be articulated in extant concepts and their languages, all the way to literal muteness. 'The true language of art is mute, and its muteness takes priority over poetry's significative element, which in music too is not altogether lacking' (*AT*: 112; *GS* 7: 171–2).

This poem, whose arresting blank music arrives virtually dead-centre in the 'Baudelaire Series''s phenomenal evocation and revisitation of a century and-a-half's lyric and social history, is by no means a last note for musicality and aesthetic experience within the sequence, where Palmer will go on to create something of a relay from the sonnet for and of Adorno to a still more broken sonnet for and of Celan. At all events, the 'Adorno' poem's virtuosically halting steps toward expression, and its semi-sounded art of halting refrain played against silently remembered, almost-heard sonnet and sonata theme-with-unbearable-variation, together *are* its semblance-expression of human suffering. That expression, emerging from the construction of a particular path into the content – and consequently moving toward a glimpse of the experience of a genuinely particularized, which is to say a genuinely available, sociohistorical content – would be unavailable without the poet's and poem's profound immersion in the long and continuing history of lyric musicality.

NOTES

For their responses to early drafts of this essay, I am indebted to Charles Altieri, Russell Berman, Norma Cole, Howard Eiland, John Felstiner, Lydia Goehr, Robert Hass, Tom Huhn, Robert Hullot-Kentor, Martin Jay, Art Strum and Susan Wolfson. A previous, slightly different version of this piece appeared in *Cultural Critique* 60 (Spring 2005), 197–216, and the essay appears in the present volume by generous permission of *Cultural Critique* and the University of Minnesota Press.

1   While such ratification appears explicitly and implicitly throughout Adorno's writings, and suffuses *Aesthetic Theory*, perhaps the most urgent and precise adaptation of the Benjaminian critique of *Innerlichkeit* appears in the opening sections of Adorno's *Kierkegaard: Construction of the Aesthetic* (1933). See also *AT*: 116; *GS* 7: 177.

2   See, for example, *NL1*: 83; *GS* 11: 98–9; and *AT*: 111–12; *GS* 7: 170–1. See also Kaufman 2002.

3   See, for example, *AT*: 57, 114–18, 138, 237; *GS* 7: 90–2, 173–80, 208, 353; and on the notion of lyric itself as the initial gestural model and base for artistic construction in general, 'The Artist as Deputy' (*NL1*: 98–108; *GS* 11: 114–26), and 'Valéry's Deviations' (*NL1*: 137–73; *GS* 11: 158–202).

4   Compare Adorno's many restatements of Benjamin's definition of aura and of what it, in its critical manifestations, enables; e.g., the experiencing of a presence that paradoxically 'moves into the distance' and as a formal consequence 'is critical of the ideological superficies of life' (*AT*: 56; *GS* 7: 89–90). See too Kaufman 2002; 2004.

5   For one example of the relationship to Frankfurt aesthetics, see the circling around Benjamin's work in Palmer 1993.

6   Makavejev recounted the Moscow anecdote on 11 March 1994, in commentary he provided during a retrospective of his work presented by the Pacific Film Archive at the University of California, Berkeley. See *W.R.: Mysteries of the Organism* (1971); the Gorky-recitation scene can also be found in the film's companion text, Makavejev 1972: 135–6.

7   The discussion again cues experimentalism to the artist's *spontaneity* [*Spontaneität*]. For Adorno's further recourse to the *Appassionata*, see, for example, *AT*: 177, 270; *GS* 7: 265, 403.

WORKS CITED

Brecht, B. (1993), *Journals*, ed. J. Willett, trans. H. Rorrison. London: Methuen.

— (1994), 'Journale 1', *Werke: Grosse kommentierte Berliner und Frankfurter Ausgabe*, ed. W. Hecht, J. Knopf, W. Mittenzwei, and K.-D. Müller. Vol. 26. Berlin and Frankfurt: Aufbau/Suhrkamp.

Gorky, M. (1932), *Days with Lenin*. New York: International Publishers.

Huyssen, A. (2002), 'High/Low in an Expanded Field', *Modernism/Modernity* 9(3), 363–74.

Jay, M. (2004), 'Is Experience Still in Crisis? Reflections on a Frankfurt School Lament', in Tom Huhn (ed.), *The Cambridge Companion to Adorno*. Cambridge: Cambridge University Press, pp. 129–47.

Kaufman, R. (2002), 'Aura, Still', *October* 99, 45–80.

— (2004), 'Adorno's Social Lyric, and Literary Criticism Today: Poetics, Aesthetics, Modernity', in Tom Huhn (ed.), *The Cambridge Companion to Adorno*. Cambridge: Cambridge University Press, pp. 354–75.

Makavejev, D. (1972), *W.R.: Mysteries of the Organism: A Cinematic Testament to the Life and Teachings of Wilhelm Reich*. New York: Avon.

Palmer, M. (1988), *Sun*. San Francisco, CA: North Point Press.

— (1993), 'Some notes on Shelley, poetics, and the present', *Sulfur* 33, 273–81.

Wordsworth, W. (1927), *Poems* [1879], ed. M. Arnold. London: Macmillan.

8

Returning to the 'House of Oblivion': Celan Between Adorno and Heidegger

Iain Macdonald

In the strange history of the Adorno–Heidegger debate – a debate that never took place – divergences generally come to the mind more easily than convergences, resulting in oppositional or, more usually, unilateral criticism.[1] It is not difficult to sketch in broad strokes what is in contention, if only to form an initial idea of the tensions that inevitably arise in dealing with this question. From Adorno's side, the central divergence between their approaches is reflected in the struggle of a historically contentful materialism pitted against metaphysical abstractions; from Heidegger's side, it could be seen as a question of fundamental versus regional ontologies, or of the history of being as opposed to history commonly understood as 'the happenings and deeds of the world' (Heidegger 1966: 79; 1959: 56).[2] The stakes of the debate are already apparent in these radically disjunctive ways of construing the divergences between Adorno and Heidegger. Thus, while it may be true for both that the essence of contemporary thought lies in a certain need or urgency [Bedürfnis, Not], the need stems from the forgotten truth of being for the one, while for the other it lies in material insufficiency, guilt and suffering. (For example: Heidegger 1999: 79, 87–8; 1975ff.: 65, 112–13, 125; ND: 5, 17–18, 408; GS 6: 17, 29, 399–400.)

But there are other ways of getting at the Adorno–Heidegger question, which perhaps avoid digging into trenches willy-nilly. The reference to the 'house of oblivion' is to a poem by Paul Celan, 'The Sand from the Urns', published in the 1952 collection, Mohn und Gedächtnis (Poppy and Memory). Celan is a remarkable figure in his own right in the history of late-twentieth-century thought, but in relation to the Adorno–Heidegger question he is of particular interest – though he presents the critic with certain difficulties in this regard. He knew both philosophers, Heidegger better than Adorno, and was both fascinated and made deeply uncomfortable by their writings, such that it is far from easy to understand how he related to them intellectually – not to mention the other way around. And while there are many implicit and explicit references to them in his poetry, prose and Nachlaß, only some of these are heavily discussed in the literature (for orientation, see Pöggeler 1986; 2000; Felstiner 1995; France-Lanord

2004). In general, a lot has been left unexplored. Certainly, there are many resonances between his thought and theirs, condensing around certain shared interests. One of these is the concept of forgetting.

HEIDEGGER

First, Heidegger. For reasons of brevity, this sketch will be limited to a few passages from *Being and Time*, though the role of forgetting is obviously paramount throughout Heidegger's career. A more complete analysis of forgetting in Heidegger would have to focus on the evolution of Heidegger's concept of truth in connection with the history of being and what he calls the abandonment of being. More modest indications will have to suffice in the present context.

As the first line of *Being and Time* has it, the question of being 'has today been forgotten' and it is made clear 'not only that the question of being lacks an *answer*, but that the question itself is obscure and without direction. So if it is to be revived [i.e. repeated]', says Heidegger, 'this means that we must first work out an adequate way of *formulating* it' (1962: §1, 4).[3] The task of fundamental ontology is therefore a task of repetition [*Wiederholung*], announced at the beginning of *Being and Time* and requiring a preparatory analysis of Dasein and the further interpretation of the results of this analysis in terms of temporality. Why Dasein? Why start with a general overview of human experience? These early sections of *Being and Time* also make the point that we *presuppose* being in a strange way, such that we have a kind of prior insight into being that allows beings to articulate themselves to us; in fact, Heidegger already claims in these passages that this prior insight is part of Dasein's essential constitution (§2, 8). In other words, Dasein in its very being is related to being and so presupposes it, understands it – if only implicitly. One could surmise, then (and one would not be mistaken, though it only becomes clear much later in the book), that the forgetting of the question of being is no accident of history, but rather an aspect – a *necessary* aspect – of Dasein's own being.

In Division II of *Being and Time*, when Heidegger is deriving temporality from the structures of existence that come to light in the first division, we discover that the individual Dasein's relation to its past in the mode of authenticity runs parallel and has a similar structure to the forgottenness of the question of being in the history of thought. Indeed, Heidegger says in §68 that 'if *being*-as-having-been is authentic [*das eigentliche Gewesensein*], we call it "*repetition*" [*Wiederholung*]', while on the other hand, the inauthentic mode of relating to one's past is called 'forgetting [*das Vergessen*]' (§68, 339). Just as the question of being has been forgotten and must be repeated, so too can the individual Dasein 'forget' its past inauthentically or 'repeat' it authentically. What is strange and difficult to grasp at first glance, however, is that forgetting is not to be understood as a simple failure to remember, a contingent or biological flaw of some kind. Inauthenticity is Dasein's 'default' mode of being, as it were (denoted by the frequently occurring expression 'proximally and for the most part', *zunächst und zumeist*). So on the contrary, forgetting has to be understood as a ' "positive" ecstatical mode of one's having-been' (§68, 339). The picture that we are presented with here is thus one in which repetition (a kind of remembering) requires forgetting as its precondition. Obviously, this is not the trivial point that to remember something, one must have forgotten it at some point. As a positive ecstatical mode of Dasein's being, forgetting has the status of a universal, necessary, and *a priori* structure. For this reason, Heidegger will say that

> only on the basis of such forgetting can anything be *retained* [*behalten*] by the concernful making-present which awaits; and what are thus retained are entities encountered within-the-world with a character other than that of Dasein. To such a retaining there corresponds a non-retaining which presents us with a kind of 'forgetting' in a derivative sense. (§68, 339)

Two points need to be made in order to clarify what Heidegger is getting at in this key passage. First, forgetting in the existential-temporal sense is not to be confused with forgetting in a derivative sense, which would include inattention, distraction, absent-mindedness, blackouts and bumps on the head leading to amnesia. None of these has the *a priori* standing of forgetting in the existential-temporal sense. The difficulty then lies in understanding what primordial forgetting is, as distinct from the derivative form. Second, then, 'primordial' forgetting is a dimension of concernful making-present whereby inauthentic Dasein deals somewhat superficially with the objects of its concern. Heidegger speaks of Dasein being 'lost' in the 'externality [*Äußerlichkeit*]' of its objects of concern (§68, 339). In plain language, primordial forgetting amounts to unreflective behaviour, the passive acceptance of ready-made possibilities, or just 'going with the flow'.

An existentialist reading of these passages would presumably stress not assuming oneself as a task. But Heidegger's argument is more general than that: it is aiming at the relation of possibility to actuality. As such, forgetting refers to the limited dealings with possibility that Dasein generally has, and to how Dasein discovers its possibilities. For example, it is one thing to watch television, quite another to be familiar with the physics of the television, and yet another to have invented the television.[4] Of course, it is not that we once knew the physics of television broadcasting and reception, only to 'forget' them subsequently; the model here is not Socratic anamnesis. It is rather that we do not generally look beyond a certain depth. We forget that we can engage with things in the world in ways other than the ways in which we normally, unthinkingly engage with them. We forget that we can discover, influence and invent possibilities. In a more general formulation of this idea, one could say that such forgetting is necessary just to get along in the world, to be able to focus on tasks and survive. That is, cognition in general *requires* this kind of blinkered relation to things, as when I hold in abeyance the noise in the street when I am sitting at home reading a book; the noise in the street presents me with a wealth of possibilities that I 'forget' in order to focus on my book. Simply put: the forgetting of possibilities explains the phenomenon of attention. For these reasons, Heidegger says that forgetting is the condition of possibility of remembering, of repeating one's having-been authentically, which amounts to saying that in order to actualize a possibility, one must be able to make explicit and intelligible what is merely implicit at a given moment in time. In short, existential-temporal forgetting corresponds to the implicitness of being.

ADORNO

Interestingly, Adorno also deploys the concept of forgetting, and in a way that lets him underscore just how much his basic position differs from that of Heidegger. But in fact his concept of forgetting is more like the mirror image of Heidegger's, and for that reason juxtaposing them sheds a great deal of light on the debate. In *Negative Dialectics*, Adorno writes:

> fighting against forgetting (meaning historical forgetting, rather than Heidegger's extra-historical forgetting within the history of being), against the prevalent expectation that one should be ready to sacrifice a formerly-won freedom of consciousness, does not entail advocating a spiritual-historical restoration ... What has been cast aside but not absorbed theoretically will often yield its truth content only later. It becomes a sore afflicting the prevailing [perception of] well-being. Changed circumstances lead back to it once again. (*ND*: 144 [trans. mod.]; *GS* 6: 147)

The first thing to remark in this passage is that Adorno situates forgetting squarely within the compass of historical experience. There is no hint of getting back behind the happenings of world history to some transcendental knowledge that conditions world events and can be investigated independently of them. Moreover, reversing historical forgetting does not mean returning to a prior golden age or to some primitive and innocent mode of life; reversing forgetting is not a process of restoration. Nor does it mean giving up the hard-won freedom of consciousness – for example, for the sake of a concept of solidarity that is all too easily perverted by party interests or the state apparatus (*MM*: 51–2; *GS* 4: 56–8). What, then, does Adorno have in mind when he talks about combating forgetting? The hint we are given in this passage is that dominant trends in history cannot fully level out and cover over what does not conform to them. Rather, 'what has been cast aside but not absorbed theoretically' festers within historical experience, such that history is haunted, as it were, by the injustices it commits, by the suffering these injustices inflict on us and on nature. The model here recalls Freud's concept of trauma, the 'return of the repressed', and what he called the repetition-compulsion. But Adorno is really harking back to the *Phenomenology of Spirit*, where Hegel demonstrates the power of thought to convict itself of its own one-sidedness (*Einseitigkeit*): 'if [consciousness] wishes to remain in a state of unthinking inertia', says Hegel, 'then thought troubles its thoughtlessness, and its own unrest disturbs its inertia' (Hegel 1977: 51; 1981: 2: 57). For Adorno, the central lesson learned from Hegel is that thought can turn back on itself, can convict itself of its own transgressions and thereby do justice to 'what has been cast aside' by the course of history. Modifying it slightly along the way, he therefore adopts Hegel's dialectical concept of experience as the process by which we must understand how thought goes wrong, how it congeals in rigid abstraction, and how it can set itself right again by the same means – that is, by diagnosing its own errors and proposing new abstractions that, with any luck, are more just than the ones they replace. Of course, this puts us in a terrible muddle because we have to see cognition as simultaneously working for and against justice and freedom, and indeed, this is why reflecting on the just life (*das richtige Leben*) is to be considered a 'melancholy science' (*MM*: 15; *GS* 4: 13).

But despite appearances, things are not all doom and gloom. What Adorno variously calls utopia, reconciliation, philosophical experience, undiminished cognition, dialectical thinking, the speculative moment and so on, all correspond (with their different accents and resonances) to the moment in which consciousness seizes on what is non-identical to it (its 'festering sore'), which constrains it and which expresses itself as a conceptual 'matter of urgency' (*ND*: 8; *GS* 6: 20). The condition of possibility for reversing forgetting, then, is the non-identical, understood as 'what has been cast aside but not absorbed theoretically'. More specifically, the true 'speculative moment of thought' is a seizing upon 'what will not have its law prescribed for it by the given facts, what transcends these facts while remaining in closest contacts with objects, and while repudiating any sacrosanct transcendence' (*ND*: 17; *GS* 6: 29). In other words, reversing forgetting involves asserting a freedom that remains immanent, tied to real existing conditions, but which posits something beyond these existing conditions – not as *outside* history, but as what is needful within history.

This may seem a little abstract, but what Adorno is describing here is just a more developed form of what we usually refer to as 'calling a spade a spade' (or sometimes even 'calling a spade a shovel'). So when Adorno says that 'concepts achieve what the concept prevents' (*ND*: 53; *GS* 6: 62), he means that we have it within our power to give shape to the felt injustices that are the result of reason gone awry, whether it be in the pursuit of special interests, in the domination of nature, in the service of an unbalanced form of historical subjectivity (e.g. the bourgeois *ratio*), or what have you. In short, we can *interpret* our historically determinate circumstances so as to give voice to the suffering caused by a specifiable injustice, to the implicit contradictions of capitalism or of communism, to the catastrophic consequences of the logic of exchange, and so on. And even though our interpretations will always be open to ideological fixity or perversion, we also have it within our power to begin the critical process anew.

A simple example should suffice to make clear what it is that Adorno has in mind. In Marx's 1843 introduction to his projected critique of Hegel's *Philosophy of Right*, we find the following passage:

> Heralding the *dissolution of the existing order of things*, the proletariat merely announces the *secret of its own existence* because it *is* the *real* dissolution of this order. Demanding the *negation of private property*, the proletariat merely raises to the *principle of society* what society has raised to the principle *of the proletariat*, what the proletariat already embodies as the negative result of society without its action. (Marx 1994: 38; Marx and Engels 1956ff.: 1: 391)

In all its historical ambivalence (manifest in hindsight), such a gesture is a typical instance of what Adorno calls the speculative moment, or the conceptual core of any reversal of forgetting. At a given moment in time, under historical pressures emanating directly from a particular system of production expanding in Germany, Europe and North America, the individual formerly conceived of as a mere *worker* became the living representative of collective interests. In the critical interpretative gesture of rebaptizing the individual worker as a representative of the *proletariat*, Marx lent a voice to processes that were in any event already redefining existing conditions. Thereby, the coherence and legitimacy of the concept 'proletariat', or the 'secret of its own existence', resided in how the German working class in 1843 had been tacitly defined by industrial capitalism. The concept 'proletariat' and everything that goes with it thereby derived its force from felt suffering and real contradictions that implicitly defined the existence of the German worker. For Marx, giving this reality a *name*, a *concept*, meant giving it effective objectivity: the concept proletariat implies not only a class, but a historical task. For these reasons, it is not just a name imposed on the worker, but the crystallization in knowledge of the reality in which he was already participating, albeit unknowingly.

But it is the logic of Marx's gesture that is of interest here. To invent a concept, or indeed a discourse, that redefines reality by giving shape to what was discovered to be wrong with reality is the essence of dialectical, utopian thinking and the innermost core of combating forgetting. Such a reversal of forgetting can and must always be concrete; that is, historically determinate. This is what gives freedom its 'bite' and what ultimately drives Adorno's critique of first philosophy and of Heidegger in particular. For Adorno, reversing forgetting means making historical processes intelligible in such a way as to liberate specific possibilities from the structures (social, ideological, conceptual) that suppress them and therefore perpetuate unfreedom. So while Adorno and Heidegger are both concerned with making possibilities intelligible, with reversing the mechanisms of forgetting that sediment them within experience, Adorno (against Heidegger) insists on the historically concrete nature of this experience.

One of the pillars of his critique is thus that while Heidegger 'secularizes' metaphysics (a healthy and necessary move, according to Adorno), he also 'ontologizes the ontic' (*ND*: 97–8, 119–22; *GS* 6: 104–5, 125–8). The end result is the mere semblance of concreteness, of a true account of human facticity. Based on what we have just seen, then, one of his most cogent criticisms is that the move from beings to being suppresses the real, determinate historical needs that motivate thought. Heidegger's approach requires that real existing conditions (what *is*, or *das Seiende*) be left unanalyzed – entailing that they are merely accepted as is and thereby condoned (*ND*: 99; *GS* 6: 107).

CELAN

For Celan, too, forgetting plays a central, if somewhat enigmatic, role in his work. The title of his first major collection provides an initial idea of what is at issue: *Mohn und Gedächtnis*, 'Poppy and Memory'. The poppy as a symbol of war and death pre-dates the tradition that began after World War I in English-speaking countries of wearing a poppy in remembrance of soldiers killed on the fields of war. This tradition may or may not have been familiar to Celan, but in any case it is not this specific association that he invokes in his poetry. So while it is true that much of Celan's work is about preserving the memory of his family and of all those who perished in the Holocaust, the image of the poppy rather pulls the title in the other direction, away from memory: the poppy (*papaver somniferum*, the opium poppy) evokes rather the dissolution of consciousness and memory. In this vein, one of the poems in the collection speaks of 'the poppy of oblivion [*der Mohn des Vergessens*]' (Celan 1975: 1: 68).[5] Also, for reasons that will become clearer in a moment, the poppy can be seen as contrasting with memory in the way that nature can be contrasted with culture, art and specifically human experience – though what is always and everywhere of interest to Celan is their inextricable entanglement, as conveyed through a multitude of liminal images that mediate between materiality and ideality. These undertones orient us in the right direction: the challenge is to understand forgetting in Celan as a kind of threshold between meaning and meaninglessness, between the immaterial plenitude of the name and the blank materiality of nature.

In order just to sketch the role played by forgetting in Celan, this section will focus on a single poem, 'The Sand from the Urns', and will then consider a few lines from his *Meridian* and Bremen speeches. In Felstiner's translation, 'The Sand from the Urns' [*Der Sand aus den Urnen*] reads:

> Mould-green is the house of oblivion.
> At each of its blowing gates your beheaded minstrel goes blue.
> For you he beats on a drum of moss and bitter pubic hair;
> With an ulcerous toe he traces your brow in the sand.
> Longer than it was he draws it, and the red of your lip.
> You fill up the urns here and nourish your heart.

> [Schimmelgrün ist das Haus des Vergessens.
> Vor jedem der wehenden Tore blaut dein enthaupteter Spielmann.
> Er schlägt dir die Trommel aus Moos und bitterem Schamhaar;
> mit schwärender Zehe malt er im Sand deine Braue.
> Länger zeichnet er sie als sie war, und das Rot deiner Lippe.
> Du füllst hier die Urnen und speisest dein Herz.]
>
>   (Celan 2000: 22–3; 1975: 1: 22)

The first thing to notice is that the central images of the poem, namely the abandoned 'house of oblivion', the minstrel, his drum and the urns are all entangled with the natural images of mould, moss, hair and sand, such that the poem's coherence stems from the balance it strikes between nature and natural processes of decay and erosion, on the one hand, and specifically human arts, on the other: architecture, music, drawing. Moreover, this entanglement happens in such a way that the natural images effectively transform and weigh down the cultural elements of humanity in the poem. The house is a house of mould and oblivion, a place where memories cannot collect or which annihilates memory. The minstrel, who is a vital and creative force, has been beheaded, though he is not dead; he is rather caught between life and death, oblivion and memory – a predicament that is reinforced by his turning blue, whether from asphyxia or exertion we do not know. His drum also signals life and death, the slow growth of moss suggesting perpetuity, or empty time kept by the beat of the drum; the 'bitter pubic hair', on the other hand, repeats and reinforces the entwinement of nature and human values: as hair it is already a liminal image, caught between living flesh and dead nature (hair is not a living organism, but rather dead skin); but as pubic hair in particular, it points to human values and emotions, and more specifically to the feeling of shame [*Schamhaar*]. The minstrel, for his part, is also an artist who, with his decaying toe, portrays a human face in the sand, transforming dead or eroded matter into human meaning (a brow, the red of lips) – though his representations are not perfect ('Longer than it was he draws it'); they are rather figurations that point to the power of art to sediment and preserve meaning in natural media, which means spiritualizing and humanizing inert nature. In the last line, the urns manifestly evoke death, cremation and remembrance, though the ashes that they would typically hold are replaced by sand; ashes – central in so many of Celan's poems – are present here only in their absence or by metonymical displacement. The sand in the urns, however, is still a sign of remembrance (and perhaps even of hope): something is taken away from the house of forgetting, saved from oblivion. But the sand-ashes' meaning is fragile, subject to the weakness and limits of human memory, partly because the sand comes from the precinct of oblivion. This fragility is further underscored by the poem itself, which volatilizes their meaning in metaphor. Ultimately, only the conventional sign of the fragile urn reminds us that what is inside it means something, something that must be remembered, something that is the same and yet different from *mere* sand, *mere* ashes. It is this commemoration of the dead – here, through poetry – that nourishes the heart, or gives solace in the face of loss at the end of the poem.

Like so much of Celan's imagery (dust, hair, crystals, snow and frost, shadows, mould, rust, thresholds, the so-called 'breath-turn' [*Atemwende*] and so on), the imagery in this poem is at once tense and fragile, wedged between life and death, order and disorder, organic and inorganic, meaning and unmeaning, memory and oblivion. There is nothing pure here, nothing that remains untainted by erosion, decay and oblivion; only art and, by extension, language, can strike an uneasy bargain with oblivion. It is art and language that save meaning, at least for a time, from loss – from moss, mould and abandonment. As in many other poems, it is as though 'The Sand from the Urns' derives its force, not from the two poles of oblivion and remembrance, but rather from oscillating between them. Oblivion does not overrun memory in the poem, but nor does memory succeed in overcoming oblivion: meaning and unmeaning are profoundly intertwined.

It should be becoming clearer that the ways in which Celan braids together forgetting and the hope of remembrance intersect thematically with how Adorno and Heidegger treat forgetting in their very different works. The *Meridian* speech, which shows obvious signs of his engagement with the work of Adorno and of Heidegger, adds more detail to the picture. In *The Meridian*, Celan further explains that 'the poem holds on at the edge of itself; so as to exist, it ceaselessly calls and hauls itself from its Now-no-more [*Schon-nicht-mehr*] back into its Ever-yet [*Immer-noch*]' (Celan 2000: 409; 1999: 32b). Here again we are kept on the threshold of oblivion, on the edge of meaning, where it risks slipping into nothingness. But Celan adds a crucial element to the mix here: the idea that it is only in the 'radical individuation' of the poem that the ego can forget itself and its limited interests and seize on something else: 'poetry, like art,' says Celan, 'moves with the self-forgotten I toward the uncanny and the strange' (Celan 2000: 406; 1999: 22b). That is, through the poem's concrete dismissal of the recognizable, of the sovereign ego and its domain of familiar experience, the poet aims at an 'actualized language' (*aktualisierte Sprache*): the Ever-yet of the poem is just such 'actualized language', says Celan, 'set free under the sign of radical individuation, which at the same time stays mindful of the limits drawn by language, of the possibilities disclosed by language' (Celan 2000: 409 [trans. mod.]; 1999: 33b). In other words, by careering along the edge of silence or by showing us the horror of oblivion in its unique constellation of images and thoughts, the poem recovers in language the 'hope of the name' (*ND*: 53; *GS* 6: 62); that is, the recovery of healing possibilities in light of the catastrophic possibility of what Celan elsewhere calls 'frightful muting', and 'the thousand darknesses of death-bringing speech' – the mutilation of language by the Nazis and, by extension, the general possibility of such mutilation and domination that language itself makes possible (Celan 2000: 395; 1983: 38). By contrast, however, the poem, 'which is not timeless' (2000: 396; 1983: 38), and which derives from 'radical individuation' – that is, real experience – is a setting-free of possibilities, where possibility itself is a figure caught between oblivion and realization, between 'frightful muting' and 'the light of u-topia', as Celan says, echoing Adorno (Celan 2000: 411 [trans. mod.]; 1999: 40b).

Between these extremes, or shuttling between them, is language, whose fragile promise is articulated in Celan's poetry. It is in this sense that language 'does not transfigure or render "poetical" ', as Celan says: 'it names, it posits, it tries to measure the domain of the given and the possible. Of course, this is never the working of language itself, of language as such, but always of an "I" who speaks from the particular inclinations of his existence [*Existenz*]. . . . Reality is not a given, it has to be sought out and won' (Celan 1986: 16; 1983: 22).[6] 'Won' – that is, won from nature, from the ravages of time, from the 'thousand darknesses of death-bringing speech', and ultimately from oblivion. Language bears the horror of oblivion within it, but it also allows us to wrest possibility from the Now-no-more of forgotten hope. Between oblivion and utopia, traversing them both: language is 'immaterial yet earthy, terrestrial, something circular, returning upon itself by way of both poles and thereby – happily – even crossing the tropics (and tropes): I find . . .', says Celan, 'a *meridian*' (2000: 413; 1999: 50c).

A MERIDIAN?

Returning now to Adorno and Heidegger, let us recall what Adorno finds most objectionable in Heidegger: Dasein's 'pseudo-concreteness' or its historically indeterminate specificity, which tacitly underwrites the brutality of concrete existence (*ND*: 75n.; *GS* 6: 82n.). So while Heidegger articulates a *general* specificity requirement (which defines Dasein in formally contentful terms, i.e. facticity), Adorno will insist on a *specific* specificity requirement, as it were, which means that for him there must be a transition to materialism and so to a mode of analysis that takes aim at real historical existence. But (and this is the rub) for the most part, Adorno's insistence on the specific is of a quite general character, for what he takes to be essential reasons: in order to remain impartial, the critical vigilance that he recommends cannot itself be tied to any specific set of prescriptions. For example, Adorno's rejection of 'orthodox' Marxism leads him to generalize the experience that Marx lent a voice to under the name 'proletariat' in order to rescue not the prescriptive content but rather the logic or the sense of Marx's gesture. But at the very moment he denies to Marxism any *definitive* truth-content, he immediately strips it of its prescriptive content: the concept 'proletariat' is no longer relevant today. This is why Adorno's materialism is 'imageless', as he himself puts it (see *ND*: 204–7; *GS* 6: 204–7). So what Adorno describes under the heading of utopia, the 'speculative moment', and so on (profoundly anti-Marxian concepts), are really ways of describing a *general* structure of historical experience: reflection has to be open, unprejudiced and untrammelled by received wisdom if it is to have a future; that is, the future of experience can neither be exhausted nor fulfilled by Marxism or any other determinate instance of dialectical thinking. So even Adorno's 'specific' specificity requirement retains a formal character that puts him at risk of falling prey to his own critique of philosophical formalism (though some measure of formalism is clearly necessary to the extent that it serves to incite broad-ranging critical vigilance). This goes some way towards explaining why there are so few specific prescriptions to be found in Adorno's philosophical writings – save perhaps one: that Auschwitz should never be repeated, that nothing similar should ever happen again (*ND*: 365; *GS* 6: 358). But as Adorno admits, even this prescription is still categorical in nature: it does not tell us in positive terms what its utopian content is; it merely says that human reason ought always to transcend its catastrophic employment.

But how then ought we to think about the Adorno–Heidegger question? Are we left in this dilemma of Heidegger's purely formal specificity and Adorno's prescriptionless demand for content? Are these not two sides of the same coin? Or, if we insist on the tensions that separate Adorno from Heidegger, could there be a meridian that connects these two poles together in their opposition? What Celan shows us is that language can work through experience in a painstaking effort to dredge up possibilities that, once made intelligible, stave off the oblivion whose limits we skirt at every moment. This is what it means to 'fill up the urns': filling these receptacles of memory with what must not be forgotten. However – and this is the key point – this filling of urns is also the primordial gesture of giving content to form in a way that no specific prescription could ever foresee. Dialectically formulated, this means speaking in a way that negotiates the general and the specific in the service of the specific, when and where the specific obtrudes in the course of things.

In this way, Celan's unique language addresses precisely the problem that keeps Adorno and Heidegger apart in their approaches: he speaks of the specific experience of catastrophic loss while at the same time recognizing that in general we cannot speak specifically, except by confronting oblivion, by pushing language to the point where it risks everything, where radical individuation faces down death-bringing speech and in a very tenuous moment gives real content to language, the purely conventional bearer of sedimented meanings. Thus the urns in the poem are the containers that hold the ashes of those killed in the Holocaust; but they are also the words and sentences of language, which Celan urges us to fill at the place where possibility drains away into the Now-no-more. He is not, however, urging us to become poets. The experience of reading Celan is perhaps enough to lead us to reflect on the way we speak, on the form of human experience today and on what this form does not adequately render.[7] What he demonstrates in his poetry is thus the act of saving possibilities from oblivion, of preserving and recollecting experiential content that marks us and determines us, often without our even being aware of it. He achieves this on two levels: on the general level of figuring how language can 'fill up the urns' and on the specific level of doing just that: filling the urns with the sand-ashes of his own experience of catastrophic loss.

In this way, Celan traces a meridian of sorts between Adorno and Heidegger, between specific and general reflections on possibility and actuality, or between specific and general demands for content. What he helps us to understand is that giving content to a language that seems no longer able to tolerate content, eking possibility out of an actuality that threatens to eclipse it – these are the gestures that bridge the gap between contentfully formal specificity (Adorno's non-identical) and formally contentful specificity (Heidegger's facticity). In other words, Celan helps us to understand better how Adorno and Heidegger converge on the question of how possibility relates to actuality by showing us how language can reach the possible in the real deployment of words around suppressed possibilities. Both Heidegger and Adorno make just this point, each in his own way, but Celan allows us to connect them together for a moment, insofar as rescuing possibility from oblivion requires that we negotiate or shuttle between prescriptionless generality and contentful specificity. Both are required in a way that could be summarized as follows: the specific requires the general to be specific (read both ways: 'to be specific, the specific requires the general' and 'to do justice to the specific, the general itself has to become specific').

Given what has emerged in the course of the preceding analyses, it should be clear that simply pitting materialism against metaphysics, Adorno against Heidegger, is hopeless as a way of getting at what is most essential in their work. But perhaps we are not faced with an ultimatum; perhaps there is no need to pick sides in the Adorno–Heidegger debate, at least on the question of forgetting and possibility. After all, we are, like Adorno and Heidegger, always caught in a struggle over a need for content that we cannot meet in advance or once and for all. We are always, every day, at the edge of a Now-no-more, hanging onto an Ever-yet that demands to be recognized 'here' and 'now'. 'Here' and 'now': the moments that describe, absolutely generally, the specific situation in which we always are. In this limited sense, the Adorno–Heidegger dispute figures the predicament that we ourselves always find ourselves in. As such, we should not – it seems to me – be taking sides.

NOTES

1 There are exceptions to the rule. For example, see Mörchen 1981; 1980; Guzzoni 1981; Dallmayr 1991; García Düttmann 2002.
2 Dual references to Heidegger, Adorno and Celan are generally to an existing English translation and to the German text, respectively.
3 Heidegger's *Sein* is rendered here as 'being' with a lower case 'b'. References to *Being and Time* follow the pagination of the seventh German edition, as reproduced in the margins of the Macquarrie and Robinson translation (1962).
4 Heidegger uses a similar example in a 1964 televised interview. Parts of the interview are shown in a later documentary film (see Rüdel and Wisser 1975).
5 'Die Ewigkeit'. See 'Corona' (Celan 2000: 28–9; 1975: 1: 37).
6 Here Celan uses the word *Existenz*. In *The Meridian*, he says '... the inclinations of his very being [*Dasein*] ...' (2000: 409; 1999: 33c).
7 This is what Celan means when he writes that 'a poem is a message in a bottle, sent out in the – not always greatly hopeful – belief that somewhere and sometime it could wash up on land, on heartland perhaps' (2000: 396; 1983: 39).

WORKS CITED

Celan, P. (1975), *Gedichte in zwei Bänden*. Frankfurt: Suhrkamp.
— (1983), *Der Meridian und andere Prosa*. Frankfurt: Suhrkamp.
— (1986), *Collected Prose*, trans. R. Waldrop. Riverdale-on-Hudson, NY: Sheep Meadow Press.
— (1999), *Der Meridian: Endfassung–Entwürfe–Materialien*. Frankfurt: Suhrkamp.
— (2000), *Selected Poems and Prose*, trans. J. Felstiner. New York: W. W. Norton.
Dallmayr, F. R. (1991), *Between Freiburg and Frankfurt: Toward a Critical Ontology*. Amherst: University of Massachusetts Press.
Felstiner, J. (1995), *Paul Celan: Poet, Survivor, Jew*. New Haven, CT: Yale University Press.
France-Lanord, H. (2004), *Paul Celan et Martin Heidegger: le sens d'un dialogue*. Paris: Arthème Fayard.
García Düttmann, A. (2002), *The Memory of Thought: An Essay on Heidegger and Adorno*, trans. N. Walker. London: Continuum.
Guzzoni, U. (1981), *Identität oder nicht: Zur kritischen Theorie der Ontologie*. Freiburg/ München: Verlag Karl-Albert.
Hegel, G. W. F. (1977), *Hegel's Phenomenology of Spirit*, trans. A. V. Miller. Oxford: Oxford University Press.
— (1981), *Gesammelte Werke*. Hamburg: Felix Meiner Verlag.
Heidegger, M. (1959), *Gelassenheit*. Pfullingen: Neske.
— (1962), *Being and Time*, trans. J. Macquarrie and E. Robinson. Oxford: Basil Blackwell.

— (1966), *Discourse on Thinking*, trans. J. M. Anderson and E. H. Freud. New York: Harper & Row.

— (1975ff.), *Gesamtausgabe*. Frankfurt: Klostermann.

— (1999), *Contributions to Philosophy: From Enowning*, trans. P. Emad and K. Maly. Bloomington: Indiana University Press.

Marx, K. (1994), *Selected Writings*, ed. L. H. Simon. Indianapolis, IN: Hackett.

Marx, K. and Engels, F. (1956ff.), *Werke*. Berlin: Dietz-Verlag.

Mörchen, H. (1980), *Macht und Herrschaft im Denken von Heidegger und Adorno*. Stuttgart: Klett-Cotta.

— (1981), *Adorno und Heidegger: Untersuchung einer philosophischen Kommunikationsverweigerung*. Stuttgart: Klett-Cotta.

Pöggeler, O. (1986), *Spur des Wortes: Zur Lyrik Paul Celans*. Freiburg/München: Verlag Karl Alber.

— (2000), *Der Stein hinterm Aug: Studien zu Celans Gedichten*. München: Wilhelm Fink.

Rüdel, W. and Wisser, R. (1975), *Martin Heidegger: Im Denken unterwegs*. Südwestfunk.

PART III:

Modernity, Drama and the Novel

9

Forgetting – Faust: *Adorno and Kommerell*

Paul Fleming

I

The composition of Theodor Adorno's 1959 essay 'On the Final Scene of *Faust*' begins with a memory. In a note appended to its publication, Adorno writes:

> I once teased Walter Benjamin about his predilection for unusual and out-of-the-way material by asking him when he planned to write an interpretation of *Faust*, and he immediately parried by saying that he would do so if it could be serialized in the *Frankfurter Zeitung*. The memory of that conversation occasioned the writing of the fragments published here. (*NL1*: xiv)

Benjamin's untimely death pre-empted the possibility that his interpretation of Goethe's *Faust* be written, much less serialized in a German newspaper. What remains is Adorno's memory of the conversation and the sense of an unrealized possibility, of an unwritten pendant to Benjamin's famous essay on Goethe's *Elective Affinities*. Adorno's text can be read then as a souvenir of and for a friend, a supplement to his friend's unwritten pages. This manifest memory, however, seems to be only half of the memento contained in Adorno's fragmentary reflections. Another, latent memory of Benjamin also most likely occasioned the essay's writing: the recollection of Benjamin's first affront. On 6 November 1934, after a period of uncomfortable silence, Adorno writes to Benjamin from his exile in Oxford:

> Since Gretel's visit you know what brought about my silence for so long; this visit as well as the indications in your letter have cleared away the difficulties. They lay thoroughly in the realm of our work; I could not suppress the most serious reservations towards some of your publications (for the first time since our association). I mean here your work on the French novel and the essay on Kommerell, which offended me uncommonly in the private sphere as well, since this author once said that men like me should be put against the wall – one doesn't need to explain more. (Lonitz 1994: 72–3)[1]

Adorno refers in this letter to the review Benjamin published of Max Kommerell's book *Jean Paul* (1933) on 29 March 1934 in none other than the above-mentioned *Frankfurter Zeitung*.[2] In this review, Benjamin describes Jean Paul as 'the most severe test of ability' and concludes unequivocally: 'Kommerell has passed the test.' Kommerell, in Benjamin's judgement, has achieved 'authority' as a literary critic (Benjamin 1991: 410). Hypothetically, one could say that instead of the desired *Faust* interpretation in the newspaper, Adorno is confronted with Benjamin's praise of Kommerell. Adorno's 'severe reservations' about Benjamin's seemingly uncritical stance toward Kommerell were not a passing offence.[3] Adorno's rancour stayed with him into his late years, as can be seen from a letter written to the German scholar Francis Golffing in 1968, in which Adorno returns to Kommerell and Benjamin's problematic relation to him:

> I knew Kommerell; we received our habilitation around the same time at Frankfurt. ... At the time, I considered him to be, I admit, a highly talented fascist, and he certainly couldn't stand me as well. ... [H]e was certainly a highly talented person, but not very appealing to me, and I never really understood Benjamin's admiration of the enemy. (Lonitz 1994: 78)

An examination of Kommerell's politics, his relation to fascism, and whether he once indeed expressed the grotesque wish that Adorno be put before the firing squad lies outside the purview of this essay.[4] Kommerell was indeed conservative, both politically and aesthetically,[5] and he was also without a doubt the most talented literary critic to come out of the George Circle. For Giorgio Agamben, Kommerell is 'the greatest German critic of the twentieth century after Benjamin, and perhaps the last great personality between the wars who still remains to be discovered' (Agamben 1999: 77). Even Adorno, in another extorted reconciliation, does not deny Kommerell's talent; he refuses to share, however, Benjamin's 'admiration of the enemy'. Talent can be both recognized and rejected, that is, critically dismantled – a task that Adorno's essay on *Faust* implicitly pursues.

Adorno never mentions Kommerell in his essay on *Faust*. In fact, excepting the two letters quoted above, the word 'Kommerell' seems to be taboo in Adorno's work. And yet, Kommerell's essays on *Faust* remain a clear subtext in Adorno's essay. Kommerell published his thoughts on *Faust* in a series of studies – 'Faust II. Teil. Zum Verständnis der Form', 'Faust und die Sorge' and 'Faust II letzte Szene' – which are collected in *Geist und Buchstabe der Dichtung* (1940).[6] For Kommerell, as for Adorno writing some twenty years later, the understanding of the otherwise inexplicable – namely, Faust's salvation at the end of Goethe's drama – lies in the question of memory and forgetting; both authors explore the extent to which oblivion can be a dynamic force, a mode of transformation and ultimately redemption.

Kommerell calls Faust 'a virtuoso of forgetting' (1991:95), and Adorno claims: 'The power of life, as a power of continued life, is equated with forgetting' (*NL1*: 120).[7] Kommerell, however, will cling fast to the transformative powers of Lethe, of forgetfulness, while Adorno will ultimately distance himself from such blissful oblivion. The last sentence of Adorno's essay reads: 'Hope is not memory held fast but the return of the forgotten' (*NL1*: 120). This line immediately calls forth, like an echoing memory, the famous conclusion to Benjamin's own essay on Goethe: 'Only for the sake of the hopeless ones have we been given hope' (Benjamin 1996: 356). In the end, Adorno uses his *Faust* essay to perform a critique of Kommerell that – to his mind – Benjamin never did, while also providing a further memento to his friend.

II

That Kommerell and Adorno both underscore the prevalence of oblivion as a determining element of *Faust II* comes as little surprise: one of the remarkable features of Goethe's Faust-figure is that he at no point reflects upon what has happened and what he has done, whether it be the making of the wager with Mephisto or the question of his soul's fate. There is no pause for thought, no introspection, no taking account of himself, no moment of memory, no conclusive turn away from Mephisto, and no hint of a turn to the divine. This oblivion persists despite the fact that the list of his misdeeds is considerable: Gretchen, her mother, her brother and their child as well as Baucis, Philemon and the Traveller belong to the list of deaths that can be attributed, at least in part, to Faust. Even the final midnight encounter with 'Worry' [*Sorge*], who wafts over to Faust from the embers of his latest act of aggression, does not result in the traditional scene of memory. Although blinded by 'Worry', Faust remains oblivious to such worry and simply strives on. In fact, Faust's infamous 'striving' [*Streben*] seems to be synonymous with his obliviousness; the only thing that Faust does not forget to do is to forget. And yet, without a moment of regret, he is saved; when he appears to lose, Faust wins.[8]

Both Kommerell and Adorno, therefore, list off the scenes of forgetting that rhythmically punctuate *Faust II*: Faust's restless sleep at the beginning of the drama, his loss of consciousness at the start of the second act, his speechlessness at the end of the third act and his blinding in Act Five (Kommerell 1991:114; *NL1*: 120). Furthermore, both agree that the continuation of *Faust I* in *Faust II* is made possible by the Lethe that bathes the hero as the sequel commences.[9] Faust's rhythm of forgetting, his lapses into oblivion which wash his memory clean therefore mark for Kommerell the formal principle of *Faust II* as a whole. Whenever Faust forgets, falls unconscious or simply experiences profound obliviousness, Kommerell notes a structural series of 'caesuras' [*Zäsuren*] or 'stops' [*Einhalte*], which he

also calls 'catastrophes' that are synonymous with 'Faust's transformations'
(Kommerell 1991: 64, 114). These caesuras provide a rhythm of interruption within Faust's development that breaks with Goethe's own notion of
metamorphosis and its 'law of imperceptible transition' and replaces it with
the 'more incalculable, more sudden, more formless element of the inner
self' (67). Instead of gradual transition, one is confronted in *Faust II* with
radical caesuras of the self, which are constitutive of Faust as a person, as 'the
principle of the person' (113). That is, the notion of the self presented in
the persistent forgetting of Faust consists in fragments, whereby such rupturing is synonymous with renewal. In opposition to the novel, particularly the
Bildungsroman, Faust II reveals a view of life, of lived experience defined as
'an eternity composed of moments . . . instead of gradual development [there
are] transformations, dazes, sleep, death' (38).

In oblivion and interruption, the structure of both the self and the drama
is revealed. Because of the formal principle of discontinuity, in which
individual oblivion maps onto and determines the dramatic structure,
Kommerell describes the project undertaken by Goethe in *Faust II* as
'a pensive fantasy about the evil and good gifts of remembering', and
Faust is one who remains 'thoroughly unconscious and non-remembering'
(Kommerell 1991:68, 69). Each moment of oblivion, each caesura is a
minor death; these intervals 'from death to death' allow Faust to be ever
again 'renewed' (74). It is then precisely Faust's ability to forget that not
only determines his transformations – opening up a 'cosmic-rhythmic view
of life against the biographical-progressive view of the novel' (73) – but also
enables his ultimate redemption: 'The question is whether one can forget.
One can – the bill is not paid, but torn up' (72). The 'bill' here is Faust's
series of misdeeds and by extension his wager with Mephisto; by forgetting
the wager one is freed of it. A pact is invalid if one of the signers constantly
transforms and is, thus, never the same. For Kommerell, Faust must forget
everything and rely on nothing but himself and his will-to-do in order to be
saved: 'It almost appears as if Faust's protection against the devil was to not
ask for a god. And even in heaven this [refusal to ask for a god] will in no
way be turned into a reproach against him. On the contrary: it is contained
in "exerting oneself in striving", in restless activity, which is the condition of
redemption' (127). Faust, in a word, prepares his salvation by pressing on
in his unwavering ambition and remaining oblivious to everything – his
deeds, their consequences, the pact, God and his soul. The possibility of
redemption lies then in a pervasive obliviousness to the question of a transcendent sphere and a relentless acting within the profane. For Kommerell,
Faust's salvation arises out of a paradox: Faust's refusal to turn to God
ultimately leads him to God. By forgetting the pact and its consequences, he
is freed from it.

Forgetting, however, is only one half of the equation in Kommerell's
interpretation of Faust's salvation. Mercy must arrive 'as the supplement to

striving' (1991: 129). This 'supplementary force' is called 'love' on earth and 'mercy' in heaven (127). But because one 'can only approach god through the world' (110), the final mercy is to be understood not as a divine act (Kommerell rejects all Christian-metaphysical readings of *Faust*) but as a human intervention: Gretchen's love of Faust. 'That Gretchen lovingly sacrificed herself for him', writes Kommerell, 'this is the beginning of the effect that is imparted to the Faust of the last scene as mercy' (126). Faust's striving, which forgets everything and remains attached to nothing, must be 'supplemented' by love, 'the profane condition of mercy' (129).

Forgetting and mercy are structurally two sides of the same coin: both announce a caesura in the prevailing continuum that allows for something new to emerge. Forgetting, one could say, is Faust's personal contribution to salvation; mercy is the contribution that comes from elsewhere. Therefore, the mercy at the end, the final forgiveness of Faust's misdeeds is everything but unexpected within the formal, poetic structure of the drama. Faust's otherwise incomprehensible redemption remains utterly consistent for the ruptured logic of the drama. In other words, the theological difficulties surrounding Faust's ultimate redemption are, for Kommerell, poetologically elucidated. What appears to be a theological question is, in fact, a poetic one. With respect to Faust's salvation, Kommerell writes:

> We are prepared for it through the drama itself, for whenever Faust was so speechless, so, as we say, unconsciously returned to himself, he experienced, whether actively or passively, the most important things; here he transformed himself. ... Certainly, the mercy in this [last] scene corresponds to something that occurred to or with Faust in those earlier scenes. For the transformation was not yet given with Faust's appropriation of the world; transformation is like a taste of death, through which the condition of a new life is won. Ergo, the danger and – in a profane sense – the mercy. (1991: 115–16)

Faust's theological enigmas are resolved in its paradoxical literary consistency, in which a structural caesura repeatedly delimits a moment of transformation and, therefore, his redemption as well – the final transformation. If the formal principle of *Faust II* is a series of interruptions, suspensions and small deaths, the ultimate mercy does not come from nowhere but is simply a continuation of this pattern. Or rather, by coming from nowhere, Faust's conclusion is utterly consistent with its rhythm of interruption. The end 'corresponds to something that occurred earlier', namely, Faust's bouts of oblivion. That is, an almost invisible continuity of discontinuity underlies and unites *Faust II* from first to last verse. The breakdown of the hermeneutic circle, in which the whole is fragmented into discrete parts, maps squarely onto the scenes of oblivion and mercy. In the continual rupture of the whole, one gleans a sense of the whole – as discontinuous but consistent all the same. The whole is composed of parts that don't fit together, that don't provide transition or continuity, and in this fragmentation of the self and the drama lies the secret to Faust's redemption: 'In so far as these caesuras help to interpret the form, they also help to interpret the drama' (73). In other words, to understand the content (the 'drama'), one only needs to look to the form.

III

Adorno's series of thoughts dedicated to the last scene of *Faust* come uncannily close to Kommerell's. Without mentioning the name of the 'enemy', Adorno's exegesis equally focuses on the productive role that forgetting and mercy play in Faust's otherwise inexplicable redemption. Adorno's reflections home in on the pact itself, whose conditions are determined in the scene 'Study' from *Faust I*. If Faust is ever content enough to utter the words 'Abide! You are so beautiful' (1,699), Mephisto can have his soul. In warning Faust about the stakes involved, Mephisto makes one promise: 'Consider this well; we won't forget it' ['*Bedenk es wohl, wir werden's nicht vergessen*'] (1,707). For Adorno, when Faust does indeed express the fatal sentence right before his death – 'May I say to the moment / "Abide, you are so beautiful!"'' ['*Zum Augenblicke dürft' ich sagen: / "Verweile doch, du bist so schön!"*'] (11,581–2) – all is lost. Philological haranguing about the conjunctive verb 'may I say', about the faux self-citation, or about the difference between the letter and spirit of the wager completely miss the point of Faust's end. For Adorno, there is no doubt: 'The wager is lost. . . . Faust has played a losing hand' (*NL1*: 118). According to the terms of the pact, which is premised on the capitalist logic of exchange – of quid pro quo and cause and effect – Faust must surrender his soul. Faust can therefore only lose and win all the same, if his salvation rests not on maintaining the principle of exchange but definitively repealing it: 'Law itself is suspended. A higher court ordains a stay [*Einhalt*] of the eternal equivalence of credit and debit' (119). In other words, the conditions upholding the validity of the pact are discarded so that an other order, an other logic can emerge. The name for this 'stay' imposed on the system of exchange is 'mercy', 'which takes precedence over law' and 'shatters the cycle of cause and effect' (119). Mercy intervenes as a 'stop' or 'stay' [*Einhalt*] and ultimately 'marks a caesura in the continuity of events' (119). Therefore, both Adorno's theoretical lexicon – 'stop' and 'caesura' – and his insistence on the fundamental role of interruption map rather seamlessly onto Kommerell's interpretation. For both authors, it is precisely discontinuity, the rupturing of a continuum that renders the last scene of *Faust* comprehensible – as that which exceeds conceptual comprehension.

   After discussing mercy in terms of suspension and caesura, Adorno provides, like Kommerell, a more profane reading of *Faust II* that highlights a different form of interruption, which is also the more probable reason for Faust's redemption – his incessant forgetting:

> Isn't the wager forgotten in Faust's 'extreme old age', along with all the crimes that Faust in his entanglement perpetrated or permitted ...? Isn't Faust saved because he is no longer the one who signed the pact? Doesn't the wisdom of the play, which is a play in pieces, a 'Stück in Stücken', lie in knowing how little the human being is identical to himself ...? The power of life, as a power of continued life, is equated with forgetting. It is only by passing through forgetting [*durchs Vergessen hindurch*] and thereby transforming that anything survives at all. (*NLI*: 119–20)

This passage in the last section of Adorno's essay could be read as a compact synthesis of Kommerell's interpretation. The notion of the subject in *Faust II* consists in non-identity, in difference from itself over time. Because Faust is not the same, the wager can be forgotten, can be, in Kommerell's words, 'torn up'. The difference of Faust from himself, this mobilization of forgetting as the structure of the non-identical subject, resurfaces in the form of the drama itself, the play made of pieces, of fragments that don't resolve into a whole. Forgetting, then, is not a lapse or failing, but the very mode of transformation and thereby the hidden key to understanding both the play and the final redemption. Were Adorno to leave his interpretation at this invocation of the transformative power of forgetting, he would prove just how 'talented' Kommerell was, for their readings differ but little.

Adorno, however, explicates the powers of oblivion carefully, as a series of questions that may be rhetorical or may, in fact, demand an answer. Furthermore, a slight but crucial difference emerges in Adorno's understanding of the function of Lethe: for Kommerell, to forget is to transform; for Adorno, it is not merely forgetting but passing through oblivion ['*durchs Vergessen hindurch*']¹⁰ that embodies the true model of transformation. In other words, Kommerell maintains that forgetting is enough, while Adorno posits forgetting as the necessary precondition of a return.

At the very end of his reflections on *Faust* – in an admittedly enigmatic last barrage – Adorno doesn't merely reflect upon the literary role of the caesura in the drama but repeatedly performs a caesura or stop of his own reading, which suspends what came before not once but twice. In other words, if Kommerell mobilizes forgetting as an interruption of the self that transforms the self, Adorno takes the additional step of interrupting the caesura itself – the negation of negation – so as to truly arrive at something else. In this dialectic of memory and forgetting, Adorno provides the first reversal of his previous reading, which until now was so close to Kommerell's:

> But when, in an affront to logic, an affront whose radiance heals all logic's acts of violence, the memory of Gretchen's lines at the city wall [*Zwinger*]

dawns on us, as if across eons, in the invocation of the Mater gloriosa as the *Ohnegleiche*, the one without equal, there speaks from it, in boundless joy, the feeling that must have seized the poet when, shortly before his death, he reread on the wooden walls of a small cottage on Gickelhahn Hill the poem, 'Wanderers Nachtlied' ['Wanderer's Night-Song'], he had inscribed on it a lifetime before. (*NL1*: 120)[11]

Adorno's delineation of the movement through oblivion and back to memory takes place through two scenes of reading: first, with the reader of *Faust II*, who recognizes in Gretchen's final invocation of the Mater gloriosa her long forgotten appeal to the Mater dolorosa in *Faust I*. Like an echo resounding out of a gorge so removed that one forgets that words were ever spoken, the attentive reader hears, after a delay akin to oblivion, Gretchen's long since spoken prayer to the Mater dolorosa.[12] In the second scene of reading, Adorno conjures up the image of Goethe himself, as reported by Johann Heinrich Christian Mahr (27 August 1831), when the aged poet finds on the walls of a forest cottage his fifty-year-old inscription of the poem 'Wanderer's Night-Song'.[13] Both scenes underscore the 'boundless joy' of recognition, the feeling of elation in rediscovering what was otherwise condemned to oblivion. Therefore, everything Adorno said before about forgetting is suspended and, indeed, forgotten with this salvo. Forgetting may prepare salvation, but only the final step of memory after an interval of oblivion produces the 'boundless joy' found in redemption. As in Kommerell, forgetting remains a dynamic force, but only as the condition of possibility of remembrance. For redemption to occur, forgetting must itself be interrupted; in this double negation, one experiences the 'boundless joy' of memory, an affront, directed at the violence of forgetting, that heals all 'acts of violence'.

This possible interpretation of *Faust*'s last scene is, however, ruptured as well. With the final two sentences, the inversion of forgetting into the precondition of memory is modified in turn. Adorno's essay concludes: 'That hut too has been burned down. Hope is not memory held fast but the return of what has been forgotten' (*NL1*: 120). The hut [*Hütte*] has multiple references: first, it points directly to the cottage where Goethe inscribed his poem (which indeed burned in 1870); then to the hut of Baucis and Philemon, who are killed in Faust's last crime, when he orders their hut burned to the ground with its inhabitants inside; and finally, if only implicitly, to the historical caesura of Auschwitz, which Adorno evokes at the beginning of the essay. If the hut has been burned down, there is no possibility of a return to the past; there is nothing left to read and therefore no 'boundless joy' to be had. All that remains is ruins. Therefore, the hermeneutic joy of recognition – of discovering a hidden connection, discovering an effaced clue, or making manifest a latent coherency within the otherwise incoherent (much like Kommerell's ingenious emphasis on the continuum of discontinuity) – is, for Adorno, no longer a possible mode of interpretation.[14] With this definitive final caesura which blocks all hopes of return, the ensuing last line of the essay – 'Hope is not memory held fast but the return of what has been forgotten' – can no longer follow the model of intervals of forgetting followed by remembrance and its attendant joy. Between the past as forgotten and the present as the locus of memory lie the ashes of the hut, an unbridgeable gap.[15] Therefore, the ruins of the conflagration mark a caesura that bars both simple forgetting and simple remembrance.

IV

Adorno provides the parameters for understanding hope as the return of the forgotten in the protocols of exegesis that he lays out in the first paragraph of his essay on *Faust*. Addressing 'the current historical situation', in which Auschwitz marks a 'boundary situation', Adorno sympathizes with 'alexandrinism', with the 'interpretive immersion in traditional texts', since, if one cannot directly express 'metaphysical intentions', one is compelled to pursue a philological exactness that locates metaphysics elsewhere, in literature, whose interpretation allows one to express such metaphysical statements indirectly (*NL1*: 111). While this taking 'refuge in texts' enables a critic to discover in traditional texts 'what remains of one's own', Adorno rejects such hermeneutic discovery missions:

> But these are not one and the same: what is discovered in the texts does not prove that something has been spared. The negative, the impossibility, is expressed in that difference, an 'if only it were so', as far from the assurance that it is so as from the assurance that it is not. Interpretation does not seize upon what it finds as valid truth, and yet it knows that without the light it tracks in the texts there would be no truth. This tinges interpretation with a sorrow wholly unsuspected by the assertion of meaning and frantically denied by an insistence on what the case is. (*NL1*: 111)

Instead of the 'boundless joy' of the above two scenes of reading, in which what had been condemned to oblivion is re-collected as a mode of salvation, Adorno underscores the ineluctable 'sorrow' that affects every interpretation that holds fast to the negative. Hermeneutics shines a light onto what it holds to be true, but can never hold that truth itself. True interpretation cannot get around the sense of 'if only it were so', a semblance of certainty that is equally aware of how uncertain all meaning is.

This is not to say that the hope invoked in Adorno's last sentence doesn't play with the possibility of memory's 'boundless joy', for the line possesses a clear 'elective affinity' to the end of Benjamin's own essay on Goethe: 'Only for the sake of the hopeless ones has hope been given to us' (Benjamin 1996: 356). After critically engaging – if only as a subtext – Kommerell's *Faust* interpretation and criticizing the notion that redemption lies in forgetting, in a striving that is oblivious to its consequences,[16] Adorno ends by echoing the words of his friend and, thereby, calling forth the memory of the conversation mentioned above as well as his affinity to Benjamin's own reading of Goethe. Hope in Benjamin's essay on *Elective Affinities* also marks a caesura in the story, but it is an interruption that neither forgets nor re-members by returning what has been lost. Rather, the caesura of hope is an interruption that at once shows just how distant one remains from reconciliation while also maintaining a relationship to such all-but-impossible reconciliation: 'This most paradoxical, most fleeting hope finally emerges from the semblance of reconciliation. ... And upon the slightest such glimmer all hope rests; even the richest hope comes only from it' (Benjamin 1996: 355). Hope does not arise from a previous reconciliation, but from its mere semblance. That is, hope is not nostalgia for something that once was and is now lost or forgotten. Rather, hope emits from a mere possibility and, thus, may rest upon nothing – a glimmer projected by an illusion. Despite the possibility of deception, one is not only 'permitted to desire the semblance of reconciliation', but more emphatically 'it must be desired: it alone is the house of the most extreme hope' (Benjamin 1996: 355). Only at the furthest remove from hope – when one is hopeless – is there not only a reason for hope, but its necessity. Hope arises precisely when there is no reason for hope. In Adorno's final invocation of Benjamin's delineation of hope, he at once offers the 'boundless joy' of memory, of a memorial to his friend, and interrupts this joy by underscoring that 'what has been forgotten' [*das Vergessene*] cannot simply mean 'what once was' [*das Vergangene*]. At the end, what returns in Adorno's hope is not what once was, for 'that hut too has been burned down'. Rather, hope is the return of what could be, but remains only a necessary possibility: reconciliation.

NOTES

1   All translations from Adorno's correspondence with Benjamin are my own.
2   The title of Benjamin's review was 'The Dipped-in Magic Wand' ['Der eingetunkte Zauberstab']. Benjamin's review of *Jean Paul* was not his first engagement with a book by Kommerell; in 1930 Benjamin reviewed Kommerell's *The Poet as Leader in German Classicism* (1928) with the ambivalent title 'Against a Masterpiece'. In discussing Kommerell's first book, Benjamin mixes praise and reproach in a manner that must have been unsettling to Adorno. 'If there were such a thing as a German Conservatism worth its salt', Benjamin begins, 'it would have to regard this book as its Magna Carta' (Benjamin 1999: 378). In a letter to Gerhard Scholem dated 18 September 1929, Benjamin describes *The Poet as Leader* as 'the most astonishing publication to have come out of the George circle in the past few years' (Benjamin 1978: 502; cf. 1999: 835).

3   Through a systematic reading of Benjamin's review of Kommerell's *Jean Paul*, Eckart Goebel has shown that the text is not as positive as it seems. Goebel also explores the complicated constellation between Adorno, Benjamin and Kommerell (Goebel 1999: 153–7).

4   For a thorough overview and examination of Kommerell's politics, see the essays by Martin Vialon and Rainer Nägele in Busch and Pickerodt (eds) 2003.

5   See the essays collected in Busch and Pickerodt (eds) 2003, particularly Eva Geulen's 'Aktualität im Übergang: Kunst und Moderne bei Max Kommerell' and my essay 'Die Moderne ohne Kunst: Max Kommerells Gattungspoetik in *Jean Paul*'.

6   The third essay 'Faust II letzte Szene' was first included in the second edition of *Geist und Buchstabe der Dichtung* from 1942. All translation from Kommerell will be mine.

7   All translation from Adorno's *Notes to Literature* will be taken from Shierry Weber Nicholsen (*NL1*) but may be silently modified.

8   Faust's ultimate redemption in Goethe's drama is doubly unexpected: first, textual evidence justifying his salvation is scarce at best and, second, it is rather exceptional in the canonical literary tradition of *Faust*: both the *Historia von D. Johann Fausten* and Marlowe's *Doctor Faustus*, for example, end in a horrific dismemberment of Faust. (There are, however, examples of a redeemed Faust primarily from the Middle Ages and the folklore tradition, in which salvation usually is attained through the intervention of a child or the Virgin Mary (see Gernentz 1988).)

9   When Faust exclaims at the end of *Faust I*: 'I wish I had never been born!' (4,596), this wish is immediately fulfilled at the beginning of *Faust II* through the cleansing powers of oblivion. As the curtains open on the Second Part, one finds Faust sleeping restlessly in a field with a circle of spirits floating about him. The Ariel sings: 'Soothe the furious battle of his heart / Remove the glowing bitter arrows of reproach, / Purify his inner state of the lived horror. ... First lower his head down upon the cool pillow / Then bathe him in the dew of Lethe's tide' (4,623–9). For Kommerell, the tone of *Faust II* is therefore offered at its beginning: 'The second part doesn't begin with introspection or taking account of what has transpired but rather with Lethe and recovery' (Kommerell 1991: 37). Adorno, almost echoing Kommerell, writes: 'This is why *Faust Part Two* has as its prelude the restless sleep of forgetting. ... [H]e no longer knows anything about the horrors that went on before' (*NL1*: 120). For both Adorno and Kommerell, *Faust I* is forgotten so that *Faust II* can begin with a clean slate. All translations from Goethe's *Faust* will be my own.

10 Shierry Weber Nicholsen's otherwise admirable translation unfortunately elides this difference by rendering '*nur durchs Vergessen hindurch*' as 'only in being forgotten'. The adverb '*hindurch*' signifies that forgetting is not a state but a process.

11 There are a few small errors in Weber Nicholsen's rendition of this passage: 1) both Adorno and Goethe refer to the Mater gloriosa as the '*Ohnegleiche*' and not as the '*Unvergleichliche*'; 2) Gretchen's previous invocation of the Mater dolorosa occurs not in the 'dungeon' but at the *Zwinger*, which is the space between the inner and outer walls of a city; and 3) Goethe didn't pencil his poem onto a 'chicken coop'. Adorno laconically locates the inscription at the 'Gickelhahn', which is a hill in the Thuringian Forest outside Weimar that Goethe often visited. In a small cottage there, Goethe inscribed his famous poem on a windowsill on 7 September 1780. See Mahr's description of Goethe's return to the 'Gickelhahn' on 27 August 1831 (Goethe 1965: 809–14).

12 In *Faust I*, Gretchen prays to the Mater dolorosa: 'Ah Incline, / You rich in pain, / Your visage mercifully towards my need' [*Ach neige, / Du Schmerzenreiche, / Dein Antlitz gnädig meiner Not!*] (3,587–9). The words of 'una poenitentium, otherwise called Gretchen' that are addressed to the Mater gloriosa at the end of *Faust II* read: 'Incline, Incline, / You without equal / You rich in radiance, / Incline your visage mercifully

toward my good fortune' ['*Neige, neige, / Du Ohnegleiche / Du Strahlenreiche, / Dein Antlitz gnädig meinem Glück*'] (12,069–72). In the manuscript, Goethe initially ascribed the lines simply to 'una poenitentium,' a penitent one, and only later added – as if to make the echo explicit – the clarifying explanation 'otherwise called Gretchen'.

13   See Mahr's description of the scene: 'Goethe read over these few lines and tears flowed over his cheeks. Very slowly he pulled his snow-white handkerchief from his dark brown coat, dried his tears, and said in soft melancholic voice: "Yes, just wait, soon you too will rest!" He was then silent for half a minute, looked out the window into the dark pine forest, and then turned to me and said: "Now let's get going again" ' (Goethe 1965: 811).

14   As Eva Geulen emphasizes in reading the line 'That hut too has been burned', a historical caesura has taken place: 'But what was still allowed to Goethe has become definitively impossible' (Busch and Pickerodt [eds] 2003: 35).

15   Goethe's hut was in fact reconstructed four years after it burned to the ground. The original poem he inscribed, however, was lost forever. In its stead one now finds the walls literally covered with versions of the 'Wanderer's Night-Song': a German transcription with its translation into fifteen different languages.

16   In 'What is the Meaning of Working through the Past', published in the same year (1959) as the essay on *Faust*, Adorno argues against a notion of working through the Nazi past that is akin to effacing memory and moving on. Here Adorno returns to the end of *Faust*, where Mephisto proclaims upon Faust's death: 'It is as good as if it never was' [*es ist so gut, als wär es nicht gewesen*]. This line expresses for Adorno the 'innermost principle' of the devil: 'the destruction of memory' (*GS* 10.2: 557).

WORKS CITED

Agamben, G. (1999), *Potentialities: Collected Essays in Philosophy*, trans. D. Heller-Roazen. Stanford, CA: Stanford University Press.

Benjamin, W. (1978), *Briefe I und II*, ed. G. Scholem and T. W. Adorno. Frankfurt: Suhrkamp.

— (1991), *Gesammelte Schriften: Band III, Kritiken und Rezensionen*, ed. H. Tiedemann-Bartels. Frankfurt: Suhrkamp.

— (1996), *Selected Writings*, vol. 1, ed. M. Bullock and M. W. Jennings. Cambridge, MA: Belknapt Harvard University Press.

— (1999), *Selected Writings*, vol. 2, ed. M. W. Jennings, H. Eiland and G. Smith. Cambridge, MA: BelknaptHarvard University Press.

Busch, W. and Pickerodt, G. (eds) (2003), *Max Kommerell: Leben – Werk – Aktualität*. Göttingen: Wallstein Verlag.

Gernentz, H. J. (ed.) (1988), *Doktor Faust und andere Teufelsbünder*. Berlin: Union Verlag.

Goebel, E. (1999), *Am Ufer der zweiten Welt: Jean Pauls 'Poetische Landschaftsmalerei'*. Tübingen: Stauffenburg.

Goethe, J. W. (1965), *Goethes Gespräche: Dritter Band, Zweiter Teil, 1825–1832*, ed. W. Herwig. Zürich: Artemis Verlag.

— (1999), *Faust: Der Tragödie erster und zweiter Teil. Urfaust*, ed. E. Truntz. Munich: Beck Verlag.

Kommerell, M. (1991), *Geist und Buchstabe der Dichtung*, 6th edn. Frankfurt: Klostermann.

Lonitz, H. (ed.) (1994), *Adorno–Benjamin: Briefwechsel 1928–1940*. Frankfurt: Suhrkamp.

10

Adorno's Aesthetic Theory and Lukács's Theory of the Novel

Timothy Hall

The Adorno–Lukács relationship is principally remembered for the vehement exchanges in the 1950s over the significance of literary modernism.[1] This debate became familiar to the English-speaking world with the publication of the 1977 collection *Aesthetics and Politics*, in which Lukács and Adorno confront each other as the champions of the realist and avantgarde novel respectively. Important as this debate is, it tends to obscure the deep influence that the works of the young Lukács exercised on Adorno – most notably the books *Soul and Form* (1910), *The Theory of the Novel* (1916) and *History and Class Consciousness* (1921). Each of these works represents a constant point of return for Adorno. Lukács's reflections on the essay form in *Soul and Form* are an important source of Adorno's reflections on the relationship between philosophy and style, and serve as a virtual template for his own 'The Essay as Form' (*NL1*: 3–23). As for *History and Class Consciousness*, it is possible to view the whole of Adorno's work, without distortion, as an extended meditation on societal reification – the key critical concept developed in this book – and the possibilities it affords for social transformation. And whilst the two thinkers had profoundly different assessments of the possibilities for change inherent in the present, there was an equally deep agreement on the nature of modern social domination and its all-pervasive and impersonal character.

My concern in this chapter is to show that Lukács's *Theory of the Novel* is an important influence on Adorno's aesthetic thought – most notably regarding the autonomy of the modern work, the conception of aesthetic form and the relationship between the 'truth-content' of the artwork and history. I will suggest, particularly on this last issue, that there is an unacknowledged but crucial affinity between their respective approaches. For both, the authentic work of art illuminates the historical present, however fleetingly. While their respective approaches are generally contrasted on account of Lukács's insistence that the authentic work of art constitutes a 'created totality', this difference can itself be explained through an elaboration of what a theory of the *modern* artwork involves. Stated schematically, Adorno offers a theory of the artwork in 'late' capitalist society whereas Lukács reflects on the fate of the literary work of art in the final phases of 'high' capitalism. For this reason, Lukács's insistence on the 'positivity' of the authentic literary work of art and its status as a 'created totality' is understandable. If theory is itself to be understood as the elaboration of the meaning of the present, then this theory, along with the categories that it employs, comes up for questioning in the face of a changing present. This is essentially what happens in the period after the First World War, the event which signals the end of capitalism in its liberal phase. Lukács's literary aesthetics is subjected to immanent critique in the face of the altered meaning of the present that is captured in works of high modernist literature, in particular, Kafka, Proust, Joyce and Beckett. At the same time, grasping the changed meaning of the present relies on an immanent critique of the historically specific theory of the nineteenth-century novel. The inadequacy of the latter in the face of the former is an important source of an adequate understanding of 'high' modernist works.

Lukács's literary aesthetics, therefore, represent a key source of Adorno's aesthetic theory. For each, the critical potential of the artwork derives from respecting the work's claim to autonomy rather than attempting to dissolve it. Similarly, each views aesthetic form as self-formed and non-dominative in character. Where they differ, on the issue of the necessarily affirmatory character of the work and the totality that it constitutes, this can be accounted for by their respective 'objects'; the late-nineteenth-century novel of 'high' bourgeois society and the 'high' modernist work of 'late' capitalist society. The critical insights into 'high' bourgeois society afforded by late-nineteenth-century novels are totalizing and affirmatory in character, in ways that critical insights into late capitalist society afforded by high modernist works are not. This change can largely be accounted for by understanding the sphere of cultural activity that comprises artistic production as subject to the same distortion and antagonism as the rest of society – what Adorno and Horkheimer referred to as the emergence of the culture industry. It is this transformation that makes it necessary to think of aesthetic form, and the critical insight that it carries, as itself contradictory.

I

The first thing to say about *The Theory of the Novel* is that, despite appearances, it is not in fact a theory at all. At first glance the book appears to insert the novel into a history of literary forms. 'The novel', Lukács writes, 'is the epic of an age in which the extensive totality of life is no longer directly given, in which the extensive totality of life has become a problem, yet which still thinks in terms of totality' (Lukács 1971: 56). Thus whilst the epic is a form pertaining to 'integrated civilisations', the novel pertains to an individualistic society characterized by a sharp separation of facts and values and the radical absence of ultimate purposes or ends in nature. The meaning of life loses its life-immanence. Whereas for the philosophers of Greek antiquity it was a question of working out what the end or specific *ergon* of the human being was, and of coming to understand one's place in a cosmic hierarchy of ends, the chasm opened up in modernity between subject and object – a subjective order of freedom and intention and an objective, causal order of things – ensures that whatever meaning or ultimate purpose is projected onto the world remains just that: a projection without an objective basis in that world. In contrasting the epic world with the modern world of the novel, Lukács reaches back behind Greek philosophy to a time in which there is no gap between appearance and essence; when essence and meaning were visible and had simply to be captured and set down by the epic poet without the mediation of the creative act. The Greek epic required neither the *dénouement* of the tragic plot to reveal the destiny of the hero nor the tortuous turns and reversals of the novel, because essence and destiny were visible. To know Achilles was to know all possible predicates that could be applied to him: that he is too quick to rage, slow to forgive, will die young and so on. For the epic poet all his actions are tinged with what has happened and what is to come as if time itself were not the medium in which his fate unfolded.

The question that immediately arises – aside from the issue of whether such an age ever actually existed – is what such a contrast is meant to establish. Lukács appears to have yoked his literary theory to a dubious philosophical history of literary forms that begins by postulating the essentiality and immediacy of the Homeric world. Moreover, in doing so, he appears to have consigned it to irrelevance for an age that does not share his metaphysical assumptions. As a number of commentators have noted, however, this turns out not to be the case, and it is not insignificant that in the passage quoted above Lukács refers to the epic *aspects* of the novel.[2] Two points in particular appear to forestall a dismissive reading: the first is the undoubted ambivalence with which Lukács views modernity; the second is the status of Lukács's work itself. While it is certainly the case that modernity is marked by a 'transcendental homelessness', in which the subject reveals itself as suspended over an abyss, the plaything of daemonic powers, it is equally the case that we have 'discovered the productivity of spirit' (Lukács 1971: 33). The fact that we are driven to *create* a totality in the absence of an extensive totality being given – a situation all but definitive for what Lukács terms the problematic of the novel – should not be taken in a purely pejorative sense. Lukács follows Kant and Hegel in taking freedom and creativity to be the reverse side of transcendental homelessness. Whilst the modern subject is in danger of losing itself, unlike the epic hero for whom the loss and rediscovery of self is not a possibility, the subject is also free and therefore in a position to create itself and the forms that structure its world. Or in idealist parlance: in the absence of any *given* end or ultimate purpose, such ends must be understood as self-legislated. The novel, for Lukács, is

principally concerned with following the course of such ideals as they
motivate the subject in its encounter with the world.

The second point refers to the status of Lukács's work. If his theory of the
novel rests on a philosophical history of forms then it would have to be
written from the vantage point of the completion of this history. The book
itself, however, ends speculatively with a consideration of the future of the
novel suggested by the late-nineteenth-century Russian novel. Moreover, as
Derwin has pointed out, Lukács's theory appears to enact the same kind of
journey to self-recognition that he attributes to the structure of the novel.
Thus rather than constituting a meta-theoretical reflection on the novel –
one that purports to account for its historical evolution and set out its
principal types – Lukács's critical essay is subject to the same truth criteria as
the novel itself. The goal of the essay is self-recognition just as it is for the
subject of the novel (Derwin 1992: 13–14). Otherwise a historical-material
account of truth would be encased in a neo-Platonist account of the truth of
a work; that is, in terms of its approximation to a pure form.

Nevertheless, Lukács does distinguish between different fundamental
'types' of novelistic form – the idealist novel, the romantic novel of disillusionment and the 'educative novel' – and it is not always clear how this is
to be read. The 'types' appear to delimit different possibilities in novelistic
form that are tied to concrete historical moments. Lukács describes the
problematic of the novel in general – its 'inner form' – as 'the individual's
journeying towards himself, the road from dull captivity within a merely
present reality ... towards clear self-recognition' (Lukács 1971: 80). As this
self-recognition is inescapably social it is routed through the other and,
further, involves an insight into the social-historical world. It is natural to
think of the separate types of novelistic form as particularizations of this
journey. Whereas the pre-modern quest represented a journey towards
essence and, necessarily, an insight into the essential structure of the world,
the self-recognition of the novelistic subject, which is intersubjective, affords
an insight into the sociohistorical world. Lukács is quick to qualify this
truth-content of the work as aesthetic only and fleeting in character:

> After such self-recognition has been attained, the ideal thus formed
> irradiates the individual's life as its immanent meaning; but the conflict
> between what is and what should be has not been abolished and cannot be
> abolished in the sphere wherein these events take place – the life sphere of
> the novel; only a maximum conciliation – the profound and intensive
> irradiation of a man by his life meaning – is attainable. The immanence
> of meaning which the form of the novel requires lies in the hero's finding
> out through experience that a mere glimpse of meaning is the highest that
> life has to offer, and that this glimpse is the only thing worth the
> commitment of an entire life, the only thing by which the struggle will be
> justified. (Lukács 1971: 80)

Lukács's claim here seems to be that self-recognition is possible in the novel although this does not amount to the dissolution of the ethical dichotomy of subject and object; rather it represents a 'maximum conciliation' between ideal and reality and one that is destined to end in failure. This turns out to be the 'biographical form' of the novel and, although Lukács describes this form as the point at which the novel overcomes its 'bad infinity', it is clear that the conciliation is restricted to the aesthetic domain (81). Through the interminable collision of ideal and reality, and the constant readjustment of each that is played out in the biographical form of the novel, a fleeting moment of self-recognition and insight into the social-historical world results.

Lukács's aesthetic resolution of the ethical dichotomy of subject and object bears certain affinities to Adorno's conception of the autonomous work of art. Like Adorno, Lukács sees novelistic form as autonomous. And whilst the formal-aesthetic problematic that constitutes it is underpinned by the ethical problematic of the dichotomy of subject and object, Lukács is careful not to confuse the aesthetic resolution of the 'bad infinity' of the novel with an ethical resolution. For Lukács the novel allows momentary insight into the social-historical world through the subject's journey to self-recognition. It is a world, however, that *remains* dirempted and contradictory. The question that immediately arises concerns the *character* of the social world that confronts the subject and what concrete possibilities for aesthetic resolution it allows. Section II of *The Theory of the Novel* ('Attempt at a typology of the novel form') is, I would suggest, an attempt to answer just this question. If the problematic of the novel in general is the individual's journey towards self-recognition, then the attempt at a typology considers the particular forms this has taken in the history of the novel and their specific problematic. Whereas the 'idealist novel' responds to a situation in which the soul is narrower than the world in which it seeks realization, the romantic novel of disillusionment pertains to the inverse situation. Its problematic is one in which the world and the objective possibilities that it contains are too narrow and restrictive for the soul (Lukács 1971: 97, 112). The hero of the idealist novel – above all represented by Don Quixote – is unable to have its subjectivity confirmed in a world that is richer in possibilities than the hero suspects; the subject of the romantic novel is unable to find fulfilment in a world altogether too constraining. What is clear is that these types and problematics are not abstract determinations of the novel in general but concrete formal-aesthetic problems relating to concrete social worlds. The idealist novel pertains to the emergence from the feudal world, the romantic novel of disillusionment to the high bourgeois society of the nineteenth century. The problematic of the romantic novel and the kinds of solutions it gives rise to relate to a time in which the institutions of bourgeois society, which held out the promise of self-recognition and fulfilment to modern individuals, reveal themselves to be constraining and alienating – in all ways insufficient 'vehicles' for the realization of an authentic life. In short, history is concealed within Lukács's typology of novel forms and, although there is some leeway in the employment of these forms, the modern novel is largely identifiable with the romantic novel of disillusionment.

The romantic novel of disillusionment is the novelistic form of a world in which our highest values have retreated inward, in which the social world no longer presents itself as a place in which these values and ideals can be realized. In contrast to the idealist novel, in which the subject is constantly seeking to prove itself in the world, the romantic novel is premised on the explicit renunciation of the world and the subject's hope of realizing itself in it. Lukács calls this the 'world of convention' or 'second nature' (62–4). The point about the world of convention is not just that we are alienated from it, but that we no longer recognize it as the product of our own sociohistorical work. To adopt Hegelian terminology, we no longer recognize ourselves in the principal social forms of family, civil society, state and religion, even though these are 'our' creations, that is, the spiritual forms in terms of which we recognize one another as kinsman, individual, citizen and brother respectively.

A notable characteristic of the romantic novel, and one that distinguishes it from its idealist forebear in the 'heroic' age of capital, is that social role or vocation is no longer significant for the destiny of the subject. As Lukács states, the world confronting the subject of the romantic novel is one 'entirely dominated by convention'; it is the 'full realisation' of the concept of second nature, a 'quintessence of meaningless laws in which no relation to the soul can be found' (131). The consequence is a lessening of the importance of vocation or profession as far as the inner destiny of the subject of the novel is concerned. The fate or destiny of the subject of the romantic novel is an inner fate because the objective forms of high bourgeois society have ceased to be the bearers of anything essential – they become the mere outward forms that clothe an inward, essential striving.

This gives rise to specific formal-aesthetic problems for the romantic novel. For although the 'retreat inward' appears to hold out the possibility of the creation of an interior life that is complete in itself, the inherent danger of this form is a slide into despairing nihilism. Significantly – particularly in respect of his relation to Adorno – Lukács holds that novelistic form must involve an affirmative moment: 'Any form must contain some positive element in order to acquire substance as form' (119). But the subject of the romantic novel can affirm neither the world of convention nor its interior psychological reality. The outcome of the former would be an accommodation with the thoughtless world that the romantic subject rises against in the first place, while the consequence of affirming interiority would be a 'formless wallowing in vain, self-worshipping lyrical psychologism' (119). Somehow the essentially contemplative subject must stake itself, even though the form of the romantic novel is premised on the inevitable failure of such a staking; it must risk its own self-understanding as though a complete self-understanding were available to it. The romantic novel overcomes this problem, according to Lukács, by showing how the subject's *'being there and being thus* coincides with his inevitable failure' (116). Lukács identifies this as the moment of hope in the romantic novel of disillusionment:

> The positive thing, the affirmation which the very form of the novel expresses no matter how inconsolably sad its content may be, is not only the distant meaning which dawns with a mild radiance on the far side of the search and the failure to find, but also the fullness of life which is revealed precisely through the manifold failures of the struggle and the search. The novel is the form of mature virility: its song of comfort rings out of the dawning recognition that traces of lost meaning are to be found everywhere; that the enemy comes from the same lost home as the knight and defender of the essence; that life had to lose its immanence of meaning so that it might be equally present everywhere. (Lukács 1971: 123)

That meaning is present everywhere testifies to the essentially literary and aesthetic character of the epic insight afforded by the romantic novel. Life as a created totality *becomes* a work of art; its principle of construction is the work of memory:

> Only in the novel ... does memory occur as the creative force affecting the object and transforming it. The genuinely epic quality of such memory is the affirmative experience of the life process. *The duality of interiority and the outside world can be abolished for the subject if he glimpses the organic unity of his whole life through the process by which the living present has grown from the stream of his past life damned up within his memory.* This surmounting of duality – that is to say the successful mastering and integration of the object – makes this experience into an element of the authentically epic form. (127, emphasis added)

The epic insight into life afforded by the romantic novel derives largely from the 'creative force' of memory, which gives form to an otherwise splintered and fragmented world. Memory transforms its objects because affect and signification no longer coincide. In the creative totality of the romantic novel, events seemingly peripheral at the time take on a greater weight and significance, and occurrences that appeared, initially, to be life-transforming, turn out to be banal and of little consequence.

For Lukács, then, the fragmented and broken world provides the 'material' for the self-creation of life in its totality. And whilst the world is *no less* fragmented and broken as a consequence of this self-creation, the specifically romantic problematic of the nineteenth-century novel does at least find a resolution. The search of the subject is an interminable one, but it is not entirely futile because an epic insight into modern life follows from it. This insight is the unanticipated consequence of the search; it would not have resulted had the subject not striven to realize his or her inner meaning in the world, but it was not the thing searched for. The accomplished romantic novel of disillusionment is one in which the meaning of the subject's life, and the inevitable failure bound up with it, spontaneously arises from the encounter with the fragmented world. This is not a meaning that is arbitrarily and wilfully imposed on the social world. (Such novels would ultimately amount to a flight from the present and Lukács cites Scott's historical novels as an example of this [115].) The affirmation generated by the authentic work of art is such *despite* the broken character of the world. Its accomplishment is that it need not falsify the social world – deny its fragmented character – for the sake of resolving its specific formal-aesthetic question. Life may be a literary creation but it is one with an immanent basis in high bourgeois society, the world of convention, which it neither affirms nor denies. What the accomplished romantic novel of disillusionment offers is both self-insight and insight into a sociohistorical world where self-realization is impossible.

It is for this reason that Lukács singles out Flaubert's *Sentimental Education* as exemplary for all novels of this type. As he remarks, in this work no attempt is made to conceal the fragmented and desultory character of the world inhabited by its central character, Frédéric. Moreover, this character is in all ways unremarkable: he is both failed bourgeois and failed bohemian, unable to affirm the conventional world (take up his estate, make a success of his legal profession) and lacking the interior 'lyric power' of some of his bohemian friends to take a stand against it (Lukács 1971: 125).[3] The epic insight into his life and the social-historical world he inhabits occurs almost by accident, as the consequence of the recollection of an abortive visit to a brothel in his adolescence. The fleeting moment of self-recognition follows the ineffectual attempts to realize his essence in the social world, but it is not a consequence of them. It is a momentary insight into the meaning of the present that springs from the involuntary work of memory.

II

Lukács's analysis of novelistic form in general and the nineteenth-century romantic novel of disillusionment in particular is influential for Adorno's aesthetic theory, which is principally concerned with the fate of the autonomous work of art. The aesthetic domain, like every other domain of human activity in modernity, *becomes* autonomous. That is to say it becomes a discrete sphere of activity. As such, it is subject to the social division of labour and participates in the general social illusion: society as nothing more than the sum of its discrete parts and their reflex in consciousness. To the extent that the work of art is complicit in social illusion, whose fundamental principle is the commodity form, its function is ideological and in need of critique. Where Adorno departs from other, contemporary 'left' aestheticians is in his denial that the artwork can *simply* be understood as ideology.[4] For the artwork is not simply autonomous in the sense that the aesthetic domain is discrete and self-regulating; it is also autonomous in a moral sense. Modern works of art claim to be valuable in themselves and not for the sake of anything else; they claim, in other words, an inner worth or dignity akin to that claimed by the moral subject as theorized by Kant. Adorno locates the critical potential of the artwork in this claim, in the work's claim to be *more than* a mere commodity, to having an intrinsic worth. For it is through this excess in the work that the possibilities of a different relation to nature and to society suggest themselves. The consequence of dissolving this claim of the work – the consequence of deleting the experience of the in-itself character of the work, or what Benjamin termed the work's aura – is the eradication of the promise embodied in the work that things could be otherwise. And in a period where society is increasingly integrated, it is the very possibility that things *could* be otherwise that has critical potential (Jarvis 1998: 115–16). The deletion of the illusion of the modern work of art's autonomy by any criticism that identifies art and ideology thus amounts to throwing out the baby with the bathwater. The relentless demystification of the work in recent literary criticism (whether Marxist, feminist, post-colonial or queer-theoretical) inadvertently liquidates what in the artwork testifies to the possibility of relating to nature and others otherwise than we do.

Adorno's concern to 'redeem' the illusion of the modern artwork might appear to open the door to a formalist aesthetics. Yet Adorno does not deny the ideological function of art, the work's complicity with barbarism; rather he sees the participation of history in the work in a different way. Instead of thinking of the work's relation to history primarily in terms of the ideological forces that it sides with, Adorno tracks history's permeation of the *form* of the work itself. Moreover, this sedimentation of history in the work is also its material moment – its 'non-posited' character:

> That by which the truth content is more than what is posited by art-works is their *methexis* (participation) in history and the determinate critique that they exercise through their form. History in artworks is not something made, and history alone frees the work from being merely something posited or manufactured: truth content is not external to history but rather its crystallization in the works. (*AT*: 133)

Thus the authentic work of art is able to effect a critique of existing social reality not through any explicit content that it takes up, but through the configuration of historical materials in its form. For Adorno a 'formal' analysis of the work in and of itself yields a critique of existing society. Here again we are reminded of the impossibility of an absolutely autonomous work, which would amount to an evacuation of any historical content whatsoever. Such a total evacuation is unimaginable, even in the most abstract of works. History is sedimented in the work and what matters is the way in which this historical content is configured. The work offers a critique of history *in and through its form*, not through the 'demystification' and dissolution of autonomous form in criticism. In fact, an unrestricted demystificatory criticism repeats what Adorno calls the dialectic of enlightenment, the process by which modern rationality reverts to myth in its attempt to control nature. By seeking to dissolve the 'residual irrationality' in the artwork – its illusory element – it reveals its will to dominate, to subsume aesthetic experience under classificatory categories. The subsumption of aesthetic experience precludes the experience of the new – the singular, unique, in-itself character of the artwork. In natural-historical terms, the artwork reaches back to a pre-historical relation to nature: the attempt to propitiate nature through its mimetic enactment in magic. There, no attempt is made to subordinate nature through a mythic system or a representative system of concepts – a system that, of necessity, reduces the qualitative to the quantitative. While the subordination of nature to a system of myth and rationality facilitates substitution and exchange respectively, the mimetic enactment of nature in magic – in the cultic fetish – is the representation of a singular, non-repeatable event. If we relate this thought to the discussion of the artwork's illusory autonomy, the promise of the possibility of a non-dominative relation to nature borne by that illusion becomes clear. The work's claim to have an intrinsic worth or dignity is part of its illusion, that is, its fetish character. In this regard, the artwork is akin to the cultic object: both hold open the possibility of a mimesis of nature which does not subordinate it to a representational system of myths or concepts. Here, however, the similarity ends. The mimetic enactment of nature in magic is pre-historical; the autonomous work of art is itself the product of the dialectic of enlightenment. The 'residual irrationality' preserved in artworks, unlike in the cultic object, is a constellated form capable of becoming rational through a broader concept of rationality (reason). Thus whereas the mimetic enactment of nature in the cultic object does not preclude the possibility of the qualitatively new, the 'non-rational' constellated form of the autonomous work of art holds open the possibility of a new *conceptualization* on the basis of the qualitatively new.[5]

The critical potential of the artwork in late capitalist society is different from its critical potential in previous times. Whereas, for example, in high bourgeois society the illusory element in the work was part of its ideological signification and therefore the subject of demystificatory critique, in late capitalist society the illusory, in-itself character of the work comes to be identified with the very possibility that things could be different; that another relation to nature is possible, that individuals could relate to one another otherwise. This is because the illusion of the commodity form becomes ubiquitous to the point of being the *real* of late capitalist society. Artworks criticize or determinately negate this reality through their constellated singular forms. Like cultic objects they embody non-dominating mimetic relations. Unlike cultic objects the mimetic elements in artworks are open to discursive elaboration in criticism. As such they are sources, if not *the* source, of new conceptualizations in late capitalist society.

III

At first glance the terms of these discussions – Lukács on the nineteenth-century novel and Adorno on the artwork in late capitalist society – appear quite different. There are, however, profound affinities between their approaches. Both offer a *defence* of autonomous works of art and both attempt to understand the work's critical potential in terms of this autonomy. That is to say, both explore the entanglement of aesthetic problems with the question of the possibility of social critique. For Lukács the solution to the formal-aesthetic problematic of the nineteenth-century novel does not imply a resolution of the ethical problem of the diremption of subject and object. The aesthetic and the ethical domains are kept separate by him. Lukács does not explore the aporia of the autonomy of the artwork to the extent that Adorno does; but this says more about the object of his enquiry, rather than any oversight on his part.

On the concept of aesthetic and novelistic form there is also significant agreement. For both thinkers, the non-dominative and spontaneous character of aesthetic form indicates the *limits* of the subject's powers of positing. For Lukács the artwork is a 'created totality', but it is not one that can afford to be indifferent to content. This is clearly indicated by the fact that the epic insight of the romantic novel into high bourgeois society is a consequence of the largely *passive* work of a memory giving form to events dispersed over time. Likewise for Adorno the truth-content of the work of art is not something posited or created. The non-posited character of the truth-content of artworks is their material moment: it is the point at which history comes to be sedimented in the artwork and it is the configuration of this sociohistorical content in the work that constitutes its critique of society. Similarly, for Lukács, the work is not something made, or, if it is, it would be better to describe it as something *self*-forming rather than a construct fashioned by the artist. This is illustrated by the exemplarity of *Sentimental Education*, which lies in the absence of any imposed form or meaning extracted from events. Instead 'the separate fragments of reality lie before us in all their hardness, brokenness and isolation' (Lukács 1971: 124). Any contrivance or imposition on the part of the author would result in a lesser work.

However, there are important differences. Adorno thinks the modern work of art both *is* and *is not* autonomous, that it both *is* and *is not* a commodity. Lukács sees the work as a *positivity* free of contradiction; while the social world encountered by the subject may be fragmented and antagonistic for him, this antagonism does not permeate the form of the novel itself. The possibility that the work might be ensnared in the same illusory immediacy as that confronting the subject of the novel – the reified world of convention – is simply not entertained by Lukács. For him, authentic works of literature contain 'epic' insights into the sociohistorical world from which they arise; this is the case even where the social world into which an insight is gained is in bits along with the subject that comprehends it, as is the case with *Sentimental Education*. It is certainly the case that artworks point towards utopia for Adorno, but they do this only negatively, through their constellated form's determinate negation of the present. They do not so much provide a glimpse of a meaningful world, or a positive view of it, as negate the idea that the present world is the only possible world.

This difference can be traced back to Adorno's analysis of the emergence of the culture industry and completely integrated society. This analysis signals, first and foremost, that late capitalist society presents no immanent stand-points from which it can be comprehended and transformed. The view Lukács expressed a few years later in *History and Class Consciousness* was that society *did* present such standpoints. However, his claim that the proletariat was the praxical subject of modernity was premised on the continuing integrity of the cultural sphere – its remaining free from reification – which allowed for its democratization. The cultural sphere was effectively the bourgeois private sphere and the forms and practices (such as novel-writing) that comprised it. It was by increasing participation in *this* sphere that the proletariat were to be able, in Lukács's eyes, to educate themselves and society generally. In an increasingly integrated society, however, the distinc-tion between private and public comes to be increasingly blurred. The 'shocks' and 'jolts' of adaptation that used to be, in high bourgeois society, the preserve of the working day come to extend into the private sphere as well, in so-called 'leisure' and related activities. In this seamless, reified continuity, autonomous works of art remain potential sources of social insight for Adorno, as we have seen. They are not, however, free of the illusion of the commodity form, and the unresolved antagonism of the social world returns in the work as its own formal antagonism (Schultz 1990: 167). That artworks are contradictory in their form is wholly consistent with the intensive and extensive penetration of reification into every sphere of human activity. For this reason, Adorno holds, they cannot represent *positivities* uncontaminated by the commodity form. Somehow they must point towards utopia without ceasing to be antagonistic in their own form.

Lukács's *The Theory of the Novel* and, especially, its analysis of the romantic novel of disillusionment are important sources of Adorno's aesthetic thought. For both thinkers, the work's critical relation to the present lies in its form rather than its ideological signification. The task of criticism is to elaborate this form and render explicit the work's critique of the present. For both, therefore, artworks are key sources of insight into the meaning of the contradictory present. Where they diverge is in Lukács's insistence that the authentic work constitutes a positivity – that it in some sense *affirms* the contradictory present without succumbing to the world of convention or abstractly opposing it in subjective lyric. Adorno, by contrast, maintains that antagonism permeates the form of the work itself, which points to the possibility of a reconciled society through the determinate negation of the present. This divergence of views itself, however, can be understood in terms of the changing meaning of the present addressed by the theories of both Lukács and Adorno. To criticize Lukács for exempting the artwork from the antagonisms and contradictions of society is to criticize him for not anticipating the emergence of the culture industry and the diremption it effects between art and entertainment. Lukács stands at the cusp of 'high' bourgeois and 'late' capitalist society. *The Theory of the Novel* is primarily a book about the nineteenth-century bourgeois novel, one which speculates on its future from the end of a period that Lukács (borrowing a phrase from Fichte) refers to as one of 'absolute sinfulness' (Lukács 1971: 18). Yet, like that of many other artists and thinkers from this period, his work points beyond this present and offers, as Adorno sees, the immanent points of departure for an aesthetic theory adequate to works of art under conditions of late capitalism.

NOTES

1 See, for example, Adorno's excoriating critique of the later Lukács in 'Extorted Reconciliation' (*NL1*: 216–40).
2 Foremost amongst these are Bernstein 1984: 69–75 and Derwin 1992: 7–34. Both show, although in marginally different ways, that Lukács's understanding of 'epic' integrated civilizations is better understood as a projection from the present, indicating a lack in the present, rather than in the context of a philosophy of history or a genealogy of literary forms.
3 See Bernstein's discussion of *Sentimental Education* (Bernstein 1984: 140–6).
4 My presentation here draws on Jarvis 1998, especially 90–147.
5 Robert Kaufman makes this link between aura and conceptual novelty clear in his discussion of the crisis of aura, which he defines as 'the crisis of the availability, in capitalist modernity, of the sort of reflective experience that in its turn makes possible a non-instrumental yet non-arbitrary potentially emancipatory capacity for constructing new conceptual-objective knowledge' (Kaufman 2005: 144).

WORKS CITED

Bernstein, J. M. (1984), *The Philosophy of the Novel: Lukács, Marxism and the Dialectics of Form*. Brighton: Harvester.

Bloch, E., Lukács, G., Brecht, B., Benjamin, W. and Adorno, T. W. (1977), *Aesthetics and Politics*. London: New Left Books.

Derwin, S. (1992), *The Ambivalence of Form: Lukács, Freud, and the Novel*. Baltimore, MD: Johns Hopkins University Press.

Jarvis, S. (1998), *Adorno: A Critical Introduction*. Cambridge: Polity.

Kaufman, R. (2005), 'Aura Still', in A. Benjamin (ed.), *Walter Benjamin and Art*. New York: Continuum, pp. 121–47.

Lukács, G. (1971), *The Theory of the Novel*, trans. A. Bostock. London: Merlin.

Schultz, K. L. (1990), *Mimesis on the Move: Theodor W. Adorno's Concept of Imitation*. Berne: Peter Lang.

11

No Nature, No Nothing: Adorno, Beckett, Disenchantment

Nigel Mapp

I

'Art, considered in its highest vocation, is and remains for us a thing of the past' (Hegel 1975: 11).[1] The end-of-art thesis appears to record, for the thinker who thought it, spirit's happy farewell to the authority of nature. Hegel's historical account of art follows the progressive freeing of humanity's self-understanding from its inadequate material instantiations. Self-determination demands the thorough sloughing off of such meaningless husks. The movement from natural to artefactual beauty, from living matter to dead materials, then through architecture, sculpture and painting to poetry and prose and, finally, out of art altogether, is precisely the story of a slow liberation from the inert sensuous medium. '[T]he work of art ... regarded as an external object, is dead' – art, we now see, was always surpassed as art, the material's appearance of living meaning due solely to the infusion or 'baptism' of spirit (Hegel 1975: 29). And yet art for Hegel *was* art, once; truth's source, not its vessel. Even as an external replication of spirit, as 'explicit' self-recognition in an object, art '[brings] what is in [man] into sight and knowledge' (32). Perhaps the goodbye is not so cheerful after all: the 'genuine truth and life' art once enjoyed is lost to us (29). Does our freedom depend on a harvesting of art, the taking in of a meaning not all our own work? A dead nature may be a murdered nature, a killing that does not enliven us. 'There's no more nature', Clov reports in Beckett's *Endgame* (1964: 16). Was nature once alive? Has spirit rightly understood its dependencies?

Art as *mere* art is born in the end Hegel diagnoses. Bricked up in the category of the aesthetic, it is denied any cognitive import and any value or normative relevance beyond that of its art-status (Bernstein 1992). Adorno thinks that aesthetic experience rebels against its incarceration; but that its prison is also a fragile refuge from the irrational rationality that menaces it. The refuge is illusion, for aesthetic autonomy is socially determined and no artwork is exempt from subsumption, exchange, commodification. Should we not then accept that art is now, as Heidegger says, a matter for 'pastry chefs' (Heidegger 2000: 140) – that aesthetics is not an autonomous category at all, its judgements highfalutin talk for what art's consumers like or dislike? Indeed, for Heidegger, aesthetics itself is to blame (Heidegger 2002: 9ff.). Its categories are those of sensory apprehension or experience, and 'experience is the element in which art dies' (50). Adorno's articulation of the problematic emphasizes experience – because it is something we do not generally have – and sensuousness, which lies under a ban. For him, the illusion of autonomy, precisely as *real* illusion, an illusion telling us something about the reality from which art is compulsorily excused, is art's chance, however perilous. It is the source of its claim against totalizing reason. Hegel's thesis, then, states a truth about society. The burial of nature is effected at the cost of a new enslavement to the identitarian concept, the exchange-principle, and society's second nature. And for Adorno, autonomy is not to be deleted in the rush to lay bare art's historical significance.

The dialectic of disenchantment is at work. Kant formulates its terms; and legislates them for eternity. Disenchanted nature, passive, mathematized and meaningless, is sundered from a disembodied, utterly empty, subject, the pure source of all knowing and valuing. To subtract all meaning from material is to subtract all substance from the subject. Freedom has no opening in the web of causality, and values float free of reality's supports (Bernstein 2003: viii–xi; 1992: 1–16). For Adorno, Hegel's uncovering of the conceptuality of Kant's 'blind' intuitions, a discovery that releases thought into the absolute, does not so much reincarnate the subject and the meaningfulness of the world as dominate the world once again – which, in turn, implies thought's capitulation to domination. Hegel saturates existence with Kant's impeccably non-dogmatic, contentless subject, which is possible only because all content is *external* to it (*ND*: 386ff.; Jarvis 2004: 73–5). As Hamm, who is both blind and empty, the disastrous identification of concept and intuition, puts it in *Endgame*: 'the bigger a man is the fuller he is. . . . And the emptier' (Beckett 1964: 12). Kant's 'block' on the absolute at least 'forestalled a mythology of the concept' (*ND*: 389). For Adorno, the regressive mythology we live under in a total exchange society is the epitome of subjective identifying rationality.

Aesthetics, because it tries to think of materials as potentially meaningful and of meaning as necessarily embodied, is an attempt to respond to this crisis. Kant's analysis of the aesthetic judgement already enciphered the difficulty of eliminating art's cognitive claim, of detaching it from the understanding and appetites (Kant 2000). A subjective feeling leads us to judge *as if* beauty were a property of the object, Kant maintains, thus modelling aesthetic judgement's distinctive character on the very machinery that has expelled it – here 'merely' subjective feeling and the objective understanding (Kant 2000: 97ff.).[2] But the fact that aesthetic judgement holds together these sundered realms, while being unable to legitimate the connection conceptually, points to the damage done to both subject and object in the tearing apart that established the claims of the subject. Perhaps feeling is cognitive, not a heteronomous datum; perhaps cognition is somatic, always a body's expression (Jarvis 2002). Perhaps, then, art's real, illusory autonomy has its truth. Art can oppose, for Adorno, the illusion of thought's self-sufficiency, criticize absolute self-determination, precisely by disturbing enlightenment rationality's monopoly of truth-telling.

Art holds open a space for the particular that the concept only categorizes – a space for non-identical sensory meaningfulness. 'The work of art', says Hegel, 'is not merely for *sensuous* apprehension ... it is essentially at the same time for *spiritual* apprehension ... it can in no way be a natural product or have in its natural aspect a natural vitality [*seiner Naturseite nach Naturlebendigkeit haben*]' (Hegel 1975: 35; 1970: 57). Here the elimination of sensuous particularity's meaning-claim is doubly insisted upon – the life in art's dead media cannot be nature's. This may speak the truth of things for us, especially when it seems that spirit, thus emptied of nature, insists on being both life *and* nature. But the tie to nature is tacitly conceded; more, and aporetically, artworks may *in their natural aspects* have some sort of vitality – a point simultaneously condemned as illusory.

The more that artworks resist discursive filleting while still calling out for interpretation and response, the more likely the claim of particularity, the limits of identity thinking, will be perceived. Enigmatic artworks demand an interpretation that we cannot fully muster. They are not (quite) dead objects, awaiting animation by the sheer idealities that may be brought to them – interpretation as imaginative add-on (see Bernstein's analysis of Lessing [Bernstein 2003: xiii]).[3] Rather, they rebuff attempts to assimilate them because they point towards a meaning we cannot grasp. Such artworks' significance is not separable and portable; they demand to be seen, heard, felt in the flesh. Thus artworks intensify the illusory, fetishizing autonomy under which they suffer. They configure their materials into a free-standing, unique, but non-conceptual whole, an illusion that figures the possibility of what rationality thwarts: reconciliation with the non-identical particular. 'Art's semblance disenchants the disenchanted world' (*AT*: 58; cf. 227).

Adorno writes in *Aesthetic Theory*:

> That works renounce communication is a necessary yet by no means sufficient condition of their unideological essence. The central criterion is the force of expression, through the tension of which artworks become *eloquent with wordless gesture*. In expression they reveal themselves as the wounds of society; expression is the social ferment of their autonomous form. (*AT*: 237, my emphasis)

Art's claim on knowing cannot be claimed by knowing – that would delete it. Yet if art fails to achieve a semblance of communication, it drops back into the world of mere things. The only space for art's truth to manifest itself is in a speech without speech, wordless eloquence. A sort of mime-language becomes the model for an expression that, were it uttered directly, would immediately be confiscated (cf. Critchley 1997: 152). Such speaking silence expresses what society has done to art, what society has done to itself – *its* 'wounds'. Such expression emerges through the tension and agitation indexed by art's illusory, but socially real, autonomy.

What sort of expression is meant here? Adorno is thinking of how the process of disenchantment has extended into language, which has been progressively carved up into signifying and mimetic elements. Horkheimer and Adorno characterize the enlightenment imperative of dismemberment thus:

> As sign, language must resign itself to being calculation and, to know nature, must renounce the claim to resemble it. As image it must resign itself to being a likeness and, to be entirely nature, must renounce the claim to know it. (*DE*: 13)

Progressive rendering-into-discourse of all meanings incapacitates thinking. But language's claim to be like its objects is not to be made good through a positive, mythic mimesis. Nor is mimesis something to be unearthed by first digging out signification and conceptuality. The mimetic is associated with the signifying, but the association is negative. Adorno seeks to decipher mimesis in its negation of schematizing discursivity (*ND*: 270; Jarvis 1998: 177–9). Adorno insists that such knowing is entwined with mimesis, and that *any* knowing depends on this inter-involvement: 'The separation of sign and image is inescapable. But if ... it is hypostatized over again, then each of the isolated principles tends toward the destruction of truth' (*DE*: 13).

Speechless expression, significant silence, is this negative mimesis: it is the sense of what discursive rationality has missed, *that* it has missed something. Language, then, is a model – because its enlightened bipartition is not yet complete, that is, has not destroyed it altogether – of the reconciliation of thought with its other, because the claims of each are necessarily woven into it (Jarvis 1998: 32–3). How, then, to 'speak according to the model of a nonconceptual, nonrigidified significative language' (*AT*: 67)? Adorno argues in 'The Essay as Form' that the essay's arrangement of language and concepts says more than the sum total of its word-meanings, propositions and deductions (*NL1*: 3–23). And art's 'affinity' to language, its 'language character', is, similarly, its appearance of meaningful ordering beyond, but through, its communicative function (*AT*: 112; 120). It is a configurative meaningfulness that demands attention because its resistance to communication appears in a form somehow *like* communication.

II

In a reading of Ibsen's *The Wild Duck*, Adorno illustrates how the good life cannot be sought through pure interiority – the reason of Kant's categorical imperative – any more than through a Hegelian responsiveness to consequences and specific realities (*MP*: 158–66).[4] The first leads to injustice (as evidenced in the actions of Gregers Werle); the latter to the cynical endorsement of existence. In fact, Adorno sees in Werle a 'concrete figure' of 'the ideal of abstract reason', a character who anticipates the existentialist imperative: 'human beings should be identical with themselves' (161). The logic of such disenchantment finally seeks identity for its own sake, and all other values evaporate. Adorno does not, in this context, explore the problem of using a play to illustrate philosophical issues, as he acknowledges (158). His 1961 reading of Beckett, 'Trying to Understand *Endgame*', addresses little else, directly or indirectly, in a reading which appears to trace how *the work itself* becomes a concrete figure of the abstract, reified subject (*NL1*: 241–75).

Adorno recommends the apparently 'inhuman' quality of Beckett's methods as an antidote for those 'whose humanness has already become an advertisement for the inhuman' (249). He has in mind, against those who demand a little hope from their art (cf. *ND*: 367–8), a sharpening of the antinomy expounded through *The Wild Duck*. Beckett's *Endgame* pushes art's claim to autonomous self-authorization and self-determination to its limits, in order to show the limits. This is achieved, Adorno thinks, through a careful construction of unintelligibility; one it is imperative to interpret (*NL1*: 242–3). He in no way, then, wishes to co-opt the play as a 'clattering machinery for the demonstration of world views' – the didactic abuse, he argues, that is the stamp of existentialist plays (*NL1*: 242). Such works take meaninglessness as their positive, meaningful doctrine, assert the necessity of becoming self-identical, and illustrate the lesson through dramaturgical forms that simply contradict it. The meaninglessness of social reality and the illusion of pure self-positing can be undermined only through a consequential process of formal construction. *Endgame* aims at the illusion of self-positing in order to breach the context of self-immanence. There can, then, be no return to natural mimesis. That would be stupefying myth. Adorno's attempt to criticize identity thinking, to mark out a space for the particular outside universal domination, is remorselessly negative. If the predicament *is* the reign of meaninglessness and the unintelligibility of social reality, expressing it, enciphering hopes for its overcoming in a way that can be experienced, requires of *Endgame* an intense formal labour. Art's illusory autonomy is to be mobilized, despite the dangers, and *Endgame* is for Adorno a configuration of a 'mode of subjectivity' that expresses its predicament (Rose 1978: 124). This mode of aesthetic subjectivity can provide, paradoxically, the semblance of the non-identical particular, what subjectivity has suppressed.

Of course, *Endgame* internalizes the antinomies of disenchantment in more obvious ways. Adorno strongly emphasizes the play's presentation of the contradictory consequences of an enlightenment unfixed from human ends (*NL1*: 271ff.; 226). He quotes the episode in which Hamm demands to be positioned, 'More or less', 'Roughly', 'Bang in the centre' – the lord of creation whose margin of movement is nil (Beckett 1964: 24; cf. *NL1*: 271). No need for telescopes and tape measures, says Hamm; they must be fetched anyway (Beckett 1964: 24). Adorno's reading, then, explores *Endgame*'s expression of the 'final history of the subject' (*NL1*: 271), claiming that Hamm represents the hubristic 'enthronement of human meaning' as creator, the ultimate, blind and crippled, product of the domination of nature. He is the man who must exterminate boys as if they were fleas or rats.[5] Hamm's duty to humanity – to stop the disaster, humanity, starting all over again – is to stamp it out (Beckett 1964: 27, 50). Adorno glosses: 'Subjectivity itself is at fault; the fact that one exists at all' (*NL1*: 271–2). Existentialism, the celebration of pure subjectivity, is exploded. The hubris is to live in the first place. Culpable self-positing is what Hamm's existence is.

Beckett's terrifying simplicity, Adorno argues, is the prosecution of disenchantment to the limit, 'an avowed process of subtraction' that reduces the subject to a quality-less 'whatchamacallit', 'the absurdity into which mere existence is transformed when it is absorbed into naked self-identity' (*NL1*: 246). Pure concreteness and pure self-positing are identical: the absolute subject as 'mollusc' (246–7; cf. 251). The speculative history of Horkheimer and Adorno's *Dialectic of Enlightenment* is extrapolated to its ongoing end in Beckett's play, after two world wars, after domination has become total, after Auschwitz (266–7). The calamity of *Endgame* is this 'infinite catastrophe' of history, not, Adorno claims, an ontological insight (273). Indeed, everything is 'corpsed', Clov reports; nature is dead to human purposes, humanity is clearly done for, and the world 'stinks of corpses' (Beckett 1964: 25, 33). Adorno, who quotes the passage, uses a translation that offers *kaputt* for 'corpsed' (*NL1*: 244–5). It seems indifferent whether the world is seen as broken machinery or dead nature. All is dead artefact. The projection of enlightened reason over nature – its mathematization – leaves it dead. 'Corpsed', however, does suggest at least the illusion that something was once alive, even if nature's purpose was only ever the thwarting of human beings, as it now appears: there are no more navigators, so at last the sea is calm (Beckett 1964: 44). Even bad theodicy has become a joke, the placid waters a derisive image of reconciliation.

The disenchantment theme immediately stimulates such thoughts about specific aspects of *Endgame*. Here there does seem to be an absolute gap between meaning and existence, just because the gap has collapsed. It appears, as Adorno suggests, that anything can be a symbol for anything else, so nothing means anything at all (*NL1*: 261). We can immediately see how this impacts on specific features and the techniques of the play. A quick list: the many game-playing and meta-dramatic references; the way speech sounds like orders given to or by an alien body ('raise hat', 'wipe' [Beckett 1964: 52]); or, perhaps conversely, the blank identification of word and action ('I'm back again, with the biscuit' [16; see also 24]). The characters are both dominator and dominated. In Kafka, as Adorno notes elsewhere, communication is blocked through the discrepancies of gesture and speech (*P*: 248–9). In Beckett, their identification, the interpenetration of move-ment and word, achieves blank unintelligibility. Speech is equivalent to the mechanical movements of matter under the rule of abstract forces. Even Clov's clumsiness or forgetfulness is quickly recouped by 'intelligence' (Beckett 1964: 47). If word and gesture utterly diverge, it is the same thing. At the play's pseudo-catastrophe when Clov announces there are no more painkillers – 'HAMM: [*appalled.*] Good . . . !' (46) – the scission may only reinforce the indifference of life and death. The clichés of obligation near the end of the play seem to exchange them *as* clichés, blank materials:

HAMM: I'm obliged to you, Clov. For your services.
CLOV: [*Turning, sharply*] Ah pardon, it's I am obliged to you.
HAMM: It's we are obliged to each other. (Beckett 1964: 51)

Especially in the context of Hamm's order to 'articulate!' (50), the omission of 'who' in these lines, after Clov's response has revealed the meaninglessness of the exchange, gives a strong sense of performing or reading a script, repeating some routine, as well as confusing us as to who is trying to say, or should be saying, what. The clichés appear to express the standstill of the master–slave dialectic (see *NL1*: 269), but the use–mention undecidability renders the lines incomprehensible. The larger, obvious question of whether the whole play is to be endlessly repeated, whether the end is just another beginning, is radicalized when the local meanings are so resistant to reading.

These are my examples. Adorno's reading builds beyond such reflections, and keeps in view the historical problematic he uncovers in the work by relating it to many examples of his own. He emphasizes from the outset that the absence of metaphysical meaning necessitates that the meaninglessness penetrate to the overall meaning of the play and, especially, into its words and sentences (*NL1*: 240–3). The logic of disenchantment saturates all elements, expressing a near-totally reified consciousness in all its contradictoriness. The language of the play is regressive. As Adorno puts it: thoughts, clichés, culture, philosophy, all become 'second order' material (243). Beckett's work reduces everything to 'bare existence', limiting itself to 'exploded facticity' (243–4) or 'forlorn particulars' (254). The stripping-down to absurdity of theme and character operates, then, through a cognate disenchantment of language. Yet the play is clearly not *just* a meaningless residuum or datum, one which we might enliven by attaching meanings, and be told off for when we do – as might seem to be the case with Adorno's addition of 'let' to 'Hamm' (*NL1*: 267; see Cunningham 2002). It is what the reified language of the play, its meaninglessness, calls out for that is important: an inter-pretation, a faithful unfaithfulness.

III

For Adorno, it seems, *Endgame* convicts reified subjective illusion by strengthening, rather than denying, its own complicity with it. Any attempt to ditch illusion backfires, as is evidenced for Adorno by Brecht's plays, which are false in a way that complements the failure of existentialism's would-be self-identities. (The argument is developed in the essay 'Commitment' [*NL2*: 76–94].) In Brecht, Adorno claims, the power of the subject, which is to be conquered in the dismantling of dramatic character and theatrical aura, returns in the character of the art form, which casts a pantomimic spell. Art strips away its aesthetic-only status on pain of enlisting with the illusion it protests against, and art must take this antinomy as its constitutive problem (*NL1*: 250).

Endgame, for example, cannot name the hope it expresses, for that is not in its power and, more damagingly, it would foreclose the specific experience of alterity it effects – wherein the hope lies. Even the difference between reconciliation and total domination is effaced: Adorno notes that Clov's wish for death, for silence and stasis (a wish for the deadened sea) is expressed in terms reminiscent of a reconciliation with otherness: 'each thing in its last place' (*NL1*: 274; Beckett 1964: 39). To make us see this *absurdity* is part of *Endgame*'s effect. These illusions of social reality can be adumbrated only by art's 'self-positing of semblance' (*AT*: 281). Art, then, is to double the stakes of its predicament. *Endgame* is explored by Adorno in precisely this way:

> although the prison of individuation is seen to be both prison and illusion – the stage set is the *imago* of this kind of insight – art cannot break the spell of a detached subjectivity; it can only give concrete form to solipsism. Here Beckett runs up against the antinomy of contemporary art. ... [U]nlike discursive knowledge of reality ... in art only what has been rendered subjective, what is commensurable with subjectivity, is valid. Art can conceive reconciliation, which is its idea, only as the reconciliation of what has been estranged. Were it to simulate the state of reconciliation by joining the world of mere objects, it would negate itself. (*NL1*: 250)

This then is why *Endgame*'s subtractive, disenchanting processes are successful, while Brecht's misfire. They express the antinomies of subjectivity in its form rather than helping themselves to an authentic voice. Art must refuse cognitive accounting, because of what has become of cognition. It presses its claim by remaining enigmatic: a negative experience of the estranged *as* estranged. This is also why the social curse can be 'spoken only in silence' (*NL1*: 249). Art achieves this speechless speech by taking all within itself, concretely constructing the illusory, solipsistic subject. Society's unintelligibility will therefore be experienced in the artwork's unintelligibility (see *NL1*: 244). But the meaninglessness, the silence, will still have the complexion of meaning; the estranged calls out for reconciliation.

What are *Endgame*'s concrete constructions? A key characteristic for Adorno is the play's relation to the dramatic tradition. *Endgame*'s precise, stringent engagement with, and negation of, this artistic tradition itself operates as if the tradition were truly autonomous (see *NL1*: 259ff.; Bernstein 1990: 179). The parodic work on past forms is crucial to Adorno, because this is what explains *Endgame*'s transcendence of 'facticity' (*NL1*: 244). The thoroughgoing inversions, the parodies of dramatic categories – Adorno slipped one of his own into the comments on Hamm's hubris, as discussed above, and another is implied in his comments on the 'catastrophe' of history (273) – give the play a determinacy that is somehow like a meaning, like the metaphysical meaning the tradition wished to express (see Zuidervaart 1993: 155). The blow-by-blow emptying of tradition's animating social experience is what constructs the meaninglessness of *Endgame* – in the image of defunct meaning. Taking these forms as its materials, the play fashions a meaninglessness that points towards meaning.

Adorno's writing offers a peculiar figuration in describing how these traditional elements, employed despite, or in order to demonstrate, their impossibility (*NL1*: 259), are given a kind of second life:

> The dramatic constituents put in a posthumous appearance. Exposition, complication, plot, peripeteia and catastrophe return in decomposed form [*als Dekomponierte*] as participants in an examination of the dramaturgical corpse. (*NL1*: 260; *GS* 11: 303)

The tradition moves from meta-theatrical import, the aesthetic tradition, to everyday personhood and, or *as*, facticity: it is now both pathologist and body. The fetishizing de-composition of artistic tradition has revealed, then, the reification of the subject.

The traditional meanings and materials resist their liquidation insofar as the meaninglessness that befalls them is structured by their demise. Their historical mortality links the play's meaninglessness with that of the social. The derangement in the play's form marks, however, the possibility of another kind of meaningful ordering, one distinct from conceptual identification (Bernstein 1990: 180). Art fashions a unique knot of 'positive nothingness', something where our not knowing what it is seems to be our problem, as well as its own (*AT*: 114). Beckett does not present us with the live nature of which we have, somewhere, lost all sense. It shadows forth, in its intensive labour on its materials, in its 'organized meaninglessness' (*NL1*: 242), a unique particularity that *should not be* nothing to us.

IV

The word *kaputt*, Adorno says, is 'snatched back from the marketplace' (*NL1*: 244). The implication is that in its transposition into art, the word speaks the truth of the marketplace, its social meaninglessness. We are entitled to ask whether this is an arbitrary conceptual translation or addition. Early in the essay, Adorno remarks that the 'cultural trash' (241), the reified language which *Endgame* gathers and configures, begins to 'fluoresce' [*fluoreszieren*] (*NL1*: 242; *GS* 11: 281). Perhaps this is what he means: in the aesthetic refuge of the play, cultural and linguistic materials reveal their deadness through a sort of surplus, an after-life of significance. Adorno sees how *Endgame* places a 'taboo' on language, but he thinks this is not sought through an attempted perfection of mimesis, a reduction to sheer sound – which would be impossible; rather, the work organizes language as 'an instrument of its own absurdity, following the ritual of the clown, whose babbling becomes nonsense by being presented as sense' (*NL1*: 262). The point once more emphasizes *Endgame*'s evacuation and inversion of theatrical tradition. The negation is determinate: configurations emerge in which the discursive aspects of meaning are forced to confess their absurdity. Indeed, for Adorno, the gamut of identitarian rational procedures is deployed by the play, demonstrating that absurdity, conflict with human ends, is the upshot of reason, not its opposite (*NL1*: 265).

Endgame takes discursive materials – whether clichés or the language of advertising – and, rather than being able to extirpate the semantic dimension, organizes them so that '[w]hat normally hides behind a communicative façade is sentenced to appear' (*NL1*: 254). The result, for Adorno, is a mimesis of the total society, one which promotes a critical experience of what is stated in the familiar verbal detritus: social meaninglessness. The play becomes 'the negative imprint of the administered world' (*AT*: 31). Adorno, more specifically, speaks of a 'physiognomy of what is no longer human' – the analysis and figuration of that which is presented as human, but is not (*NL1*: 254). From this physiognomy, which is a relational, contoured pattern formed in and between the materials absorbed into the play, a fragile, normative link to the human is, however, preserved. 'Physiognomy' recalls a leitmotif of Adorno's comments on Beckett: 'the only face left is the one whose tears have dried up' (*NL1*: 290); elsewhere he invokes 'human beings' who 'look mutely out from [Beckett's] sentences' (*NL2*: 90; see also 252). The rigorous construction of solipsistic consciousness allows a pattern to emerge from its concrete meaninglessness, a trace of what cannot be produced conceptually. Adorno claims that Hamm with his handkerchief over his face at the play's opening is a sign, wrested from the quotidian and familial, of the face's loss of identity: for he is possibly dead, a mere body (*NL1*: 254–5). This 'sign' reveals an important dimension of Adorno's approach to Beckett. The language and characters are for him a mask (cf. 251) precisely when they identify what they are masking. In *Minima Moralia* he speaks of film corpses as 'allegories of what they already are' (*MM*: 233). A moment of non-identity inheres in the claim to close it off: Beckett's 'sign' holds a place open for a life we cannot yet think. The play itself, Adorno says, is an 'allegory whose intention has fizzled out' (*NL1*: 269). He is thinking of the play's end, and the question of Clov's departure. The thought suggests that an incomprehensible space between sign and meaning has been opened *in* its fizzling out: 'Aesthetic transcendence and disenchantment converge in the moment of falling mute: in Beckett's oeuvre. A language remote from all meaning is not a speaking language and this is its affinity to muteness' (*AT*: 79). The misidentification of persons and things is indicated through its consequential unfolding. Beckett's meaninglessness transfixes attention through the semblance of what has been muted: our humanity, a meaningfulness outside.

NOTES

1   The writings of J. M. Bernstein and Simon Jarvis have been a crucial resource for this essay. My first paragraph owes much to Bernstein's 'Freedom from Nature? Post-Hegelian Reflections on the End(s) of Art' (forthcoming), which the author kindly forwarded to me.

2   See Bernstein 1992: 17–65; 1990: 178.

3   The disenchanting idea that artworks need their beholder's imagination to animate their otherwise dead materials can be illustrated through Freud's 1914 account of Michelangelo's 'Moses' (Freud 1990). Freud reads from this figure the events that lie behind Moses' current situation – his discovery of the Golden Calf, his wrath, his near-dropping of the tablets of law. If Freud is right, and although he thinks the necessity of such intense speculation may be a flaw in the work (280), the sculpture encourages us to think that what we make of it is just what we have put into it. To make it art, interpretative imagination must set to work. Showing Moses at the peak of his anger, shutting off the enlivening projection of meaning, would, however, somehow lose this point about both art and idols – that their power is not theirs, but ours – by killing the sculpture completely.

4   See *NL1*: 261; *AT*: 346; *MM*: 152, 179.

5   In the German edition of the play that Adorno refers to, Hamm orders Clov to 'wipe out' the boy Clov claims to see (cited *NL1*: 272); in the English version, Hamm holds back, for unclear reasons (Beckett 1964: 49–50).

WORKS CITED

Beckett, S. (1964), *Endgame: A Play in One Act followed by Act Without Words: A Mime for One Player*. London and Boston: Faber and Faber.

Bernstein, J. M. (1990), 'Philosophy's Refuge: Adorno in Beckett', in D. Wood (ed.), *Philosophers' Poets*. London: Routledge, pp. 177–91.

— (1992), *The Fate of Art: Aesthetic Alienation from Kant to Derrida and Adorno*. Cambridge: Polity.

— (2003), 'Introduction', in *Classic and Romantic German Aesthetics*, ed. J. M. Bernstein. Cambridge: Cambridge University Press, pp. vii–xxxiii.

Critchley, S. (1997), *Very Little ... Almost Nothing: Death, Philosophy, Literature*. London and New York: Routledge.

Cunningham, D. (2002), 'Trying (Not) to Understand: Adorno and the Work of Beckett', in R. Lane (ed.), *Beckett and Philosophy*. Basingstoke and New York: Palgrave, pp. 125–39.

Freud, S. (1990), 'The Moses of Michelangelo', trans. J. Strachey, in *Art and Literature: Jensen's 'Gradiva', Leonardo da Vinci and Other Works*, ed. A. Dickson. London: Penguin, pp. 251–82.

Hegel, G. W. F. (1970), *Vorlesungen über die Ästhetik I*, ed. E. Moldenhauer and K. M. Michel. Frankfurt: Suhrkamp.

— (1975), *Aesthetics: Lectures on Fine Art*, trans. T. M. Knox, vol. 1. Oxford: Clarendon.

Heidegger, M. (2000), *Introduction to Metaphysics*, trans. G. Fried and R. Polt. New Haven, CT: Yale University Press.

— (2002) 'The Origin of the Work of Art', trans. J. Young, in *Off the Beaten Track*, ed. J. Young and K. Haynes. Cambridge: Cambridge University Press, pp. 1–56.

Jarvis, S. (1998), *Adorno: A Critical Introduction*. Cambridge: Polity.

— (2002), 'An undeleter for criticism', *diacritics* 32(1), 3–18.

— (2004), 'What is speculative thinking?', *Revue internationale de philosophie*, 63(227), 69–83.

Kant, I. (2000), *Critique of the Power of Judgment*, trans. P. Guyer and E. Matthews. Cambridge: Cambridge University Press.

Rose, G. (1978), *The Melancholy Science: An Introduction to the Thought of Theodor W. Adorno*. London and Basingstoke: Macmillan.

Zuidervaart, L. (1993), *Adorno's Aesthetic Theory: The Redemption of Illusion*. Cambridge, MA: MIT Press.

12

Late Style in Naipaul: Adorno's Aesthetics and the Post-Colonial Novel

Timothy Bewes

> Artworks are archaic in the age in which they are falling silent. But when they no longer speak, their muteness itself speaks.
>
> Theodor Adorno (*AT*: 286)

> What has made it impossible for us to live in time like fish in water, like birds in air, like children? It is the fault of Empire! Empire has created the time of history. Empire has located its existence not in the smooth recurrent spinning time of the cycle of the seasons but in the jagged time of rise and fall, of beginning and end, of catastrophe. Empire dooms itself to live in history and plot against history. One thought alone preoccupies the submerged mind of Empire: how not to end, how not to die, how to prolong its era. By day it pursues its enemies. It is cunning and ruthless, it sends its bloodhounds everywhere. By night it feeds on images of disaster: the sack of cities, the rape of populations, pyramids of bones, acres of desolation.
>
> J. M. Coetzee (2000: 146)

What could it mean to understand the historical moment as one in which failure becomes precisely the 'measure of success' of an artistic work? Adorno's theory of 'late style' offers one optic through which to appraise the contemporary poetics of disconnection, inorganicity and alienation; yet Adorno's idea seems encumbered by certain problematical cultural assumptions, the most obvious being a motif of historical 'exhaustion' attending existing artistic forms – a sense of decrepitude which does nothing to disrupt the Eurocentric logic of historical pre-eminence at its origin. Can the theorization of artistic failure contained in Adorno's work on lateness be salvaged from the imperialist relation to chronology and temporality that it seems to presuppose? 'Lateness', the epigonal superstition as Nietzsche called it, implies a literary development narrative, much like the one that emerges out of Conrad's *Heart of Darkness*: the European novel, moribund, sepulchral, is counterposed to the vibrancy of 'new literatures', the most prominent means by which the literary academy persistently revivifies itself.

Yet Adorno's framing of his theory of late style, particularly the ambiguities and reversals with which he approaches its chronological aspects, also has resonances with more recent currents in aesthetics, such as Gilles Deleuze's similarly ambiguous historical framing of the development of modern cinema as an irruption of formal incommensurability into the filmic text. Both narratives, I shall argue, have as much significance for recent developments in literature as they do for the specific artistic forms they describe; both, furthermore, are elaborated in ways that complicate any attempt to read them in purely developmentalist, Eurocentric terms.

Adorno's theory of 'late style' was developed not in relation to literature, but to musical composition; indeed, apart from a short essay on the final scene of Goethe's *Faust* (*NL1*: 111–20), almost all his references to 'late style' refer to Beethoven's so-called 'Third Period' between 1816 and 1827. During these last years, Beethoven produced works characterized by a lack of formal consistency so glaring that the only unifying principle available for their interpretation seems to be the fact of their origination with the composer himself. As a consequence, writes Adorno in the essay 'Late style in Beethoven', the work has been received more as a biographical 'document' than as a work of art. Late works are typically 'furrowed, even ravaged'; they resist 'mere delectation' and lack 'the harmony that the classicist aesthetic is in the habit of demanding from works of art'. In the most usual understanding of this phenomenon, the subjectivity or 'personality' of the artist haunted by death finally 'breaks through the envelope of form to better express itself, transforming harmony into the dissonance of its suffering, and disdaining sensual charms with the sovereign self-assurance of the spirit liberated' (*EM*: 564). Such is the explanation for the difficulty and 'bitterness' of late works offered by biographical criticism, the tendency that, according to Adorno, enjoys an almost total monopoly on the commentary on Beethoven's late works.

Adorno's emphasis is completely away from such 'biographical' or 'psychological' interpretations – approaches which are only possible by ignoring the actuality of the works under discussion: the proliferation of conventions *qua* conventions, the relative absence of 'expressive' elements, and the apparently perpetual withholding of signification. What distinguishes late from middle period Beethoven is principally that the composer's attempt at a subjective and artistic 'transformation' of the traditional formal and thematic elements 'according to his intention' is abandoned. Rather, conventions appear 'in a form that is bald, undisguised, untransformed' achieving expression, finally, as 'the naked representation of themselves' (*EM*: 565, 566). The psychological critical approach, conceiving of the work as a vehicle for subjective expression, misses entirely the fact that death is not an actuality that may be read through the work of art, no matter how brittle the work in question may seem. The idea of death that is present in late works is not the impending expiration of the individual writing, but the altogether other death that Blanchot writes about as always present: 'the limit of your self-possession' (1982: 91). Death is an emblem of that which cannot appear in the work at all except in a highly 'refracted' mode. The force of late works derives from the thought of death, certainly, but purely negatively, as the confrontation of art with its own impossibility. The psychologistic interpretation reduces impossibility to merely biographical or egoistic significance, and death to the positive image of death we foster in life. The 'thought of death' that is present in late works tells us nothing whatever about death; it speaks eloquently, instead, of the necessary failure of art itself. To read late works as 'documents' through which the subjectivity of the artist is finally visible violates the principle insisted upon by Adorno, that 'the content of art always consists in mere appearance' (*EM*: 566).[1] The 'necessity' of art's failure apparent in late works, therefore, amounts to the removal of art from the binary logic of aesthetic success and failure, communication and its breakdown, altogether:

> The power of subjectivity in the late works of art is the irascible gesture with which it takes leave of the works themselves. It breaks their bonds, not in order to express itself, but in order, expressionless, to cast off the appearance of art. Of the works themselves it leaves only fragments behind, and communicates itself, like a cipher, only through the blank spaces from which it has disengaged itself. Touched by death, the hand of the master sets free the masses of material that he used to form; its tears and fissures, witnesses to the finite powerlessness of the I confronted with Being, are its final work. (*EM*: 566)

The astonishing import of this passage is that late works are characterized by *the disappearance of the work from the work as such*; by the dematerialization of the work, its liberation from the inadequacy of its material form. Not only that, but that this eventuality represents the highest fulfilment of the work itself. The 'exhaustion' of artistic forms is here not an active historical *process* at all; 'exhaustion' rather refers – in a purely nominal, abstract sense – to the condition of possibility of all art in the modern period. In modernity, the disappearance of meaning from art – what Adorno calls its 'enigmaticalness' – is dramatized by the corresponding fetishization of 'meaning' at the expense of 'form'. Lateness, difficulty, is the character of all artistic activity in modernity, which thus begins its irreversible trajectory towards volatilization, abstraction. The idea has its origins in Hegel's philosophy of history; 'late works' are a distinct form, characteristic of a particular historical situation, and subject to certain 'formal laws' that may be interrogated and understood. It is undeniable that Adorno's lateness is in some sense a temporal hypothesis. Yet Hegel's philosophy of history, as Adorno's book on him makes clear, is not one of decline, and the same should be said of the 'lateness' motif in Adorno (*H*: 53–88). As Edward

Said, discussing the 'late style' essay, observes: 'It is the *Zeitgeist* that Adorno really loathed and that all his writing struggles mightily to insult' (Said 2002: 207). Yet – rather contrary to Said's implication – it is not any particular *Zeitgeist*, but the *category* of the *Zeitgeist*, contemporaneity itself, that antagonizes Adorno's aesthetics. Said appears to forget – perhaps on account of the 'obvious personal reasons' with which, coyly, he explains his own interest in the theme, months before his own death (Said 2004: 3) – that Adorno's conception of lateness was developed in fierce opposition to biographical criticism. Said imbues late style, or the late stylist, with a 'prerogative' that is difficult to dissociate from the dignity accorded the dying: 'to render disenchantment and pleasure without resolving the contradiction between them' (Said 2004: 7). 'Late Style in Beethoven', however, was produced not when Adorno was himself facing death but early on in his career, in 1934. Adorno later claimed that most of his ideas about music originated in his youth, long before he developed them in his writing (*GS* 17: 9). The detail is worth noting, given Adorno's own understanding of the temporal dimension of 'late' works, and the nature of the 'death' or 'exhaustion' by which they are haunted.

In this regard, the bleakness imputed to Adorno's thought by the wide dissemination of his best-known statement about art – that to write literature after Auschwitz is barbaric – is thoroughly misleading. Its context is an essay on precisely the complacencies of a cultural criticism devoted to the denunciation of civilization. Entitled 'Cultural Criticism and Society', Adorno's essay is a critique of that form of reification which idealizes both 'culture' and 'the present', which takes one or the other as an object of criticism as such. It is also, therefore, a critique of the ideology of lateness conceived in temporalizing, idealizing terms: as cultural decline. 'What appears to be the decline of culture is its coming to pure self-consciousness. Only when neutralized and reified, does culture allow itself to be idolized. ... Cultural criticism rejects the progressive integration of all aspects of consciousness within the apparatus of material production. But because it fails to see through the apparatus, it turns towards the past, lured by the promise of immediacy' (*P*: 24).

'Neutralization of culture' is one of many synonyms for reification in Adorno's work. It refers to the reduction of artworks to objects stripped of any 'vital relationship' with the observer, as in art museums or performances of Mozart 'by candlelight', which constitute a doomed attempt to undo the process of neutralization by supplementing the work with period details (*P*: 175–6). Neutralization is not a tendency to be lamented but an objective situation that demands and generates new artistic forms. Adorno's 1959 assessment of the *Missa Solemnis* – a work performed only twice before Beethoven died – begins with the statement that 'every now and then' a work appears 'in which the neutralization of culture has expressed itself most strikingly' (*EM*: 569). The *Missa* 'offers no justification for the admiration accorded it'; it is this enigmatic incomprehensibility at the level of content, combined with its 'uncontested place within the repertoire', that speak of the release of the work from the limits of form itself – a release achieved in its insistently 'archaic' character, its constitution by 'sections imitative in themselves', and its 'peculiar character of quotation' (*EM*: 574, 575).

The sentences which immediately precede and follow the famous statement about Auschwitz, but which are rarely quoted alongside it, provide the logical apparatus for conceiving of the *Missa* as in some sense a post-Auschwitz work:

> The more total society becomes [*Je totaler die Gesellschaft*], the greater the reification of the mind and the more paradoxical its effort to escape reification on its own. Even the most extreme consciousness of doom threatens to degenerate into idle chatter. Cultural criticism finds itself faced with the final stage of the dialectic of culture and barbarism. To write poetry after Auschwitz is barbaric. *And this corrodes even the knowledge of why it has become impossible to write poetry today.* (*P*: 34, emphasis added)

'Auschwitz' names and marks the condition of modernity itself as one of incommensurability between the ethical obligation to speak and the availability of aesthetic forms which can do justice to that obligation; yet for Adorno the conception that Auschwitz inaugurates the break is a further symptom of an inability to grasp the full implications of this incommensurability. 'Auschwitz', seen as the catastrophe that makes meaning meaningless, emblematizes the tendency to cling to ideology critique, or cultural criticism, long after both have become obsolete. Dialectics, he says – by which he means 'immanent' as opposed to 'transcendent' critique, Hegelian phenomenology rather than the Kantian division into categories – amounts to an 'intransigence towards all reification' (*P*: 31), including all vehicles of the expressivist delusion (such as Edward Said's 'prerogative' of the dying artist, or the phrase 'mere ideology') (*P*: 32). In late capitalism, the ideologies of decline, deterioration, lateness itself, even meaninglessness, are as much vectors of reification as those of freedom, culture and national identity, or 'mind, life and the individual' (*P*: 23); indeed, the definition of the late period, for Adorno, is that in it, lateness is revealed to be no longer a viable chronological hypothesis.

Lateness, then, is a self-rescinding concept: a periodizing hypothesis which is abolished as such by the forms in which it is expressed, along with the categories of cultural decline, subjective expression, death as calamity, and linear temporality itself. Late works are the 'catastrophes' in the history of art, says Adorno (*EM*: 567). And chief among their casualties is the notion of catastrophe as the end of anything. In *Negative Dialectics*, rethinking his own earlier statement about Auschwitz, Adorno writes: 'After Auschwitz, our feelings resist any claim of the positivity of existence as

sanctimonious, as wronging the victims; they balk at squeezing any kind
of sense, however bleached, out of the victims' fate' (*ND*: 361). The
impossibility of poetry 'after Auschwitz' is – paradoxically – susceptible to
a 'positivist' reading which betrays its refusal of the thesis in the form of
its wholehearted adoption. The sentimentalization of meaninglessness, an
eventuality which must once have seemed unlikely in the extreme, is the
most effective means of dissipating its actuality altogether.

In what follows, I will discuss the transferability of the categories of
lateness and late style to literature – in particular the novel, and specifically
to V. S. Naipaul's novelistic meditation on lateness, *The Enigma of Arrival*
(1987). In Naipaul's work several apparently distinct aspects of lateness
combine. Yet the question of the applicability of the concept of lateness to
the novel form is complicated, to say the least. If lateness is a theme which
Adorno inherits from Hegel, one of the primary transmitters of the
inheritance is Lukács's *The Theory of the Novel*, a work which, Adorno once
declared, 'established a standard for philosophical aesthetics that still holds
today' (*NL1*: 151). For Lukács, the novel is a form that, *tout court*, expresses
and incubates lateness. The novel emerges in a world in which the 'natural
unity of the metaphysical spheres' – a unity expressed in the pure, sensuous
immediacy of the epic – has disappeared forever. An ethical rupture at
the heart of the novel separates content from form, meaning that ethics
in the novel is always a matter of reflection rather than of sensation,
materiality. 'A totality that can be simply accepted is no longer given to the
forms of art,' writes Lukács; 'therefore they must either narrow down and
volatilize whatever has to be given form to the point where they can
encompass it, or else they must show polemically the impossibility of
achieving their necessary object and the inner nullity of their own means.
And in this case they carry the fragmentary nature of the world's structure
into the world of forms' (Lukács 1971: 37, 38–9).

Lukács's *The Theory of the Novel* looks here like an instance of the idealizing, periodizing hypothesis that Adorno's work seeks to dismantle. Both
options – 'volatilization' and 'polemical impossibility' – are, in a chronological sense, late forms; only the second, however, describes what Adorno
conceives of as the late work. Indeed, the late work actually abolishes the
category of the late as a mode of 'exhaustion' or historical 'obsolescence'; it is
this latter which, by the process of 'volatilization' (i.e. self-deception), is able
to maintain the values of 'classicist aesthetic harmony'. In either case, the
work is constituted by failure, although in the case of 'polemical impossibility' failure is precisely its 'measure of success' (*EM*: 581). Furthermore,
late style *as such* is actually abolished – *aufgehoben*, we should say – in the
development of Adorno's own *Aesthetic Theory*, where it is absorbed as a
constituent element of aesthetics itself: 'The unsolved antagonisms of reality
return in artworks as immanent problems of form', writes Adorno in the
opening chapter of that work, echoing Lukács's second, 'polemical' solution

to the loss of totality: form as an index of impossibility. 'The moment a limit is posited it is overstepped and that against which the limit was established is absorbed' (*AT*: 6). It is at this late stage in his thought that Adorno becomes, in Said's phrase, 'lateness itself' (Said 2002).

The Enigma of Arrival as a novel, then, is *condemned* to lateness. For Lukács, the novel cannot not be a meditation on lateness, on failure, on death – events which, in the 'contingent' (i.e. inorganic) world of the novel, become inflected through what Lukács calls the central category of the 'problematic individual'. For Lukács, the novel appears at a moment when the outside world and the ideas of the individual become incommensurable, leading to the elaboration of the ideas into 'subjective facts – *ideals* – in his soul' (Lukács 1971: 78). *Enigma* is certainly a novel in this sense, organized as it is around the mysteries of the writing life, and the intense shame that has accompanied the narrator-protagonist's pursuit of it, and that now infuses his recollections (Naipaul 1987: 245). The narrative of the book concerns his loss of faith in the possibility of literary *creativity*, and his subsequent attempt at a reformulation of what that activity entails: no longer the recording or the projection of an 'inward development' (146), but an openness to the world and to its volatility, an openness which requires that he suspend even the apparent certainty of subjective perception. The incommensurability talked of by Lukács, which he names 'transcendental homelessness', has here been radicalized to the point at which the sense of disconnection between the world and the self becomes the very substance of their relation. Shame, subtraction of the self, replaces egoistic projection as the operative principle of the writing subject. The work is present only as an absence, as the book's very substance becomes an index to the question of its own possibility.

Not only is lateness explicitly thematized, then; *The Enigma of Arrival* also meditates at length on the inseparability of this condition of lateness from the situation of the novel as such, and that of the novel writer. As in so many of Naipaul's books, the writer at the centre of the text is intensely aware of the peculiar compulsions and frustrations of the literary enterprise itself. At the beginning of the book, Naipaul's author-narrator has recently moved to a cottage in Wiltshire, near Stonehenge – the ancient origins of England – where he seems weighed down by a morbid sense of destiny past, of 'glory dead' (Naipaul 1987: 53). England, the country of arrival, is a post-Imperial world, still coming to terms with its economic decline and the loss of cultural influence, both of which find a kind of symptomatic, consolatory expression in the idea of cultural and artistic 'exhaustion' – an idea which Naipaul's narrator is seduced by, even as he sees through its attractions. At almost every moment *The Enigma of Arrival* manifests an awareness of the obsolescence of temporality as linear progression (that is to say, the obsolescence of obsolescence). The temporality of the novel is never simply that of the time narrated, but is always allied to the time of the narration itself. Consider the following pair of sentences from the introduction to 'Jack's Garden', the novel's first section: 'Jack lived among ruins, among superseded things. But that way of looking came to me later, has come to me with greater force now, with the writing' (Naipaul 1987: 15).

Lateness, then, has the distinct quality of 'belatedness', in the sense intended by Frantz Fanon when he ventriloquizes the racist temporality of the relation between white Europeans and blacks in *Black Skin White Masks*: 'You come too late, much too late. There will always be a world – a white world – between you and us' (Fanon 1986: 122). In Naipaul, this awakening to belatedness is paralleled by the trajectory of his transposition from Trinidad to England – from the status of a colonial whose relation to history is purely 'abstract' (Naipaul 1987: 143) to that of latecomer (or in other words, novelist). For Naipaul, it seems, lateness is not primarily a temporal category; or rather, it is a geographical, existential and world-historical category as much as it is a temporal one. The immigrant is always belated, not only culturally but – as a racially distinctive figure – *in respect of his own first impression*. Late at night on the boat to Southampton, a black passenger from tourist class is introduced into the superior cabin that Naipaul's narrator, through 'a wonderful piece of luck', occupies alone: 'I was … ashamed that they had brought the Negro to my cabin. I was ashamed that, with all my aspirations, and all that I had put into this adventure, *this was all that people saw in me* – so far from the way I thought of myself, so far from what I wanted for myself' (125–6). Shame is an experience of time as aberrant, out of joint; the temporal dimension of shame is precisely belatedness. Sartre writes: Shame is the consciousness of being irremediably what I always was: 'in suspense' – that is, in the mode of the 'not yet' or of the 'already-no-longer'. Pure shame is not a feeling of being this or that guilty object but in general of being *an* object; that is, of *recognizing myself* in this degraded, fixed, and dependent being which I am for the Other. (Sartre 1989: 288) This misrecognition is an experience of temporal disjunction, which cannot not result in shame, since one's every conceivable expression and utterance is thereby condemned to anachronism. Adorno finds a similar quality in Beethoven's *Missa* – the impotence 'not merely of the mightiest composer but of an historical position of the intellect [*des Geistes*] which, of whatever it dares write here, *can speak no longer or not yet*' (*EM*: 580, emphasis added). This impotence should be located not in the composer but in the consciousness, the 'spirit', that is coterminous with the work. If the 'disengaged' subjectivity of the work speaks of its *belatedness*, however, the same work is *premature* as well; Beethoven's *Missa*, inasmuch as it is a post-Auschwitz work, is also – the logic of Adorno's work would suggest – presciently post-colonial.

'Belatedness', perhaps – paradoxically – is what provides *The Enigma of Arrival*'s most convincing claim to modernity. The sense of belatedness of Naipaul's narrator is expressed as a deep ambivalence towards the age of empire, a period in which the model of art as the organic imposition of the artist's 'vision' was still intact (Naipaul 1987: 187). As always in this text, the apparent nostalgia exists alongside an awareness that the organic vision, as enjoyed by artists such as John Constable and E. H. Shepard, no longer affords anything other than 'a modern picturesque' (187); furthermore, that in that world of organic immediacy, 'occurring at a time of empire', there would have been no place for a man like Naipaul (52). Not only is *The Enigma of Arrival* a meditation on lateness; it is a meditation on the unreliable consolations offered by, precisely, the meditation on lateness: 'I had always lived with [the] idea, ... even as a child in Trinidad, that I had come into a world past its peak. ... Already I lived with the idea of death, the idea, impossible for a young person to possess, to hold in his heart, that one's time on earth, one's life, was a short thing' (23). The great innovation of Beethoven's *Missa* is to renounce the obligation to innovate, to wrest any scrap of subjective affirmation out of subjective defeat. Liturgy, says Adorno, is left in its conventional, archaic form, undeveloped; the classical is exposed 'as classicizing' (*EM*: 580). In Naipaul, the refusal of affirmation has a similar effect, cutting loose the subjective element from the objective forms that are available to it in the text itself. 'The noblest impulse of all', he writes – 'the wish to be a writer, the wish that ruled my life – was the impulse that was the most imprisoning, the most insidious, and in some ways the most corrupting. ... To be what I wanted to be, I had to cease to be or to grow out of what I was' (Naipaul 1987: 245). In these passages, it seems, the propensity of the text is towards liberating subjective expression from the objective arena of the artwork, which includes all categories of 'narrator', 'authorial voice', 'meaning', 'interpretation', and so on.

Nevertheless, late works, for all the reasons spelled out in Adorno's essay, are particularly liable to be read in the confessional mode. On the manuscript of the *Missa*, above the Kyrie, Beethoven wrote the words '*Von Herzen – möge es zu Herzen gehen*' ('From the heart – may it go to hearts') – 'a confession', writes Adorno, 'the like of which one may search for in vain in all the other printed editions of Beethoven's works' (*EM*: 571). Yet, as Rose Subotnik has observed, precisely Beethoven's recourse to these words amounts to 'an admission of their futility' (Subotnik 1976: 265). In Adorno's reading, the work itself – particularly its use of repetition in the most sacred and 'personal' section of the Mass, the Credo – effectively undermines any suggestion of either subjective piety or the opposite, a kind of abstract 'Unitarian' religiosity, stripped of its doctrinal elements and made universal. With its insistent, jarring incantation of the word 'Credo', for Adorno it is 'as if the isolated man had to assure himself and others of his actual belief'. For the secular humanist Beethoven, the real question is not located on the subjective level – belief or atheism – at all. 'Expressed in more modern terms, it is a matter for Beethoven of whether ontology, the objective intellectual organization of existence, is still possible' (*EM*: 577).

The Enigma of Arrival too appears to solicit, and has in any case been frequently subjected to, such 'confessional' readings. Parts of the book are intimately self-exposing: 'For years ... I had dreamed of coming to England. But my life in England had been savorless, and much of it mean. I had taken to England all the rawness of my colonial's nerves, and those nerves had more or less remained, nerves which in the beginning were in a good part also the nerves of youth and inexperience, physical and sexual inadequacy, and of undeveloped talent' (Naipaul 1987: 101–2). It is these passages that have led the most prominent critics of the book to subject it to the kind of biographical interpretation that Adorno's interlocutors imposed upon Beethoven's late works. Indeed, the same qualities of 'irascibility' and 'bitterness' recur amongst the epithets hurled by these critics in Naipaul's direction. Salman Rushdie writes that the 'bitter taste' of Naipaul's middle period fiction has in *Enigma* been replaced not only by 'sadness', but by the author's secession from the demands of art: 'when the strength for fiction fails the writer, what remains is autobiography' (Rushdie 1992: 150). Rushdie introduces a distinction between technical and spiritual accomplishment, as he describes the 'delicate, precise' and yet 'bloodless' prose of the novel – testament, says Rushdie, somewhat presumptuously, to 'a life without love' (151). Caryl Phillips modifies this distinction into one between writerly virtuosity and 'likeability' (Phillips 2001: 204). Incessantly invoking the 'lateness' theme, he writes that Naipaul's 'subject is himself. But his theme is a tender and delicate one: it is death. Naipaul is engaged in rumination of the most superior kind as he waits for the inevitable' (199). With the 'autumnal' novels, Naipaul 'has cleared the way for a fuller reconciliation with his past and with himself' (200). Even Said, a critic intimately familiar with Adorno's writings on Beethoven, speaks of 'an increasingly bitter and obsessive strain in Naipaul's writing' since the early 1970s (Said 2000: 99). A common theme in both Said's and Phillips's readings is the absence of 'tenderness', 'affection' or 'compassion' from Naipaul's treatment of the post-colonial world (Said 2000: 100; Phillips 2001: 209, 208). All three writers acknowledge Naipaul's technical 'brilliance' (Rushdie 1992: 150; Phillips 2001: 195); Naipaul, says Said, is 'in the end too remarkable and gifted a writer to be dismissed' (Said 2000: 103), a verdict which establishes and presupposes a radical separation between the ethical and aesthetic dimensions of literature. It is difficult not to read this inexplicable reference to Naipaul's 'undismissibility' as a moment of critical defeat in Said's essay: the moment when it encounters the unthinkable actuality of Naipaul's text in respect of those categories of ethics and aesthetics, or of 'success' and 'failure'. Faced with the late work, Said acknowledges there is something he is simply not comprehending.

The critical embarrassment evinced in these readings is the inverse of that which Adorno detected in the reception of late Beethoven, yet it is identical in its effects. Naipaul's critics are reduced not to uncomprehending

'pronouncements of awe about an immortal *chef d'oeuvre*' (*EM*: 570), but to
an equally idealizing orgy of ululation over the withering of a 'gifted talent'.
Certainly, *The Enigma of Arrival* has none of the literary flamboyance that
we find elsewhere in Naipaul: in *A House for Mr Biswas*, for example, or *The
Mimic Men*. Yet, contra Phillips, this is precisely what establishes this work
in a continuity with Naipaul's earlier writings, which have implemented a
gradual distance from the confectionary appeal of the literary phrase at least
since *The Mimic Men*. In *Guerrillas*, for example, everything strains to escape
the merely verbal; passages of pure visual description contrast with the
emotional and intellectual dependence of each of the characters on totemic
phrases, most obviously the writer-character Jimmy Ahmed, hopelessly
aware that the failure of his writing is apparent in its inertness ('words
alone'), its refusal to leave the page (Naipaul 1975: 35). Even this 'middle
period' work of Naipaul's, therefore, invites comparison with Beethoven's
late sonatas, where the 'mere phrase' becomes 'a monument to what has
been, marking a subjectivity turned to stone' (*EM*: 567). In a reading which
takes issue with Said's condemnation of Naipaul for presenting a 'cliché-
ridden' third world, Sara Suleri proposes that Naipaul's subject is not the
'actualities' of the third world, but the 'anxiety of empire' – that is to say, in
part, the perpetual complicity of the literary itself in the colonial project: 'his
fascination with the cliché and the readily available colonial myth may be his
only means to arrive at an idiom in which to address his perception of
himself as a postcolonial cliché' (Suleri 1992: 158).

Among *Enigma*'s claims to originality, indeed, is the way it sets about
dismantling the category of literary originality. As in Beethoven, Naipaul's
late reformulation of the idea of artistic activity involves replacing the artist's
'sensibility' and the subjective transformation of one's 'material' – 'ideas
bred essentially out of empire, wealth and imperial security' (Naipaul
1987: 146) – with 'the worlds I contained within myself, the worlds I lived
in' (147). If the *Missa* is a work that aims at the *elimination* of the subjective
intention, the same is true of the abandonment of literary originality in *The
Enigma of Arrival*. In a passage that could almost, *mutatis mutandis*, have
been lifted from Adorno's essay on late style, Suleri anatomizes the
characteristics of Naipaul's later work: the arrival of incomprehensibility as
legitimate subject matter of the work; the retreat from – and castigation
of – ethical commentary; the interest in cliché as a dramatization of the
limits of discourse; the collapse of faith of the text in its own viability. For
Suleri, the 'problems' in Naipaul's work speak to the fact that it inhabits and
embodies the very pathos that it describes:

> Naipaul's mature writing no longer conceives of the literary as a recourse
> from the political, but instead internalizes the imperial tradition repre-
> sented by both modes into *a dazzling idiom that no longer needs to indicate
> the referents of its discourse*. As a consequence of this condensation, such a

language will never clearly identify the object of its indictment. Its burden is, of course, to demonstrate the objectlessness of postcolonial indignation, as that discourse seeks to establish the parameters of its suffering. (Suleri 1992: 155, emphasis added)

This shift in perspective in Naipaul's work is inseparable from his awareness of 'that great movement of peoples that was to take place in the second half of the twentieth century' (Naipaul 1987: 141), the significance of which he failed to notice when he was directly caught up in it, but which left the stability of identity, on which the possibility of the writer's subjective transfiguration of his 'material' depends, in tatters. 'The flotsam of Europe not long after the end of the terrible war, in a London house that was now too big for the people it sheltered – that was the true material of the boardinghouse. But I didn't see it' (141). Among the ideas which become untenable in the wake of this movement is that of the organic work, emanating out of a stable, identifiable historical world-context, and in ultimate justification of the 'literary' approach to experience: what Naipaul painstakingly discredits in the course of *Enigma* with terms such as the 'literary eye' (18), 'sensibility' (146, 256), 'inward development' (146, 147), and the 'writer's personality' (288).[2]

The transition narrated over the course of *The Enigma of Arrival* is thus from one idea of lateness to the other: from a chronologically driven sense of decline and decay ('the idea, which I had had even as a child in Trinidad, that I had come into a world past its peak' [23]) to something closer to Adorno's idea of the late work ('I began to be awakened by thoughts of death, the end of things ... it was only out of this new awareness of death that I began at last to write' [*EM*: 343–4]); from one idea of writing – the subjective transformation of one's 'material' – to another – 'the writer defined by his writer's discoveries, his ways of seeing, rather than by his personal adventures' (*EM*: 343–4). Naipaul writes himself out of the logic of imitation and mimicry and towards a logic of immanence.

Homi Bhabha has written that colonial discourse is defined by a 'splitting' into two regimes, two 'attitudes towards external reality': one, that 'takes reality into consideration', and another, that 'disavows it and replaces it by a product of desire that repeats, rearticulates "reality" as mimicry' (Bhabha 1992: 91). The upshot of Bhabha's essay is a reversal in the meaning of mimicry itself. The mere fact of mimicry as a disciplinary technology in the colonial world, registered in 'the difference between being English and being Anglicized' (89–90), exposes its contradictions; mimicry operates subtly, in the apparatus of colonial power, to undermine the very 'monumentality' on which its authority depends – and the same might be said of the deliberate archaism and 'peculiar character of quotation' of Beethoven's *Missa Solemnis* (*EM*: 576, 575). Identity and meaning – reality itself – are rendered unstable by their *imitability*. The idea offers one explanation for the gradual appearance in Naipaul's work of a fascination with cliché, with the corrosive appeal of the totemic phrase, and his relentless interrogation and implication of the literary register – not only in *The Enigma of Arrival* but in 'middle period' works such as *The Mimic Men*, an important point of reference for Bhabha's essay.

Bhabha's discursive 'splitting' may be mapped approximately onto Gilles Deleuze's distinction between two 'regimes of the image' in cinema: an 'organic' regime and a 'crystalline' regime. The first is representational – what Deleuze calls 'kinetic', insofar as images always relate to movement, to action, and 'organic' since it concerns 'a description which assumes the independence of its object'. The second is a description which 'stands for its object, replaces it, both creates and erases it', and which is 'chronic' in the sense that time is liberated from its subordination to movement, and becomes perceivable 'in itself' (Deleuze 1989: 127). Deleuze describes a shift from one to the other regime after the Second World War. In the work of directors such as Ozu (who anticipates the shift), Rossellini, Antonioni and Godard, 'a cinematographic mutation occurs when aberrations of movement take on their independence; that is, when the moving bodies and movements lose their invariants' – the points of stability which orient and organize them.

> There then occurs a reversal where movement ceases to demand the true and where time ceases to be subordinate to movement: both at once. *Movement which is fundamentally decentred becomes false movement, and time which is fundamentally liberated becomes power of the false which is now brought into effect in false movement.* (Deleuze 1989: 143)

While its logic requires that it play out similarly across different aesthetic forms, the 'crystalline' regime is most easily understood in relation to cinema, where its clearest manifestation is the appearance of 'purely optical and sound situations detached from their motor extension'. At such moments, the linear temporality of the plot-driven narrative is suspended; the focus upon a moment of pure sensory (visual or aural) perception creates 'crystals' of time that cut across the representational, narrative boundaries of the filmic utterance. No longer simply a neutral 'flow', time becomes 'crystalline', attains a sensory actuality, and actually replaces the narrative event as the object of the image.

This 'cinematographic mutation' is not restricted to a few cinematic texts. In fact, insists Deleuze, the mutation is metaphysical and historical as much as it is cinematographic (Deleuze 1989: 142); the category that remains fundamentally untenable, or at least radically altered, is ontology itself. If, for Naipaul, the transition from one idea of writing to another is explicable in terms of his own geographical and historical transposition from the periphery to the centre, those same 'historical' reasons – summed up in Naipaul's phrase 'the flotsam of Europe' – feature amongst those that

Deleuze puts forward to explain the appearance of the time-image (Deleuze 1986: 206). Yet Deleuze's discussion, in particular the simultaneity of the 'historical' and the 'metaphysical', offers a way of conceiving the loss of the 'organic' connection between work and world (Lukács's 'transcendental homelessness') in positive rather than negative terms; indeed, one might consider the centrality of cinema to Deleuze's analysis as another version of the almost systematic discrediting of the 'literary approach to experience' that we find in Naipaul.

The distinction between 'organic' and 'crystalline' narration illuminates both the formal complexity of Naipaul's fiction and, therefore, the 'chronic' – non-chronological – aspect of Adorno's category of the late work. Naipaul's 'middle period' novel *The Mimic Men* (1967) is narrated by Ralph Singh, a former colonial politician in exile in London, writing his memoirs, which comprise the text of the novel. Thus, there are two books in the novel: Naipaul's work of fiction, which we hold in our hands, and Singh's memoir, heterogeneous to the text we are reading, yet whose boundaries coincide with it. The two books are indistinguishable, yet non-identical. At certain moments the incommensurability defining their relation attains a 'crystalline' quality. In several sequences, Singh, in the 'present', remembers himself imagining himself seen through a camera lens located in the sky – imagining himself, that is to say, viewed from a future perspective represented *in the present-day narration of the book we are reading*: 'I saw the scene as though I had already been removed from it and it was occurring in memory, in a book' (Naipaul 1967: 209). Singh is 'marked' by this experience, not only for survival, but for a meaningful life in exile (134); he sees the episodes as *having guaranteed* him a future away from the 'disorder' of the Caribbean island of his birth (141) – but only retrospectively, from the point of view of *having already attained* that future: in London, in the present, and *in the pages of the book we hold in our hands*. As in *Enigma*, belatedness and prematurity coincide; time is presented 'in itself', abstracted from the linearity of past–present–future.

The psychopathology so often ascribed to Naipaul, most recently and explicitly by Pascale Casanova, but implicitly in Said's, Rushdie's and Phillips's readings also, is that of 'assimilationism'. Naipaul is, in Casanova's understanding, exemplary of the 'lowest level of literary revolt'; his is 'the obligatory itinerary of every apprentice writer from an impoverished region having no literary resources of its own' (Casanova 2004: 207). This charge presupposes a linear narrative of history, bounded at either end by precocity and belatedness. Casanova attributes to Naipaul that 'possessive, intolerant kind of love' for the metropole that Adorno attributes to all 'latecomers and newcomers' (*MM*: 52–3).[3] Naipaul's traditionalism is 'the direct conse-quence of [his] pathetic search for identity' (Casanova 2004: 212).

Yet Casanova's account has failed to notice the 'crystalline' elements in Naipaul's work; has neglected Naipaul's formal, as opposed to historical, lateness; has succumbed to the delusion that its brittleness renders it permeable and decodable – that the writer's weakness, vulnerability and shame are perceivable *through* (or despite) the work; has, finally, imposed an ideological and conceptual stability upon the work – an ontology of failure, rather than an opening to potentiality. The shame that permeates Naipaul's texts, furthermore, is read as a symptom that underlies and explains his writing, rather than an affect that appears alongside it, that is inseparable from and simultaneous with it. Like the reversibility of recollection and premonition, shame in Naipaul is a 'crystalline' motif: an affect produced in and by the very moment of 'confession', and in which the text we are reading is entirely implicated. Shame, in other words, is a pure 'time-image': an element in the text that cuts across the time of the narration and the time narrated – that can be reduced neither to the fiction nor to the fictionalization.

Near the beginning of *The Mimic Men*, Ralph Singh recalls first conceiving of his memoir as a work that would be undertaken 'in the evening of my days', and that would 'give expression to the restlessness, the deep disorder' of the movements of decolonization across three continents. 'But this work will not now be written by me', he says; 'I am too much a victim of that restlessness which was to have been my subject' (Naipaul 1967: 38). The passage is exemplary of the kind taken by critics of Naipaul as simple truth-statements. Yet the question of attribution of the failure and the shame – whether to Naipaul's book or to Singh's – is here radically indeterminate. Suleri refers to the 'striking parallels between the nature of colonial shame and that of literary mortification' in Naipaul's work. Both 'become instances in a failure in language' (Suleri 1992: 158); a statement that suggests that Naipaul's real subject is neither shame, nor colonialism, nor even writing, but the incommensurability which defines the relation between these things.

In *The Enigma of Arrival* the structural complexity of the work is even more elusive, since the incommensurable elements are formally unmarked as such in the text. The books that Naipaul's narrator has written in the past, for example, are indistinguishable from those Naipaul himself has written. As in *The Mimic Men*, references to the process of writing 'the present book' are difficult to separate, even conceptually, from the book we are reading (Naipaul 1987: 97, 343–4, 354); and yet, as Adorno's 'theory of art' insists, we are obliged to register the separation, even in its indiscernibility. In all these instances, Naipaul's 'late work' shares the characteristics that Deleuze attributes to the 'new kind of image' in post-war cinema: the replacement of a unified, 'organic' situation with a 'dispersive' one; the irruption of incommensurability, or 'ellipsis', into the substance of the tale, rather than remaining a mode of the telling; the introduction of an open stroll/voyage narrative form in place of the closed quest/search form; a strong, irresolvable consciousness of clichés; and the expansion of this consciousness to such a level that all possibilities of a meaningful whole become suspect.[4]

To read Adorno, the philosopher of negation, in alliance with Deleuze, the philosopher of affirmation, might seem perverse. And yet, in order to grasp the reversibility of terms and concepts implied in Adorno's concept of lateness it is necessary that we think also of the identity or simultaneity of opposites. The terms 'positive' and 'negative' need themselves to be stripped of their positivism, as do the terms lateness and infancy. Furthermore, the comparison with Deleuze's 'time-image' clarifies the atemporal, 'crystalline' quality of Adorno's 'late style', a quality that becomes more apparent in Adorno's own thought once he suppresses the category of 'late work' in *Aesthetic Theory*. 'Every artwork is an instant,' he writes there, 'every success-ful work is a cessation, a suspended moment of the process, as which it reveals itself to the unwavering eye' (*AT*: 6).

Naipaul's project in *Enigma* is not entirely successful, even as a work which hopes to transcend the logic of artistic 'success' and 'failure'. The author's own peculiar prejudices and biases are present, particularly in the final pages, where he lapses into the denunciatory register, and the work does indeed take on a brittle, friable quality. And yet, to imagine that it could be 'successful' is to subject the text to a conception of aesthetic harmony that would be immediately self-defeating. For all the 'dissatisfactory' qualities of the text – in fact, both because of and irrespective of these problems – *The Enigma of Arrival* overcomes the notions of 'crisis', 'decline', 'success' and 'failure' – all concepts embedded in a Cartesian organicism – and approaches a practice of writing as 'event', a writing capable of giving form to the *simultaneity* of belief and unbelief, of success and failure, experience and recollection, lateness and infancy, nostalgia and prolepsis.[5] *Enigma*, that is to say, undertakes the same interrogation of ontology that Adorno locates in Beethoven's *Missa Solemnis*. Naipaul's most lucid statement on the results of that interrogation is offered near the beginning of the text: 'I liked the decay, such as it was. It gave me no wish to prune or weed or set right or remake. It couldn't last, clearly. But while it lasted, it was perfection. To see the possibility, the certainty of ruin, even at the moment of creation: it was my temperament' (Naipaul 1987: 52). As in Beethoven, what we see in Naipaul is not the fragile envelope of form broken apart by the bald assertion of a subjectivity in its encounter with death, but a material-ization of the negative dialectic of form itself. 'Lateness' converges with the immediacy of perception that Lukács ascribes to man's pre-novelistic 'infancy', in a direct presentation not of the 'decline' but of the 'coming to pure self-consciousness' of the novel form as such.

NOTES

1   Artworks, writes Adorno, 'participate in enlightenment because they do not lie: They do not feign the literalness of what speaks out of them. They are real as answers to the puzzle externally posed to them' (*AT*: 5).

2 This demolition of the 'literary imagination' in *The Enigma of Arrival* is most complete in the portrayal of Alan, a 'literary friend' whose 'literary approach to experience' is as much a cause of falsification as was the narrator's own as a young man (Naipaul 1987: 288–90).

3 For a subtly counterintuitive reading of this fragment, which offers a way of recuperating its apparent 'Eurocentrism', see Lazarus 1999.

4 These five characteristics are summarized in Deleuze 1986: 207–10.

5 Ian Baucom has called Naipaul's nostalgia a 'proleptic nostalgia' which 'does not see wholeness in the ruin, but the promise of ruin in the whole' (Baucom 1996: 280).

WORKS CITED

Baucom, I. (1996), 'Mournful histories: narratives of postimperial melancholy', *Modern Fiction Studies* 42(2), 259–88.

Bhabha, H. (1992), *The Location of Culture*. London: Routledge.

Blanchot, M. (1982), *The Space of Literature*, trans. A. Smock. Lincoln and London: University of Nebraska Press.

Casanova, P. (2004), *The World Republic of Letters*, trans. M. B. DeBevoise. Cambridge, MA: Harvard University Press.

Coetzee, J. M. (2000), *Waiting for the Barbarians*. London: Vintage.

Deleuze, G. (1986), *Cinema 1: The Movement-Image*, trans. H. Tomlinson and B. Habberjam. London: Athlone.

— (1989), *Cinema 2: The Time-Image*, trans. H. Tomlinson and R. Galeta. London: Athlone.

Fanon, F. (1986), *Black Skin White Masks*, trans. C. L. Markmann. London: Pluto.

Lazarus, N. (1999), 'Hating tradition properly', *New Formations* 38, 9–30.

Lukács, G. (1971), *The Theory of the Novel*, trans. A. Bostock. London: Merlin.

Naipaul, V. S. (1967), *The Mimic Men*. New York: Knopf.

— (1975), *Guerrillas*. New York: Knopf.

— (1987), *The Enigma of Arrival*. New York: Knopf.

Phillips, C. (2001), 'V. S. Naipaul', in *A New World Order: Essays*. New York: Random House, pp. 187–219.

Rushdie, S. (1992), 'V. S. Naipaul', in *Imaginary Homelands: Essays and Criticism 1981–1991*. New York: Penguin, pp. 148–51.

Said, E. (2000), *Reflections on Exile*. London: Granta.

— (2002), 'Adorno as lateness itself', in N. Gibson (ed.), *Adorno: A Critical Reader*. Oxford: Blackwell, pp. 193–208.

— (2004), 'Thoughts on late style', *London Review of Books*, 26(15), 3–7.

Sartre, J.-P. (1989), *Being and Nothingness*, trans. H. Barnes. London: Routledge.

Subotnik, R. (1976), 'Adorno's diagnosis of Beethoven's late style: early symptom of a fatal condition', *Journal of the American Musicological Society*, 29(2), 242–75.

Suleri, S. (1992), 'Naipaul's arrival', in *The Rhetoric of English India*. Chicago, IL and London: University of Chicago Press, pp. 149–73.

13

After Adorno: The Narrator of the Contemporary European Novel

David Cunningham

Ubiquitous and culturally central as it may apparently continue to be, to what extent is the novel a *present force*? Have its narrative functions finally been usurped by its younger twentieth-century competitors: film, TV, video? Is it the case that for the most important writers today, as the late W. G. Sebald wrote in 1993: 'My medium is prose, not the novel' (Sebald 2005: xi)? Is the 'novel' itself now a redundant critical category?

These are active questions, in the sense that they exert a particular pressure on contemporary 'literary' culture, whether inside or outside the academy. Since the 1960s, and the proselytizing of New Journalists and avant-gardists alike, the novel has seemed subject to a ceaseless anxiety, threatened from all sides, whether by best-selling memoirs, travelogues or video games. To talk of the 'death of the novel', writes the literary editor of a 'quality' British newspaper, 'in the season in which [Ian] McEwan's *Saturday* has been breaking all previous records for serious fiction and in which the Booker Prize longlist includes important new books by Ishiguro, Barnes, Ali Smith and Salman Rushdie', is 'perverse, even baffling' (McCrum 2005). Yet the culture industry criteria of sales figures and publicity cannot disguise the concerns that such assertions implicitly articulate.

Of course, questions regarding the novel's health have accompanied its development throughout the twentieth century. T. S. Eliot, in a famous 1923 review of *Ulysses*, wrote: 'If it is not a novel, that is simply because the novel is a form which will no longer serve. ... Mr. Joyce and Mr. [Wyndham] Lewis, being "in advance" of their time, felt a conscious or probably unconscious dissatisfaction with the form' (Eliot 1975: 177). Nonetheless, over the last few decades, such 'dissatisfaction' has certainly seemed to be felt with a new intensity. In his influential 1991 book on postmodernism, Fredric Jameson, for example, suggests that, confronted with the 'impossible totality of the contemporary world system', the novel 'is the weakest of the newer culture areas, ... considerably excelled by its narrative counterparts in film and video' (Jameson 1991: 38, 298). Arguably, as Jameson goes on to observe, 'in the Third World, of course, all this falls out very differently' (298). Yet the distinctiveness of certain 'non-western' contemporary forms of the novel, of their own particular 'unstable formations' and 'paradoxical fusions', is clearly the historical product of what is itself a very distinct *social* development (Moretti 1998: 194). What it means for the European novel itself, the source of such 'diffusion', is less clear.

In fact, beyond the products of the instrumentalized 'craft' of creative writing courses, and its prize-winning celebrity practitioners, the 'serious' European novel today appears defined, in some fundamental sense, by its *crisis*, manifested in a troubling of any conventional distinctions between narration and commentary, storytelling and essayism, reportage and autobiography; a troubling through which the traditional distance separating author from narrator presents itself as simultaneously disturbed and ironized. From Iain Sinclair to J. G. Ballard, Sebald to Michel Houellebecq, the very boundaries demarcating individual works prove porous, apparently opening the novel out onto a continuous practice of writing, revising the same obsessive concerns, and digesting and hybridizing different genres in a way qualitatively different to that synthesis both Bakhtin and Lukács saw as constitutive of the novel in general. Writers directly incorporate into such works the literary (and 'sub-literary') styles and practices of the diary entry, biography, travel writing, journalism, polemic, philosophical reflection, advertising copy, pornography, scrapbook and so on; often, as in Ballard, with self-conscious clumsiness. Art and documentary, 'fiction' and 'fact', collide, and refuse their disentanglement.

THEORY OF THE NOVEL

Written in 1954, and originally composed as a radio talk, Adorno's one text devoted to 'the current status of the novel as a form' presents itself as the essayistic 'compression' of some more general investigation of the novel's changed meaning in a post-war present. To turn to it today may well seem odd, even perverse. Predating post-colonialism, magic realism and the American 'postmodernism' of a Pynchon or Doctorow, Adorno's text looks already dated at the time of its composition. Entitled 'The Position of the Narrator in the Contemporary Novel [*zeitgenössichen Roman*]', every one of its principal subjects – Joyce, Proust, Kafka, Musil – was, with the exception of Thomas Mann (who was to die a year later), long dead when it was written. As such, it can very easily seem to accord with what its first English translator argued of *Aesthetic Theory*: that it 'was obsolete to begin with . . . welded to artistic tendencies that came to an end with the first half of this [the twentieth] century, if not earlier' (Lenhardt 1985: 147). Yet, I want to suggest, it remains an interesting and critically productive text, despite some obvious limitations, and one, moreover, that indicates a keen awareness of 'tendencies' constituting something of the pre-history of our own contemporary condition.

As a summation of sorts, Adorno's 'remarks' in fact 'compress', not only his own thoughts on the novel, developed from the 1940s onwards (see, for example, *DE*: 35–6), but also the central theses of a far broader history of its earlier twentieth-century theorization – one which goes, most significantly, via both Georg Lukács's *The Theory of the Novel*, written in 1914–15, and Walter Benjamin's 1930s essays on the likes of Kafka, Proust and Leskov. Indeed Adorno's opening judgement on the essential 'paradox' that defines the contemporary 'position of the narrator' – that 'it is no longer possible to tell a story, but the form of the novel requires narration' (*NL1*: 30) – is directly lifted from the beginning of Benjamin's 1936 essay on Leskov. For Benjamin, the rise of the novel is already the 'earliest symptom of a process whose end is the decline of storytelling' (Benjamin 1973: 87); an assertion which indicates what, for both, most crucially delimits the novel – that it has a specific history. As a literary form, Adorno asserts, the novel is *essentially* defined by its modern, alienated character, directing itself towards the (historically new) 'inner experience' of the bourgeois subject.

If such an account can ultimately be traced back to Hegel's *Aesthetics*, its more immediate source is Lukács's *The Theory of the Novel*, which Adorno first read as a student in the early 1920s, and which is constructed around an historicized distinction between the classical epic, as the product of a social reality whose 'homogeneity' cannot be 'disturbed' by any 'separation between "I" and "you"' (Lukács 1971: 32), and the novel, 'born' in the 'solitary individual', able to express only the 'profound perplexity of the living' (Benjamin 1973: 87). For Lukács, a writer like Dante already marks a 'historico-philosophical transition from the pure epic to the novel', because his 'figures are already individuals' (Lukács 1971: 68). As for the novel proper, it can only ever be the epic of what Hegel calls a 'world of prose'; that social world in which

> occupations and activities are sundered and split into infinitely many parts, so that to individuals only a particle of the whole may accrue. . . . This is the prose of the world, as it appears to the consciousness both of the individual and of others: a world of finitude and mutability, of entanglement in the relative, of the pressure of necessity from which the individual is in no position to withdraw. (Hegel 1975: 149–50)

Seeking to recover the epic's range and 'wholeness', what the novel necessarily lacks is 'the occurrence of an action which in the whole breadth of its circumstances and relations must gain access to our contemplation as a rich event connected with the total world of a nation and epoch' (Hegel 1975: 1,044). For it is, on Hegel's account, a structural feature of modernity, as regards its potential mediation by the artwork, that it resists formation as a collective totality which might be embodied by any particular individual subject. The individual subject acts as 'only involved' in society, 'and interest in such a figure, like the content of its aims and activity, is unendingly particular' (194). While the 'whole' may determine individual reality, it is ineliminably opaque to any individual subject's capacity of understanding, and much as any 'story' might strive for universality, it will always resolve back into the particular and the contingent. In Lukács's still essentially idealist terminology of 1914, the epic and the novel 'differ from one another not by their authors' fundamental intentions' – for the novel 'still *thinks* in terms of totality' – 'but by the given historico-philosophical realities with which the authors were confronted' (Lukács 1971: 56, emphasis added). The novel *qua* novel is born of a uniquely modern cleavage of subject and object, fact and value, which it can never, in itself, reconcile.

If then the novel's 'inner form' *in general* is that of 'the individual's journeying towards himself' (Lukács 1971: 80–1), it is what Lukács calls the romantic 'novel of disillusionment', in particular, that will inaugurate the more radical inward turn of twentieth-century modernism; a move towards a focus on individual interior consciousness, and the 'interior space' of the text, which yet cannot escape the 'soul's' imbrication with a social reality beyond its control. And the obvious danger that it will harbour is a 'disintegration' of the novel form itself into a mere 'nebulous and unstructured sequence of moods and reflections about moods' (113). As Adorno writes in the contemporary novel essay:

> Realism was inherent in the novel; even those that are novels of fantasy as far as their subject matter is concerned attempt to present their content in such a way that the suggestion of reality emanates from them. ... [But] today, this mode of proceeding has become questionable. Where the narrator is concerned, this process has occurred through a subjectivism that leaves no material untransformed and thereby undermines the epic precept of objectivity or material concreteness [*Gegenständlichkeit*]. (*NL1*: 30)

Yet the movement delineated here away from the epic's devotion to the concrete – 'having *what is* as its topic', in Hegel's words (Hegel 1975: 1,044) – is not, for Adorno, as it largely is for Lukács, one simply to be lamented, but is, rather, an aspect of a changing social reality that requires and generates new literary forms. Originally rooted in an emergent bourgeois secularism and empiricism, which sought to privilege the individual and the concrete, the narratorial form of the modern novel comes, necessarily, to find itself forced into an incipiently paradoxical position: 'Nowadays anyone who continued to dwell on concrete reality the way Stifter, for instance, did ... would be guilty of a lie: the lie of delivering himself over to the world with a love that presupposes that the world is meaningful' (*NL1*: 30). If human reality can no longer be taken to have an inherent meaning or necessity, then the meanings and logical patterns imposed upon it by novelistic narration must necessarily appear as artificial and arbitrary (something clearly foregrounded in, for example, Joyce's *Ulysses*), thus making questionable any conventional claim to 'realism'. The 'illusion' of 'objective purity' accorded by the novel is irrevocably broken apart by the limitations inherent in its subjective shaping and design, rendering the novel necessarily ironic, and opening up a disjunction between its form and content: 'The more strictly the novel adheres to realism in external things, to the gesture that says "this is how it was", the more every word becomes a mere "as if", and the greater becomes the contradiction between the claim and the fact that it was not so' (*NL1*: 33).

If this would draw the novel down the path of its 'dissolution in extreme subjectivism', it is, at the same time, part of an objective *social* development which, according to Adorno, also comes to problematize, and even 'liquidate', the very category of the *individual* itself, around which the novel was historically constituted. Today, in the 'administered world', any 'implicit claim' – whether by author or narrator – that 'the course of the world is still one of individuation' becomes inescapably 'ideological in itself' (*NL1*: 31). Spurious as might be Adorno's tendency here to speak in totalizing terms of the 'reification of *all* relationships' (see Cunningham 2003), given this, one can understand why, in the case of the story as a specific narrative and social form, its present *impossibility* is traced, by both Adorno and Benjamin, to the same historical 'event': 'The identity of experience in the form of a life that is articulated and possesses internal continuity – and that life was the only thing that made the narrator's stance possible – has disintegrated' (*NL1*: 31). A modern author such as Proust necessarily 'depicts a life bereft of meaning, a life the subject can no longer shape into a cosmos' (*NL1*: 181). Yet, neither for Adorno nor Benjamin, is the 'process' described here entirely new (even if massively accelerated by the social formation of individuality as 'eternal sameness'). Rather it is, in some fundamental sense, present in the very beginnings of the novel *as such*. The 'category of the contingent' is, Adorno writes, one Proust 'shares with the great tradition in the novel' (*NL1*: 181).

Indeed, Adorno argues, the novel has, since the eighteenth century at least, *always* 'had as its true subject matter the conflict between living human beings and rigidified conditions'. Such 'conditions' entail that, ultimately, 'alienation itself' must become 'an aesthetic device for the novel', in particular through the figure of the narrator (*NL1*: 32). Hence, against Lukács's simultaneously melancholic and utopianist musings on the potential *return* of the epic, the modern novel is logically affirmed by Adorno precisely as a qualitatively new kind of *negative* epic; one in which 'an unleashed subjectivity turns into its opposite through its own momentum': the objective 'witness to what has befallen the individual':

> The literary subject who declares himself free of the conventions of concrete representation acknowledges his own impotence at the same time; he

acknowledges the superior strength of the world of things that reappears in the midst of the monologue. (*NL1*: 35)

If alienation 'needs to be called by name', the novel, Adorno asserts, is 'qualified to do so as few other art forms are' (*NL1*: 32).

FORM, HYBRIDITY AND THE NOVEL

Why, then, is the novel so qualified? What accords it this apparent, perhaps unexpected, privilege? Despite his well-known disagreements with Lukács's later critiques of modernism, and the undoubtedly mythicized character of the depiction of epic totality in *The Theory of the Novel* itself, what Adorno took from him was a compelling thesis concerning the *historical* character of the novel form *as such*. It is this concern for the novel's particular historicity which sharply contrasts Lukács's account with that of another great early-twentieth-century theorist of the novel, Mikhail Bakhtin, who, as a seminal figure for so-called 'post-structuralist' criticism during the 1980s, has probably had the larger influence on recent literary studies. For Bakhtin, the novel appears as an *always* protean and 'subversive' disruption of literary authority, ever new in whatever era it emerges, from Heliodorus to Dostoevsky. In its relations to other genres, writes Bakhtin, the novel is a perpetually renewed site of 'indeterminacy', 'a living contact with un-finished, still-evolving contemporary reality' (Bakhtin 1981: 7). While this imparts a powerfully generalized, affirmative 'modernity' to the novel, in so doing it deprives it of what is so key to Lukács's theory: the novel's *specific* relation to (capitalist) modernity in a broader social sense, as – unlike, say, the lyric – 'the literary form specific to the bourgeois age' (*NL1*: 30). It is this difference that crucially inflects the divergent accounts of what, nonetheless, *both* Lukács and Bakhtin take to be definitive of the novel form: its essential heterogeneity or hybridity. As a genre, the novel is inherently anti-generic: an anarchic, mongrel 'genre' possessing only a 'negative' identity, made up of unsublatable fragments and combinations of other forms. Yet, for Lukács, the 'homelessness' of such dissonant hybridity – where '[a]rtistic genres now cut across one another, with a complexity that cannot be disentangled' (Lukács 1971: 41) – has a much more definite set of historical coordinates than it does in Bakhtin. If the novel is 'the literary form specific to the bourgeois age', it is so, not only as a 'reflection' of such an age, but as an effective 'model' of it, a formal equivalent to its *social* being. For much as it might strive to be a positive repetition of epic totality, the novel can, by virtue of its social character, only ever be 'the paradoxical fusion of heterogenous and discrete components into an organic whole which is then abolished over and over again' (Lukács 1971: 84), a translation of 'the fragmentary nature of the world's structure into the world of forms' (38).

It is, arguably, one potential of this 'paradoxical fusion' – the capacity to immanently articulate a demonstration of 'the impossibility of achieving [its own] necessary object' (Lukács 1971: 38–9) – that Adorno extends, in his own later writings, to the character of the autonomous modern artwork per se: the refusal to present 'what is not reconciled as reconciled' (*AT*: 110). Moreover, it is an argument which, famously, Adorno will come to turn against Lukács himself in their dispute over literary modernism (see *NL1*: 216–40). Ultimately, it will simply define what the artwork *qua* artwork is:

> No artwork is an undiminished unity; each must simulate it, and thus collides with itself. Confronted with an antagonistic reality, the aesthetic unity that is established in opposition to it immanently becomes a semblance. The integration of artworks culminates in the semblance that their life is precisely that of their elements. However, the elements import the heterogenous into artworks and their semblance becomes apocryphal. In fact, every penetrating analysis of an artwork turns up fictions in its claim to aesthetic unity. (*AT*: 105)

The *authentic* artwork is, then, that which does not conceal this immanent non-identity of its elements, nor its importing of the heterogenous as a condition of the ongoing *renewal* of its very autonomy. Indeed Adorno suggests, in his last work *Aesthetic Theory*, contemporary art is increasingly *compelled* to foreground such reliance on the heterogenous, as part of a productive logic of non-identity to prevailing norms that is a prerequisite of resisting a 'socially affordable' aestheticism: 'Currently art stirs most energetically where it decomposes its subordinating concept. In this de-composition, art is true to itself: It breaks the mimetic taboo on the impure and the hybrid' (*AT*: 182 [trans. mod.]). It is only art's immanent (as well as 'external') relations to its others – those forms or practices that are pre-sented, in the contemporary, as *non*-aesthetic – that make it socially *critical* rather than *mere* 'social fact'. Great literature, Adorno writes in a 1960 essay on the avant-garde novelist Hans G. Helms, 'owes its greatness precisely to what is heterogenous to it. It becomes a work of art through the friction between it and the extra-artistic; it transcends that, and itself, by respecting it' (*NL2*: 99). Such an inherently problematic dialectic entails, therefore, a realization of the potential for productive tension to be found in the novel's 'incorporation' of 'non-literary' linguistic practices. Yet – and here is my key point – in the case of the novel form, this is, in some sense, simply to extend its own essential character, as an 'anti-generic' genre always already *defined* by the 'cannibalization' of others.

It is in this way that the novel remains the exemplary form of modern(ist) artwork generally – the basis for what Bakhtin describes as an increasing 'novelization' of *all* art forms within capitalist modernity (Bakhtin 1981: 5). Yet, and such is Adorno's evident dilemma, this essential dissonance and hybridity also, necessarily, renders the 'integrity' of the novel itself, as a form, *ipso facto* problematic; and thus threatens its very autonomy as *art*. This can be seen most clearly in the skewed relation between reflection and narration that Adorno identifies in several modern novels, including Proust, in whom 'commentary is so thoroughly interwoven with action that the distinction between the two begins to disappear'. This tendency of reflection to break through 'the pure immanence of form' has, as Adorno points out, nothing to do with the essentially 'moral' judgements characteristic of 'pre-Flaubertian reflection' as a commentary on characters (*NL1*: 34). Rather it amounts to an immanently tendential destruction of the 'traditional aesthetic distance' that defines the very relationship between narrator and reader. If this 'decomposition' is both necessary and inevitable as a condition of the art of the novel remaining 'true to itself' – a 'requirement of form itself' – this, at least, is not subject to an unqualified affirmation by Adorno however. For where 'conscious deliberations' on this actually 'enter the novelist's reflections', there is, he cautions, 'reason to suppose' that 'it is not to the advantage of the work of art' (*NL1*: 32).

Perhaps the clearest instance of this is to be found in his ambivalence concerning Musil's great unfinished work *The Man Without Qualities*. In a letter to Webern, written soon after the novel appeared, Adorno asserted that it was affected by a surfeit of 'thinking' and too little narration or character (see Jonsson 2004: 140). Yet, as Jonsson points out, in some respects Musil's novel is readable as 'a virtual textbook' in an 'aesthetics of negativity', resisting any 'normative definitions of the cognitive or aesthetic functions that a novel is supposed to perform' (Jonsson 2004: 140). More to the point, such defiance of 'normative conventions' can plausibly be understood as itself the mark of Musil's holding to the 'truth' of the novel's historical form. As Jonsson puts it, in Musil's hands the novel as 'genre burst from its own internal pressure', from its own tendency to present itself as 'a discourse of discourses that could contain all other linguistic registers and rhetorical codes: scientific, colloquial, narrative, religious, political, poetic, social, visionary, sexual, legal and more' (140). By these means, as an impossible totality that would immanently defy (if not resolve) the modern social divisions of artistic and intellectual labour, Musil's monumental work incarnates a formal freedom that actually constitutes the formal distinctiveness of the novel itself. Like Hegel's modern individual subject, the novel is (formally) free to create itself in the absence of any *given* end. Yet this is itself the direct corollary of Lukács's 'transcendental homelessness'. Its freedom, in this sense, is defined, both formally and socially, by a certain inevitable *emptiness* that threatens its very 'integrity' as a work of art.

Adorno's concern with the 'integrity' of the novel form here is not, however, a kind of pseudo-Greenbergian defence of artistic purity. First, because the 'autonomy' that is, for Adorno, necessary to the artwork (including the novel) is not, as it is in Greenberg or the New Critics, restricted to the self-reflexively formal meaning of the artwork itself, but is the historical product of the social relations that constitute 'art' as such within capitalist modernity – meaning that the artwork is always *both* autonomous *and* 'social fact' (*AT*: 225–9) – and, second, because such autonomy cannot, in itself, necessarily rely upon the purity of any *specific* art in a generic sense, least of all in the novel. Rather, this 'destruction of form', Adorno writes, 'is inherent in the very meaning of form' (*NL1*: 34).

THE CONTEMPORARY EUROPEAN NOVEL

Such destruction of form must be understood in a properly dialectical sense if we are to grasp Adorno's argument at this point, or to consider what it may have to communicate as regards the condition of the novel today. What, in a late essay, Adorno refers to as a 'fraying' [*Verfransung*] of the boundaries dividing different arts or genres (*AA*: 371) has been taken up by some recent critics as a theoretical resource for thinking through post-1960s developments in installation and intermedia art. Yet it has some pertinence also in regard to the novel, as do Adorno's particular hesitations with respect to its significance. For, despite a strong sense of the 'authentic' logic of such a tendency, Adorno is equally clear that the 'authenticity' of any particular work remains dependent upon its emergence from, and its ongoing value in respect to, the internal pressure of 'genre' itself. The (perpetually incomplete) 'dissolution' of 'normative definitions of cognitive or aesthetic functions' must itself be the product of demands originating within the immanent logic of specific forms.

It is perhaps in this way that the novel, 'in some sense dialectically', as Jameson puts it, 'regenerates itself out of its own impossibility' (Jameson 1971: 352). Following, as they do, the novels of early-twentieth-century modernism, the most 'progressive' of contemporary prose texts are compelled to register immanently, within their own forms, their bringing into question of the novel. Yet, at the same time, they must rely upon such a category for their own historical intelligibility. This is the double bind of the modern artwork, of which the novel is exemplary, which must gain its meaning from its relation to past works, as a determinate negation of what precedes it. Such antagonism, generated in a negative dialectic of artistic and extra-artistic that it can never resolve, is *inherent* to the historical dynamic of the modern work of art itself, as well as to its social character.

It is in this light that I want to conclude here with some extremely brief and summary remarks on the position of the narrator in a contemporary writer, W. G. Sebald, whose work would seem to represent one specific pole of the novel's contemporary development. In fact, an 'Adornian' critical engagement seems apposite here, if only because of the frequency with which Sebald himself cites Adorno's work (see, for example, Sebald 2005: 126–7, 222n., 226n.). More generally, if implicitly, his writings are widely perceived as the products of an authorial will to confront the question of how to write literature 'after Auschwitz'. This is true up to a point, although it should be said that, for the most part, such engagement with the Holocaust is indirect, and appears as part of a broader range of historical catastrophes. If anything would seem 'thematically' to unite Sebald's *oeuvre* it is rather an obsessive and overwhelming preoccupation with *memory*; the 'art' of writing defined as 'a struggle consisting in the constant transfer of recollection into written signs', in which 'the artistic self ... engages personally' (Sebald 2003: 176–7). Characteristically afflicted by a kind of hypersensitivity that borders on debilitating anxiety – Sebald ventures an implicit comparison with the Kafka of the diaries; the latter's 'wretched state', 'seized by a creeping paralysis' and by 'mounting despair' (Sebald 1999: 142–7) – the Sebaldian narrator embodies a new degree of sub-jectivism in the novel 'that leaves no material untransformed'. Tacitly encouraging a confusion of the relationship between narrator and author – Sebald reproduces snapshots of himself among the images incorporated into his books – Sebald effects an elision of traditional 'aesthetic distance' that results in a mode of writing in which narration and reflection, commentary and action, are so thoroughly intertwined as to be ultimately indistinguishable. It would thus be easy, indeed plausible, to read this as the final moment in a process whereby the novel form itself dissolves into a 'nebulous and unstructured sequence of moods and reflections about moods' (Lukács 1971: 113).

Yet, evidently, as Sebald writes of Peter Weiss, what appears as a dissolution in 'extreme subjectivism' is also pursued in the belief that, through the work of memory, what the narrator thereby 'discovers' is not merely 'the *partie honteuse* of his own life', but a certain 'objective nature' of 'society': '[P]rivate suffering increasingly merges with a realization that ... grotesque deformities have their background and origin in collective social history' (Sebald 2003: 188). In this sense Sebald does indeed identify him-self with something very like an 'Adornian' conception of modernism's will to express subjective experience in such a way as to acknowledge 'the superior strength of the world of things that reappears in the midst of the monologue' (*NL1*: 35). But it is also what brings the 'integrity' of the novel form itself under renewed questioning in his work.

In his writings on immediate post-war German literature, Sebald precisely affirms that which 'breaks the mould of the culture of the novel' in favour of the recognition of 'historical contingency' to be found in 'experiments with the prosaic genre of the report, the documentary account, the investiga-tion' (Sebald 2005: 80–1). Such a 'break' is most obviously manifested in Sebald's own promiscuity with regard to established generic boundaries. His prose works present an idiosyncratic formal hybrid of memoir, scrap-book, travelogue, criticism and historical document. As in other con-temporary writers such as Iain Sinclair, the boundaries between 'fiction' and autobiographical 'fact' are rendered indeterminate. His commentary on Alexander Kluge's *Neue Geschicten. Hefte 1–18* (1977) stands as an effective summary of Sebald's own writing: a non-integrated combination of 'textual and pictorial material', which, nonetheless, does 'not invalidate his subjective involvement and commitment' (Sebald 2005: 89). Yet the historical intelligibility of such a constellatory form is itself dependent – despite the insistence that his 'medium' is simply 'prose' – upon its critical relation to the novel's history; simultaneously inscribing its ruination *and* reiterating and continuing its essential formal openness. The novel form is not so much erased as re-presented as 'opaque images of broken rebellion' (Sebald 2005: 67) held together by little more than a certain narrative *tone*. It is for this reason that, despite an apparent emphasis on the singular, and an openness to what Adorno calls 'the priority of the object', the manifest 'content' of Sebald's texts often appears strangely interchangeable; reducible to a series of lists of 'things' which, on the one hand, darkly parody instrumental rationality, but, on the other, are all-too-obvious placeholders for an unachievable encyclopaedic concreteness and totality (see, for example, the single sentence on the Theresienstadt ghetto which runs for nearly twelve pages in *Austerlitz* [Sebald 2001: 331–42]). Nowhere is this clearer than in the figuration of 'literature' itself in Sebald's texts. What the narrator usually recollects, in the geographical wanderings that provide the momentum for his thoroughly 'painful' labour of transferring 'recollection into written signs', are other literary texts. Essayistically reflecting, often at considerable length, upon the great works of an irrecoverable European tradition – Stendhal, Conrad, Swinburne, Kafka, Chateaubriand and so on – 'literature' itself takes on material form as a vertiginous archival ad infinitum, an infinite series of fragments, 'stacks piled high on the floor and the overloaded shelves' (Sebald 2001: 43), or in bibliographical catalogues that, like Thomas Browne's imaginary *Musaeum Clausum* in *The Rings of Saturn*, resist all totalization (Sebald 1998: 271–4).

If something of the novelty of his texts is to be found in their incorporation of 'real', 'extra-artistic' material, it is, nonetheless, Sebald's persistent use of narratorial reflection, overwhelming all narrative momentum, that is, above all, employed to generate their claim to autonomy as *art*; a claim which must be made at an historical moment in which the illusory character of such autonomy ever more impinges on the work's construction, by virtue of the seemingly universal reach of the exchange value form. Yet such subjectivism, and the self-consciously 'poetic' (even archaic) diction in which it is expressed, may simply result in – perhaps cannot avoid – a problematic disengagement from contemporary social reality altogether, a regression into 'literary' solipsism. As one critic has observed, it is noticeable that, inhabiting a kind of 'leisure time', the eyes of Sebald's narrators are in fact, more often than not, 'averted from the explicit processes of contemporary capitalist exploitation and commodification'.

What proposes itself as an 'art of memory' thus threatens to become an 'art of forgetting' of the present (Martin 2005: 195, 182).

In his essay on Leskov, Benjamin saw the novel, which had once deposed the story as a 'present force', being itself displaced by a 'new form of communication', characterized by the newspaper (as, today, by television and the Internet): a form he called 'information' (Benjamin 1973: 88). In Sebald's last book, *Austerlitz*, travelling to Paris to 'search for traces' of his father, mourns the loss of the 'silent harmony' of the old National Library. Confronted with the 'inexorable spread' of that form of 'processed' memoration which is the 'electronic data retrieval system', he can only turn away, abandoning his research and retreating into the pages of Balzac (Sebald 2001: 398, 392). It would be worth contrasting this ambiguous return to the novel, in the midst of its 'disintegration', with the path apparently pursued by other contemporary writers, like Ballard or Houelle-becq, who imply a kind of irresistible submission of the novel's narrative modes to newer informational forms, interpolating the present-tense styles of advertising copy, pornography or technical brochures into the very fabric of their works. By contrast, Sebald can seem to articulate a mode of resistance which risks slipping into 'socially affordable' aestheticism. Yet if the destruction of form 'is inherent in the very meaning of form', it is evidently not a simple matter here of choosing. As Adorno writes, in a situation in which all 'authenticity' is suspect, it is not up to the novelist 'to determine whether the goal of the historical tendency they register is a regression to barbarism or the realization of humanity' (*NL1*: 35).

WORKS CITED

Bakhtin, M. (1981), *The Dialogic Imagination*, trans. C. Emerson and M. Holquist. Austin: University of Texas Press.

Benjamin, W. (1973), 'The Storyteller', in *Illuminations*, trans. H. Zohn. London: Fontana, pp. 83–107.

Cunningham, D. (2003), 'A time for dissonance and noise: on Adorno, music and the concept of modernism', *Angelaki* 8(1), 61–74.

Eliot, T. S. (1975), '*Ulysses*, order and myth', in *Selected Prose*, ed. F. Kermode. London: Faber and Faber, pp. 175–8.

Hegel, G. W. F. (1975), *Aesthetics: Lectures on Fine Art*, 2 vols, trans. T. M. Knox. Oxford: Clarendon Press.

Jameson, F. (1971), *Marxism and Form: Twentieth-Century Dialectical Theories of Literature*. Princeton, NJ: Princeton University Press.

— (1991), *Postmodernism, or the Cultural Logic of Late Capitalism*. London and New York: Verso.

Jonsson, S. (2004), 'A citizen of Kakania', *New Left Review* 27, 131–41.

Lenhardt, C. (1985), 'Reply to Hullot-Kentor', *Telos* 65, 147–52.

Lukács, G. (1971), *The Theory of the Novel*, trans. A. Bostock. London: Merlin.

McCrum, R. (2005), 'Want to know what's happening? Read a novel', *The Observer*, review section, 4 September, 19.

Martin, S. (2005), 'W. G. Sebald and the modern art of memory', in D. Cunningham,
    A. Fisher and S. Mays (eds), *Photography and Literature in the Twentieth Century*.
    Newcastle: Cambridge Scholars Press, pp. 180–201.
Moretti, F. (1998), *Atlas of the European Novel 1800–1900*. London and New York: Verso.
Sebald, W. G. (1998), *The Rings of Saturn*, trans. M. Hulse. London: Harvill.
— (1999), *Vertigo*, trans. M. Hulse. London: Harvill.
— (2001), *Austerlitz*, trans. A. Bell. London: Hamish Hamilton.
— (2003), *On The Natural History of Destruction*, trans. A. Bell. London: Hamish Hamilton.
— (2005), *Campo Santo*, trans. A. Bell. London: Penguin.

Index

Printed in Great Britain
by Amazon.co.uk, Ltd.,
Marston Gate.